Ethics in
American Adoption

Ethics in
American Adoption

L. ANNE BABB

Foreword by Randolph Severson

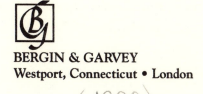

BERGIN & GARVEY
Westport, Connecticut • London

(1999)

Library of Congress Cataloging-in-Publication Data

Babb, L. Anne (Linda Anne), 1957–
    Ethics in American adoption / L. Anne Babb ; foreword by Randolph
Severson.
        p.   cm.
    Includes bibliographical references and index.
    ISBN 0–89789–538–X (alk. paper)
    1. Adoption—Moral and ethical aspects—United States.   2. Child
welfare—Moral and ethical aspects—United States.   3. Professional
ethics—United States.   4. Social ethics—United States.   I. Title.
HV875.55.B335   1999
174′.9362—dc21   98–30988

British Library Cataloguing in Publication Data is available.

Library of Congress Catalog Card Number: 98–30988
ISBN: 0–89789–538–X

First published in 1999

Bergin & Garvey, 88 Post Road West, Westport, CT 06881
An imprint of Greenwood Publishing Group, Inc.
www.greenwood.com

Printed in the United States of America

The paper used in this book complies with the
Permanent Paper Standard issued by the National
Information Standards Organization (Z39.48–1984).

10 9 8 7 6 5 4 3 2 1

Copyright Acknowledgments

The author and the publisher gratefully acknowledge permission for use of the following material:

Extracts from personal communications by L. Anne Babb with Annette Baran, Kevin McCarty, Margaret Lawrence and Jean Paton. Used with permission.

Extracts from G. William Troxler, *State of the Sabbatical: Midway to Marianne*, unpublished report to the trustees, faculty, and board of Capitol College, May 5, 1994. Used with permission of G. William Troxler.

For my husband, Dirk, truly a man of integrity.

The righteous walk in integrity, blessed are their children after them.
—Proverbs 20:7

Contents

Tables   ix

Foreword *by Randolph Severson*   xi

Acknowledgments   xxi

Introduction   xxv

Part I: Foundations   1

Chapter 1   Living the Experience   3

Chapter 2   Values in Adoption   27

Part II: Explorations   71

Chapter 3   Ethical Inquiry   73

Chapter 4   Ethical Codes Influencing Adoption Practice   95

Part III: Contentions   115

Chapter 5   When Professional Values Collide   117

Part IV: Recommendations   133

Chapter 6   Recommended Model for Ethical Standards in Adoption   135

Part V: Challenges   161

Chapter 7   Challenges to Change   163

Appendix A: Resources   201

Appendix B: Are You Considering Adoption? Information for
             Expectant Parents   203

Appendix C: Texas Child Protective Services Supervisor Competencies   209

Glossary   211

References   217

Index   227

Tables

Table 4.1 Frequency and Percentage Distribution of the Types of
Organizations   98

Table 4.2 Frequency and Percentage Distribution of Membership Types
Among Adoption-Related Organizations   99

Table 4.3 Frequency and Percentage Distribution of Membership Types
Among Total Population   100

Table 4.4 Should Certain Types of Adoption Be Allowed?   101

Table 4.5 Determinants of the Best Interest of the Child Standard 104

Table 4.6 Fair and Reasonable Adoption Fee in Healthy Infant
Adoption   107

Table 4.7 Areas in which Policy or Practice Changed as a Result of
Employee, Client, or Membership Disagreement   110

Table 4.8 Confidentiality and Adoptee Access to Birth Certificates in
Adoption   113

Table 5.1 Before an Adoption, Who Is the Adoption Worker's Client? 118

Table 5.2 Relationship between Identified Client before an Adoption
and Adult Adoptee Access to Original Birth Certificate   121

Table 5.3 Adult Adoptee Access to Original Birth Certificate   129

Foreword

In education and clinical orientation I'm an existential-phenomenological psychologist. Existentialism is a philosophy that emphasizes choice and personal responsibility and that thinks much of our distress in life results from our attempt to deny our freedom, to run away from it, to lose ourselves in the comforting distractions and illusions of ordinary, routine existence, or to rationalize our flight from freedom by locating the cause of our actions in factors external to the Self. The tragic irony is that these denials, which begin as efforts to reduce tension, in time become enslavements, depleting life of its pleasure, stimulation, and joy, dehumanizing it into a hollow, meaningless futility. Existentialism further maintains that we find fulfillment in life, find what existentialists call "authenticity," when we face that freedom—face it together with the other great imponderables of human existence, such as Death, Loneliness, Despair, Suffering, Illness, Hope and Joy, with all the anxiety, the fear and trembling, and the Dread, to which this encounter with the truth about ourselves inevitably gives rise. Then, with the "Courage to Be" as Tillich says, we recognize and affirm our freedom and assume our responsibilities in what another existentialist, Gabriel Marcel, calls "creative fidelity" to transcendentals whose claims we are always free to renounce or embrace. Authenticity imparts dignity, strengthens resolve, gives a spine to character, materializes as a desire to dwell, tend, cultivate, and care in community.

Phenomenology is an attitude, or "method," that supposes the best means for arriving at truth is through a description and reflection upon ordinary experience whose discipline unfolds through an attentive wondering and respectful, almost reverent "musing" presence more akin to a spiritual meditation than a statistical analysis.

I came to adoption as a psychologist interested in what phenomenology calls the theme of "embodiment" and what a religious consciousness might refer to as the mystery of Incarnation, that is to say, how is it that a human being can exist simultaneously as spirit, soul, heart, and consciousness on the one side, body, blood, flesh, history, biology, and genetics on the other? I was interested in the mind-body split that has crippled Western culture at least since Descartes and that seemed to me the fundamental issue for adult adoptees in search of their birth parents. My goal was to provide an existential-phenomenological background to this biographical struggle and perhaps to provide a possible road map for healing.

But what began as a philosophical quest became a quite personal one characterized by emotional involvement as I found myself repeatedly gripped by the emotional rawness and vulnerability of adoption. I remember the first adoption conference I attended, a regional conference of the American Adoption Congress, where, expecting to encounter the usual conference schedule of mildly interesting papers combined with panel discussions, I was instead overwhelmed by the intensity and passion of the presentations. Many were stories told by triad members themselves—adult adoptees, birth parents, and adoptive parents—whose honesty disarmed me, whose palpable, but often wordless, uncomprehending suffering moved me to tears and whose humanity restored to me some of my own humanity, lost, I think, or maybe bartered away in exchange for success, by too many years spent as an "expert," a "professional" whose understanding remained detached from the "object" of his study. Their words struck deep into my vitals, went clear, as Yeats said, to "the deep heart's core." I found myself touched, and my own issues surfaced. As I reflected upon this experience I realized that these adoption issues—abandonment, loss, power, identity—were ultimate human issues, issues, again to quote Tillich, of "ultimate concern" for all of us.

And this impression, this indelible impression into the core of my being, ran deeper rather than being effaced when I returned from this conference to recommit to my clients and commit now unreservedly to "adoption," to making every effort to understand the adoption experience and to relieve that suffering through the origination of a therapy that could speak to adoptees in the language they spoke, a language of story, of meaning and beauty, of suffering and loss, of the spirit and hope. From that commitment ten years' work developed.

Elie Wiesel said that God made us because He loves a good story. He or She must really love adoption because it makes a great story. Adoption throws into sharp relief so many of our virtues and vices, our topmost successes and worst failures as human beings—abandonment, exposure, loss, separation, division, the soul and body split, sex, illegitimacy, orphanhood, power, society, institutions, money, mystery, men and women, conflict, deception, lies, self-love and possessiveness, search and reunion—so that they can be known not as abstract themes but in a living human face, the face in whose mystery and limitless expressiveness the existentialist Levinas saw as the source of transcendence and ethics.

I came back from the conference and the stories with a commitment to help, seeking understanding from the adoption literature. But with a few exceptions such as David Kirk's *Shared Fate* and Baran and Pannor's *The Adoption Triangle*, the professional literature disappointed me. In its characteristic academic representatives it seemed arid, abstract, aloof—and on the whole not very helpful. When I turned to the search and reunion literature, the testaments of personal experience, I once again encountered the emotion I had met at my first conference but it seemed almost "compulsive"—automatic, insatiable, and repetitive—in the telling of its tales. In these books the emotion never seemed to crystalize into understanding or a comprehensive vision of the meaning of adoption. The writer, the teller of the tale, reminded me quite often of the Ancient Mariner in Coleridge's famous poem who is condemned to repeat his tale again and again to anyone within hearing.

Mind and heart. Intellect and emotion. The field divided into two categories of expression just as, I guessed, adoptees themselves were sundered. I wondered if the literature and, through the literature, the profession itself was becoming isomorphic with the subject of its study and perhaps was even in some profound sense responsible for the adoptee's self-division. How could adoptees ever find healing and dignity if the chief theories in the field and the practices built upon those theories could never seem to integrate heart and head in their language and approach? If ideas have consequences, then maybe the failure to develop a truly integrated vision of the meaning of adoption produced the old closed adoption system, which then, through its policies, practices, and procedures, afflicted adoptees with the selfsame split.

I said I came back with a commitment to help that was afterwards disappointed by the professional literature and its alienation from search and autobiographical stories. As I became more deeply invested in adoption I also became more and more enraged at the mediocrity of the system—the corruption of the lukewarm that pervades it and the corrupting effect the self-regulation of the system exerts, particularly on adoption professionals.

Who really "does" adoption? Who are the professionals upon whose "expertise" clients must rely? From the point of view of the client, whose needs are so great, whose judgment is so disoriented, unbalanced by crisis, the average adoption worker is a sorry spectacle, almost totally incapable of doing her job, while from the perspective of years of adoption experience, she is an entirely understandable and predictable phenomena. In all likelihood she is young, from her middle twenties to late thirties, from a middle-class, religious, respectable, comfortable, and reasonably affluent background, where a premium was put on education. At some point, usually because of the influence of an unacknowledged sexism, she decided that she was too smart to be a secretary but not smart enough to be a lawyer, but she didn't want to teach, wanted professional status, a "safe" income, flexibility in employment, and an opportunity to do meaningful and altruistic work. So she became a social worker without any thought or intention of becoming an adoption social worker. In school, several courses may have touched on adoption but not a single course was exclusively devoted to the subject. These courses tend to be taught by career academics who may have done some "field work" but have spent most of their careers trying, on the basis of politics and the occasional article—comprised mostly of rehashing other articles—to scramble up the academic ladder. While in school or just after graduation, she married, and either as her first job or subsequent to several other "placements" she landed in adoption as an agency worker. Though married and settled, she is very likely to be childless herself, but intending to begin her family soon, usually as soon as her husband succeeds enough in his career to make her income disposable, and on the basis of her background, education, or lack thereof, and her current life situation, brimming as it is with dreams of an ideal marriage and family life, she bubbles with enthusiasm about her new job, "building families" and "finding new families for children."

Then, she smacks into reality. Adoption isn't about building families at all. It's about tearing them apart. It's about poverty, exploitation, incredible pain and need. It's about young women, not much younger than herself, sitting in her office, sobbing, choking back the tears, trying to figure out a way, any way to keep their baby. It's about stone-faced parents or grandparents blinking back the tears as they see their daughter or their son torn apart, to face a lifetime of grief and loneliness and arms and breasts that ache to hold and nurse a phantom infant. It's about birth fathers who want to do the right thing but don't know what it is, who are pilloried, connived against, locked out of the system. It's also about birth fathers who don't care, are callous and irresponsible. It's about infertile couples who have suffered almost every conceivable indignity a human being can bear without surrendering hope. They too have been torn apart by disappointments, anguish, by the phantom child that arms yearn to hold, by being prodded, poked, bent over, humiliated, legs up in the stirrups, ejaculating into jars, had their sex life drained of intimacy, joy, spontaneity, trust, and finally ardor. They've been dehumanized and now must go to meet a future that they didn't want, never intended, and rebel against in their murmuring wishes, even now. Or parents of older or special need adoptees, unable to meet or cope with their children's needs or unable to understand them, overwhelmed, isolated, filled with self-recriminations, or shocked, incredulous, floored—often because of their lack of preparation and the absence or expense of available services—by their children's deviance. And the child . . . the children, whether separated at birth or later from their parents, victims of society, impulse, the foster care system, abuse, neglect, with a wound inside that may never quite heal—even if the child never "remembers" anything—unattached, with anger boiling, primitive impulse and need spilling over, torturing a pet, sexually abusing an infant, smearing feces on the wall, lighting fires, running away, repeating the cycle of abuse and victimization with others as often as he can.

And, occasionally, it works a miracle. Both birth parents are involved, they do make the right decision, the adoption is open, the adoptive parents join their families and their hearts to the birth family, to the child's history and need to know and love and touch the people who gave him life and birth, and the child grows up, nurtured, honored, loved, cherished, knowing who his parents are, that is, the ones who picked him up when he fell down, cleaned up the bathroom when he threw up, rocked him to sleep at night, and checked in on him once or twice to make sure he was all right, who walked him to his class that first day, who took him to the doctor, swelled with pride at his accomplishments and comforted and sympathized when he failed, the ones who are always there and always will be, even while he also loves and cares for his birth parents. Even the unattached child finally gets the security and discipline and consistency and limits and love that he needs. Birth parents know themselves as lifegivers who did what they could. Adoptive parents know that it's love, not the law, that makes an adopted parent real as truth, beauty, and goodness. And a child grows up with both identities, birth and adoptive, joined to become the adult everyone dreamed and prayed he or she would be.

But it doesn't happen often. Not nearly often enough, and the social worker—now learning everything she can, now totally invested in her clients, putting herself out and on the line, doing the best she possibly can, taking cases home at night, dreaming about them, sweating and crying and fretting over them, trying to be fair, look ahead, make good judgments and decisions—discovers the system is against her. The system needs infants, healthy and white if possible, or with special needs or of color if necessary, to maintain itself. She discovers that the agency board, or the administrators, or the lawyer she works for don't really want her to do too much or look too hard at any of the human losses and issues. They just want her to expedite the process of getting affluent adoptive parents the commodity they want—for it becomes a commodity, despite the best efforts of the adoptive parents not to think of the baby, their baby, that way. Sensibilities are blunted. Feelings numbed. Moral instincts atrophied. Initiative petrified. The whole system is awash with greed, the need to perpetuate itself, with an ugly core disguised by layer after layer of self-righteousness, sentimentality, and hypocrisy. And, of course, a new building. The status quo prevails.

And the older workers, the colleagues and supervisors to whom she turns for support and advice? They're drained and burned out by the same system that is destroying her now. If they're still in adoption, they sold out years ago, don't want to know too much, urge her just to do her job and keep up with the paperwork. Move on.

In frustration, she hangs on. But not for long. She gets out, moves to another job or has a baby or, desperate to hang on to the job for whatever reasons, accepts a promotion into management where she begins to do unto others what has been done unto her. When she leaves or is promoted, ethics often vanish. The best and the brightest get out quick or, if they're too vocal, are fired. The worst amass power and seniority. They lack all conviction and are passionately intense only about time sheets.

But what if, despite all this, she does hang on, confirmed rather than deterred in her commitment by the near hopelessness and despair of the situation? What if she covets wisdom, wants to improve her knowledge base? In the literature she will meet the same division I did, the same split between head and heart, between disembodied abstractions that don't really apply to any one living individual and the intimate personal confessional stories of triad members whose narcissism and exhibitionism she may find mildly repellant. And if she desires to improve her clinical skills through continuing education? She will find herself in expensive tutelage to an adoption elite comprised mainly of one-trick ponies, with one big idea, one big technique, or one big story to tell that is endlessly repeated, in stellar performances, in the trainings and workshops and annual conference circuit. Many presenters try to privilege their views through their status as triad members (though it is hard to understand why an adoptee, for example, could be assumed to be a reliable interpreter of the birth parents or adoptive parent decision of which she herself, depending on her view, is either the victim or beneficiary, it is not at all hard to understand why birth and adoptive parents and adoption professionals would flock to hear an adult adoptee speak in hopes of receiving through this symbolic substitute of their own child, or the children they place, relief and forgiveness for their own ambivalence and guilt) but as any good detective knows, eyewitnesses to any event are notoriously unreliable. To piece together the motive, the meaning, and the "what" of "what really happened" requires the artistry of interpretation, and this is a gift honed by study and reflection. As a student of the field and onetime one-trick pony myself, I don't know whether to laugh or cry, to sound the alarm, or just die of shame. The current state of the field, in terms of its most influential texts and most popular speakers, with a few ameliorating and one or two stellar exceptions, is disgraceful. Ethical considerations rarely prompt reflection; almost never compel decisions.

This scenario may sound like an exaggeration or exception. It's not. It happens every day, all across the country, to the consternation and detriment of the clients adoption is supposed to serve.

Can this be changed? Can real, meaningful adoption reform succeed? How?

One way of describing what my work in adoption has been is a collaboration with a few other colleagues in the genesis of a new myth, or mythos of adoption. Because the word "myth" is bandied about so often today and used in such a variety of ways, many of which are pejorative, let me define what I mean by the word. A myth is a story addressed to the whole person, body, mind, spirit, senses, heart, and soul: a statement that through symbols, narrative, and meanings, some of which can be quite abstract; (1) enunciates a view of the meaning and the mysteries of life; (2) espouses an ethic, that is, the principles of right actions; and (3) present inner psychological and spiritual realities and dynamics. Thus every true mythology articulates a philosophy or metaphysics, an ethics, and a psychology. A vision that is genuinely "mythic" in scope and intent incorporates all three dimensions.

A myth provides a form in light of which and in terms of which we interpret our experience—make meaning or sense of it. The shared meanings—norms, customs, observances, ideals, laws, practices, rituals, etc.—created by these conscious interpretative acts make up culture. To the degree that a myth reflects or is open to the transcendentals or the "spiritual," its effects will be positive; it predisposes thought, affect, and behavior towards the Good. According to this standard not all cultures are equal or at least not equal to themselves, that is, successful in the job of maximizing their own potential for goodness. There's always room for growth and improvement. By this standard some specific cultural practices deserve condemnation as bad or even evil.

Transform the myth, transform the culture. Poets, as Shelley said, really are the unacknowledged legislators of humankind, the voice and conscience of the tribe. The mythmakers. A family therapist, working with a family culture, must be a kind of poet to initiate change in the family. By a similar dynamic, a writer or researcher addressing a particular field can, if her writing is persuasive, illuminating, and transforming enough, speed transformation.

Much of the important work done in adoption during the last two decades can be understood in terms of this formulation of a new myth. My hope is this: change the adoption myth, change the adoption culture. Change adoption culture, change adoption policy, procedures and practice. Change practice, change lives for the better.

And now this author enters with a cogent, comprehensive, and timely new contribution to ethics.

Ethics: the determination of right action. The principles of right conduct. What is right action in adoption? What is the right relationship between the adoption professional and the various clients she serves? What is the right thing to do in a crisis situation? What is right in law and practice, in professional codes of conduct? What is right in infant and special needs adoptions? When conflict arises, who should decide and on what basis? What is right for a client to expect from a social worker? These are some of the questions the author considers and answers.

She can tell a good story, starts out with case examples that are chilling in their awfulness—their tragedy that could have, should have, been averted. She ranges widely across opinions and theory, demonstrating a sophisticated grasp of the best available and most philosophically complex classical and modern ethical theories together with an appreciative familiarity with what tops the best seller list. She pleads for integrity, for truth, honesty, and justice and outlines concretely how such abstract notions can be translated into specific reforms and practices. She softens her most polemical points with a human touch and sensitivity, and yet they retain verve and propulsion. Her abstractions are couched in human terms and are made on human grounds. She speaks with a logician's clarity, a prophet's authority, and a philosopher's subtlety and vision. Most critically—and unusually—she understands adoption and adoption practice.

I've known Dr. Babb slightly for the last five years, exchanging an infrequent letter and meeting on two occasions, but I'm much more familiar with her writings, her political activism (which includes a term as president of the American Adoption Congress), her dedication to the cause of truth and honesty in adoption, her work as a professional in the field and as an adoption agency director. She is also an adoptive mother—not that this last fact automatically substantiates her views, but it does yield the strength that comes from being solidly rooted in the earth of personal experience. In her prolific writings, her activism, her conscientious professional work, in her family life, and in her devout religious faith, Dr. Babb exemplifies the integrity that she has made the heartbeat of her work. Although it may seem too trite a phrase, I am in awe of her—astonished at her energy and competence, admiring of the strength of her convictions and style, and attuned with her, I think, to the same voices, the many voices of the adoption experience, voices of pain, hurt, trust, and love, voices that cry out for understanding, help, hope, and justice.

Those voices, which haunt the field, find a tribune here, a spokeswoman, a writer, an intellectual and professional worthy of them. The ideas presented here have weight and consequence. Their integrity has impact. They contribute to a new myth. Without a new myth, the tragedies in adoption will continue and multiply while the occasional "happy ending" proves nothing so much as the power of love to sometimes conquer in spite of everything.

—Randolph Severson

Acknowledgments

I am deeply indebted to a number of professionals, philosophers, and experts in adoption whose contributions to this book as a work in progress were invaluable. Dr. Leroy Cordrey advised me throughout the process of researching and writing my doctoral dissertation on ethics in American adoption. On several occasions Brent Neiser sent me research on professional certification and talked with me about certification of adoption professionals. Also during the course of my doctoral research, the suggestions I received from Hope Marindin, director of the National Council for Single Adoptive Parents, and from Dixie Davis, director of the Adoption Exchange Association, were priceless.

Victor Groza helped me distill hundreds of pages of doctoral research into a cogent book chapter on adoption ethics, coedited by Karen Rosenberg, which later served me as I wrote this book.

Social worker, philosopher, author, and adoptive mother Margaret Rhodes can only be described as the midwife of this book, having witnessed its gestation and birth and advised me in all matters philosophical. Randolph Severson and James Gritter, brilliant men with hearts of gold, also advised me in philosophical and practice matters and answered my countless questions, taking time from their busy schedules to help.

I'm indebted to Lois Melina for her advice and for putting me in touch with Madelyn Freundlich of the Evan B. Donaldson Adoption Institute and to Madelyn for involving me in the Institute's work on adoption ethics. I extend a note of gratitude to the members of the Institute's ethics committee, all of them doing the trailblazing work of defining what ethical adoption practice means. Likewise, I'm grateful to Adoptive Families of America's Education and Policy council for allowing me to eavesdrop on a few of their meetings, and to Linda Lynch, editor of *Adoptive Families Magazine*, for trusting me to explain adoption ethics through the pages of the magazine. Writing about adoption ethics in 2,000 words or less did much to clarify my thinking and hone my communication skills.

Betty Jean Lifton and Annette Baran reviewed the manuscript and made suggestions. Their mentoring over the years and their examples have taught me so much about what ethics is about. Likewise, Bastard Nation activists Shea Grimm, Alfia Wallace, and Marley Greiner advised me on ethical issues specific to adoptees of all ages and made suggestions that became part of the book. College president and late-discovery adoptee G. William Troxler contributed by describing in nearly poetic beauty what it means to have one's identity information torn and hidden from oneself by people who take access to their own records for granted.

Former presidents of Concerned United Birthparents Janet Fenton and Carole Anderson advised me in the early stages of my research. Poet, birth mother, activist, and friend, Mary Anne Cohen read the manuscript, offered suggestions, and through her fierce loyalty to what is right in the face of unbelievable betrayal by so-called friends taught me something about honor.

Theologian John W. "Jack" Sweeley's love of research, all things biblical, and of doing the right thing was a support during the final months of copy editing and manuscript revisions. Jeanette Wiedemeier Bower, of the North American Council on Adoptable Children, and Tim O'Hanlon, my favorite bureaucrat, are national treasures in assisting children with special needs, the parents who adopt them, and the administrators and front-line social workers who are supposed to serve them. Without their mentoring in the field of special needs adoption I'd still be a babe in the woods.

While I decry the wrongness of the many state agency administrators, social workers, and state's attorneys whose wrong decisions in special needs adoption assistance I've helped appeal and overturn, I am nevertheless grateful for the tutelage wrangling with them has provided. Right-headedness is easier to discern when one is confronted with such blatant wrong-headedness.

I cannot adequately express my gratitude to Rita Laws and Nancy Diven, whose understanding of right and wrong and whose deeply held desires for justice in biblical proportions helped me to believe that I was in very good company, indeed.

Through her acceptance of the manuscript and her skillful editing, Greenwood Publishing Group editor Lynn Taylor breathed life into what was formless and void.

Finally, my life has been changed by the love of Anna Katharina Fey, my Omi ("little grandmother"), who understood my love of children and particularly my desire to adopt children who needed parents. Years ago she told me that many children bring many blessings, and she was right. I never knew my Omi to express hatred or mean-spiritedness toward another human being. In spite of experiencing years of hardship, widowhood, and want in Nazi Germany, she came through with an indomitable spirit, teaching me by rare example that justice is meaningless unless we can love, forgive, and have mercy upon our enemies.

Introduction

The research on ethics in adoption shows that adoption, more than any other human service, is rife with conflict of interest. Adoption agency social workers and attorneys routinely represent both the birth and adoptive families party to the same adoption. Agencies whose very existence is based on fees paid for consummated adoptions claim to offer unbiased "crisis pregnancy" counseling to expectant mothers.

Professionals have yet to develop uniform ethical standards in adoption or to make meaningful attempts to monitor their own professional behavior. Instead, our own clients and former clients have had to impose an ethic of honesty and disclosure onto the profession from the outside. The development of open adoption, the open adoption records movement, and the tort of wrongful adoption are three examples of what happened when birth and adoptive parents and adoptees did what we said we wanted them to do all along—become self-determined.

The research also shows that professionals, especially in social work, the profession most likely to be involved in adoption, have been unable to translate ethical principles into behavior. This failure, I believe, is at the root of many of the problems with adoption services in the United States. this book addresses not only the historical problem of unethical behavior among professionals in adoption service delivery but also examines current practices, existing standards, and the problems we still have in adoption practice—and suggests solutions.

Professionals cannot hope to serve adoption clients, nor can their clients hope to be well-served, until they establish discrete standards for service to *each corner* of the adoption "triad"—birth parents, adoptive parents, and adoptees. Our "one size fits all" approach to adoption standards has not worked, and the outcry has spawned a national debate about what constitutes ethical adoption practice and how we can do the right thing in adoption. To that end, I hope this book can advance discussion and research into adoption ethics so that future generations of American children do not have to grow up in an adult-centered adoption system governed by a hodge-podge of laws and ethical values so ill defined or misunderstood that they are nearly useless to the people most personally affected by them.

Part I

Foundations

Chapter 1

Living the Experience

When Charles and Joanie Hall's ninth foster child left their home for an adoptive family, the couple found their sorrow stronger and their adjustment to having fewer children more difficult than it had been for them before. Their two daughters, six and five, wept inconsolably over the loss of their foster brother and asked why their parents had sent him away.

Charles and Joanie asked their social worker, Anita Davies, to enroll them in the state's foster-adopt program and completed adoptive parent training and an adoption home study process. They asked Anita to forward their adoption study to the state office and to keep her eye open for children who might fit into their family.

The Halls had parented infants, toddlers, and teenagers, including children who had been physically or sexually abused. Their experience with a former foster child who acted out sexually and their concern for their young daughters led them to tell Anita that they could not accept a child with a known history of sexual abuse or sexual acting out. Perhaps when their daughters were older, they said, they could consider adopting such a child.

Anita Davies lent the Halls some photolisting books, notebooks containing photographs and descriptions of children waiting to be adopted. The Halls went home with their state's current photolistings and a regional photolisting book, listing adoptable children from a number of states.

That night, Charles and Joanie sat up in bed and pored through hundreds of photographs and descriptions of waiting children. The number of adoptable children in their region seemed overwhelming. After an hour of going through the books, Joanie had pulled out the listings of over thirty children or sibling groups, telling Charles, "They all look like Halls to me!"

As Joanie's excitement grew, Charles became quiet. He set aside his stack of listings, turned off his bedside lamp, and turned away from his wife. Joanie nudged her husband, "Look at this one, honey!"

"I don't want to look at one more page!" Charles snapped. Taken aback, Joanie put the books away and cuddled with her husband, asking him what was wrong. "There are just so many kids who need parents! How am I supposed to pick just one or two? How can I play God like that with children's lives, when so many need a mom and a dad?" Joanie could hear the anguish in her husband's voice. "Honey," she said, "we can't do this by ourselves. We have Anita, and we have God. Let's pray for God to send us just the right kids." In the dark, they prayed for God's guidance and wisdom and fell asleep peacefully, each of them trying to imagine what sort of child would come their way.

Joanie returned the books to Anita at the Department of Human Services (DHS), explaining with a laugh that she and Charles had been overwhelmed and would probably borrow the books again in a few weeks. She asked the social worker to call if any new photolistings came in of children who made Anita think of them.

A few weeks later, Anita called. "Joanie? You have got to see this photolisting that just came in with the regional updates! I'm looking at two little angel-faced boys who have 'Hall' written all over them!"

Joanie's heart soared. "When can we see them?" she asked. Joanie agreed to pick up the photolisting at the front desk and grabbed her car keys. "Oh, Lord, let these be the ones!" she prayed.

At DHS, Joanie tore open the envelope marked with her name. The faces of two curly-headed boys smiled out at her from the photolisting. "Eric, 7, and his brother Anthony, 6, are active and energetic boys. Eric loves to read and likes animals. Anthony, a real live wire, likes cars and wants to be a cowboy when he grows up. The children have lived with the same foster parents for three years and have a history of abuse. They need a patient and understanding two-parent family." The listing gave the name and telephone number of Eric and Anthony's social worker several states away.

All the way home, Joanie's heart sang. "The minute I saw those boys," she would later say, "I knew they were my sons!" From home she excitedly called Charles at work, then called several of her closest friends to tell them about Eric and Anthony. When her daughters came home from school, Joanie showed them the photo of the boys and was thrilled to hear them ask, "When can we go and get them, Mommy?"

Later that night, Charles agreed that they were "fine-looking boys" and asked Joanie to have Anita Davies call for more information about them. Joanie did, and a few days later heard from Anita that Eric and Anthony's social worker had requested their home study.

Soon the Halls received a thick envelope containing more photographs of Eric and Anthony and their social and medical histories. The boys had been raised by a single mother whose father had beaten her severely while she was pregnant with the younger child, Anthony. There was a history of alcoholism and criminality on both sides of the family. Eric's arm had been broken by his mother, and a boyfriend had threatened to cut Anthony's penis off. The information made Charles and Joanie sad and angry. "What kind of people would treat little kids that way?" Charles stormed. That these boys could still smile after all they'd been through made the Halls all the more eager to bring them home.

Their social worker expressed some concerns, though. "These boys have had some severe abuse," she said, "and I think Anthony sounds hyperactive. I'm concerned about their ability to attach and I think we should ask more questions." Joanie followed Anita's advice and wrote the boys' social worker a long letter, asking about specific abuse, whether either boy had ever been sexually abused or had acted out sexually, if either boy set fires, and how they treated other children and small animals. The Halls knew the signs of attachment disorder (Reactive Attachment Disorder of Childhood) and wanted to have all the information they could get about Eric and Anthony.

Within a week, they received not only a written response from the social worker, but from Eric and Anthony's foster mother as well. Both women wrote about the boys in glowing terms and reassured the Halls that the boys had no known history of sexual abuse or sexual acting out. The foster mother, whom Eric and Anthony called "Nana," said that she and her husband would have adopted the boys themselves if they weren't already in their fifties. The letters were so reassuring that Charles and Joanie decided that day to adopt Eric and Anthony. Within weeks the Halls were on an airplane to meet their new sons.

The boys' social worker, Carmel Jones, arranged for six days of visits between the foster parents and the boys, beginning with a two-hour meeting the first day and ending with an overnight visit and a trip back home. When Joanie and Charles met Eric and Anthony at Carmel's office, the boys nearly flew into their outstretched arms, crying, "Mama! Daddy!" Charles laughed and said he guessed there would be no worrying about what the boys would call them while they got to know one another.

The boys seemed excited and a bit unruly at the foster home, where the Halls met "Nana" and "Papa" Jefferson, Eric and Anthony's foster parents. "They're so excited!" chuckled Mrs. Jefferson, "They can't sit still for nothin'!" As the foster and adoptive parents sat down for dinner, Eric and Anthony darted in and out of the dining room, snatching food off their plates and running outside with it. Anthony ran up to Joanie with a piece of fried chicken in each hand, planted a greasy kiss on her cheek, and cried, "I'm glad you're my mom!" before running outside again. Later, during their drive to the motel in their rental car, the Halls discussed the boys' undisciplined behavior, concluding that the Jeffersons had acted more like doting grandparents than parents. They agreed they had their work cut out for them but were encouraged that the boys were so open and affectionate.

Over the coming days, Joanie and Charles saw more and more of Eric and Anthony, spending time sightseeing and shopping. Both boys ate voraciously and Anthony seemed to run everywhere rather than walk. One day during a shopping trip, the couple was horrified to watch helplessly as Anthony ran into traffic ahead of them, narrowly missed by an oncoming car. The shaken driver yelled out the window to them, "Can't you people control your kid?!" Charles realized with a start that Anthony seemed to control them, rather than the other way around.

Even so, the Halls were pleased with the boys. They called both social workers and told them they felt the placement was right and they were ready to take the boys home. Carmel arranged for a parting ceremony at the local Department of Human Services the day the Halls were to fly home. There, for the first time, Joanie and Charles met Eric and Anthony's teachers and day care providers. They had asked to meet them before, but Carmel had said there simply hadn't been time to arrange a meeting.

Eric and Anthony said tearful good-byes to Nana and Papa Jefferson and their teachers and friends, then pressed tearstained faces to the windows of the Hall's rental car as their new dad drove out of the only town they had ever known.

At home, the introduction of Eric and Anthony to Amanda and April, the Halls' daughters, went well. The children happily played together and settled into what the social worker called a "honeymoon" period. At the end of a week, Anita Davies visited the Hall home and asked the new adoptive parents how things had been going. Charles and Joanie exchanged looks and answered, "The honeymoon's over!" Eric, it seemed, was doing well. He was compliant, played well with the girls, and seemed comfortable with his new parents. His only problem was that he ate too much and a few times vomited at the table, but judging from his eating habits in the foster home, the Halls concluded that their retraining would take time.

Anthony, on the other hand, was more than a handful. He had regressed in his toileting and was soiling and wetting his pants several times a day. Anita told them this was to be expected and that it would probably soon pass. She arranged another postplacement visit in six weeks, and told the Halls that if they had any problems, they should call her any time. Weeks passed and the problems with Anthony continued. He soiled and wet his pants no matter what rewards or punishments the Halls tried. They caught him hitting the family's dog and pinching their younger daughter, April. Neighborhood children complained that Anthony was "mean and stinky" and refused to play with him. Eric continued to do well, and Charles and Joanie began to wonder how two brothers raised in the same circumstances could be so different. They knew they could parent Eric, but worried about raising Anthony.

At Anita's next visit the couple expressed their concerns and frustrations with the social worker. They had caught Eric and Anthony stealing at school, but Eric had seemed remorseful. Anthony had been picking and eating the paint from the walls, gouging the insides of his arms with his fingernails, and urinating in the corners and wastebaskets until their whole house, Charles said, smelled like a urinal.

Their social worker told them that Anthony's behavior indicated more serious abuse than had been divulged to them and said she would call Carmel Jones and ask for more information. She told them that Anthony's behavior was consistent with a diagnosis of attachment disorder and bluntly asked them if they wanted to disrupt the placement.

Shocked, Joanie and Charles turned on their social worker. "We never said we wanted to send them back! We're just needing some support, not this kind of a solution." Anita apologized and soon ended the visit. A few days later, the Halls asked Anita Davies's supervisor to assign a more understanding social worker to them who could support them in a difficult placement.

Months passed and Joanie and Charles found themselves in a seemingly endless pattern of good kid–bad kid behavior with Eric and Anthony. Anthony seemed to be the designated "bad kid," while Eric looked on with dismay. Every now and then Charles or Joanie would catch Eric stealing, lying, or surreptitiously kicking one of their girls under the table. But he seemed to do fine at school, and their biggest concern continued to be Anthony. They began to take the whole family to therapy at the suggestion of their new social worker, Mrs. Cox. It helped Joanie and Charles to vent their frustrations, but Anthony did not improve.

A week or two of calm would pass, and then one boy or the other would precipitate another crisis. Eric broke their dog's leg "on accident," he said.

Amanda's tearful report was that she had seen Eric maliciously kicking the dog while the dog yelped in pain. Joanie dismissed Amanda's story when faced with Eric's wide-eyed, sorrowful expression and heartfelt apologies. He was usually so good that she couldn't believe he would purposely hurt the dog.

After six months, an exhausted Charles and Joanie hospitalized Anthony. The therapists at the hospital said he was hyperactive and prescribed medication. They suggested that Charles and Joanie were failing at home, since the boys had lived with them for nine months and no noticeable improvement had occurred in Anthony.

Eric's behavior deteriorated with Anthony's hospitalization. He became angry and belligerent. The Halls felt that hospitalizing Anthony had been a mistake, arousing all of Eric's feelings of abandonment and insecurity. They were relieved when Anthony was released and decided to legalize the adoption in court, in the hopes that this would reassure the boys that the Halls were their "forever family."

Some three weeks after the adoption was finalized, Joanie received a phone call from a neighbor. "Joanie," she said sharply, "you'd better come down here and get your boys." Joanie rushed down the street and into her neighbor's yard to see Anthony standing on top of a child's slide, pants around his ankles, urinating down the slide. Eric stood nearby, his pants around his knees, pointing at his penis and yelling, "Eat my dick! Eat my cock!" as the neighbor's children huddled around their mother. Red-faced with shame and anger, Joanie yanked the boys' pants around their waists and marched them home.

That night, Joanie dissolved into tears while describing the scene to Charles. "Honey, we have got to get them some real help," she sobbed. The Halls agreed to find expert help for adopted children in the next few weeks. They talked for hours about their hopes and dreams for their new sons and about how to help Amanda and April cope with the chaos the little boys generated.

As Charles showered before bed, Joanie went to check on the children before turning in. When she opened her daughter Amanda's bedroom door, she was confronted with a sight she would never forget. In the dim light of Amanda's Barbie night-light, Joanie saw Eric poised above Amanda's prone form, pumping rhythmically back and forth, and grunting under his breath, "Take that, you bitch, take that, you whore," while Amanda lay beneath him, wide-eyed with terror. Joanie's gasp startled Eric, who leaped out of Amanda's bed and cowered in a corner. Crying, "Oh, my God! Oh, my God!" Joanie pulled Amanda by the wrist into the master bedroom, bumping into an alarmed Charles.

"What is going on?!" Charles asked. "Charles, you go and get Eric right now and you take him to his room," Joanie cried, "because if I have to touch him I swear to God I'll kill him!" Joanie bundled Amanda into their bed and then brought a sleepy April into their room also.

Two days later, the adoptive parents drove Eric and Anthony to a children's psychiatric hospital several hours away, the closest program they could find experienced in treating foster and adopted children. They learned from their daughter Amanda that Eric had repeatedly molested her, sticking pencils, crayons, and his fingers into her anus and vagina and attempting anal and vaginal intercourse. Months afterward, the Halls learned from neighbors and close family friends that Eric had similarly molested other children.

Ten months later, the treatment team at the hospital recommended against returning Eric and Anthony to the Halls, saying that the boys should be placed separately in therapeutic foster homes without younger children. The Halls dissolved their adoption of Eric and Anthony, wondering why they had failed with these two little boys when they had succeeded with so many foster children. They felt sick at heart, and Joanie cried until she felt her heart would literally break.

"We've just become one more set of parents who have let these little kids down," Charles told their social worker, "but we have to protect our girls, too. We will never foster or adopt again. We must have been crazy or stupid, or both."

A few months after the adoption failed, Joanie received a long-distance telephone call from Eric and Anthony's home state. A woman whose voice wasn't familiar introduced herself as Alma Rankin, the day care director from Happy Days Preschool, "where the boys went before they were transferred to Small World Day Care." Confused, Joanie asked if Alma had been at the farewell ceremony, thinking that in the emotion of the moment she might have overlooked the day care director.

"Oh, no, honey, you didn't meet me at DHS," Alma replied. "You didn't meet me at all. They didn't even tell me about the adoption 'til I ran into the foster mother at the store one day and asked how the boys were. She told me they had moved out of state with you, and gave me your phone number. I can't imagine why those boys spent three years here, and only four months at Small World, and they wouldn't even let me say good-bye to them." Puzzled, Joanie asked Alma Rankin why Eric and Anthony had been transferred from Alma's preschool to Small World.

"Well, hon, I hated to do it, because I really loved those little boys. Why I'm the one that found Eric with his arm broken when his mama put him outside because of his screaming. But those boys were a danger to our other children, we just couldn't have them acting like they did and keep the day care safe. I had to call Miz Jones and ask her to get them into another day care."

Gripping the phone, Joanie asked what reason Alma had given to Carmel Jones for dismissing the boys from Happy Days Preschool. "Anthony was out of control, tore up the whole day care more than once," Alma Rankin replied. "He would pee on the walls, other kids, and himself and once even stuck his head in the commode and it seemed he was trying to drown himself. But Eric, he was the one that put icing on the cake. The poor little guy kept dropping his drawers and trying to have sex with the little girls, and sometimes the boys. He would imitate the sex act 'til we all knew someone had really showed him how to do it, and had done it to him, and he would stick things up his bottom and stick things up the girls, too. We just had to let him go. It about broke my heart."

Joanie's mind reeled with the impact of this information. She shook her head as if to shake some sense into it. "Mrs. Rankin, I just have to ask you again, did you tell all these things to Miss Jones, Carmel Jones, Eric and Anthony's social worker?"

"Oh, yes, sure I did. As a matter of fact, I had to put it in a written report on our day care's stationery before DHS would release me from the day care contract on the boys. I even gave a copy to Mrs. Jefferson, the boys' foster mother and told her all about it the day we moved the boys. Didn't they tell you?"

* * *

The adult daughter of an abusive, alcoholic father, Kathy Tucker ended her first marriage after four years, a broken jaw, and two children. Fearing her husband's violence, Kathy left him and established a new life in another state, vowing to regain custody of her two little girls.

While working at a grocery store in her new community, Kathy met and fell in love with a clerk who seemed to be all that her ex-husband was not. Carl was attentive, kind, and sympathetic about her longing for her daughters. He told a sad story about how his first and second wives had taken his children from him, too. The couple grew closer and eventually moved into an apartment together.

Within a few months, Kathy was pregnant with Carl's child. As her body changed, so did their relationship. Carl, once considerate and caring, became moody, irritable, and verbally abusive. He became jealous and controlling, and demanded that Kathy quit her job. Finally, one night after several hours of drinking, Carl hit Kathy and broke her nose. Five months pregnant, broke, and homeless, Kathy moved into a girlfriend's house and asked herself what she could do for the child she was carrying. She had no home, no money, no transportation, and, she felt, no future.

Kathy decided to give her baby up for adoption to a couple she would choose, in a type of placement called open adoption. She would choose and meet the adoptive parents of her baby and establish an ongoing relationship with them.

Some months later, having chosen a couple to adopt her baby on the basis of a personal ad, Kathy was ready to deliver. The adoptive parents, who lived several states away, sent Kathy to an attorney in her community and arranged to have a grief counselor work with her after the adoption. They agreed to stay in contact with Kathy by telephone and letter, and to let her come and visit them and her child once or twice a year.

By Cesarean-section, Kathy delivered a healthy baby boy into the waiting arms of Robin and Dan, the adoptive parents. Robin and Dan stayed at the hospital and cared for the baby while Kathy recuperated from the surgery. They showered Kathy with gifts, including a lacy gown and robe with matching slippers, gourmet chocolates, and a dozen roses. "You guys are the best friends I could have hoped for," Kathy told Robin, "and the best parents I could have found for my baby."

Five days later, Kathy went home with empty arms after signing a consent to adoption in front of a judge who came to her hospital room and asked her to sign the papers. The attorney the adoptive parents had arranged for Kathy wasn't able to appear at the hospital room "hearing," but, anxious to be released from the hospital, Kathy signed the papers before the grandfatherly judge and a beaming Robin and Dan. After posing for photos, Kathy left the hospital with her friend, and Dan and Robin took the baby, whom they had named Parker, to the motel room they had rented while waiting for completion of the paperwork that would allow them to leave the state with their new son.

Like many mothers who plan adoption for their unborn children, Kathy was unprepared for the grief she felt upon surrendering her little boy. The medications she took in the hospital after her Cesarean-section had taken the edge off of her physical and emotional pain. Watching Robin and Dan, the adoptive parents who had waited so long to have a baby and would never have children of their own, made Kathy feel proud that she could give such a gift to people who so clearly cared not only for her baby, but for her as well. The generosity and kindness of the couple had overwhelmed Kathy, who had never been so pampered. Kathy felt good that she would be able to stay in touch with her baby and know that he was healthy, loved, and doing well in Robin and Dan's home.

Without having had preparatory counseling, however, Kathy was ill-informed about the impact giving up her baby would have on her. Having already experienced the hurt of parenting her little girls as a noncustodial parent, Kathy thought that she would be prepared to give up her little boy. But the grief of giving up another child, especially her first-born son, was overwhelming. When Robin and Dan called on Kathy to see how she was doing, she dissolved into sobs. Torn between their love for their new baby and compassion for Kathy, Robin and Dan contacted an adoption counselor experienced with open adoptions and urged Kathy to call the counseling center.

Kathy finally called the agency after another day, asking tearfully for Marilyn, the counselor recommended by Robin and Dan. Marilyn's first question, "How are you doing?" elicited muffled sobs. For a few moments, all Marilyn could hear on the other end of the telephone line was Kathy's crying. Trying another approach, Marilyn asked, "What can I do to help? What is it you want?" Kathy's answer: "I want my baby back!"

Marilyn asked Kathy to think about her original reasons for relinquishing her son, and how circumstances had changed. Kathy said she was simply unprepared to lose another child and wanted to make a new start in life. "This baby gives me every reason to not make the same mistakes I've made before. I know I can be a good mom!" Kathy insisted. Marilyn suggested that Kathy call the adoptive parents and attorney and tell them that she had changed her mind about the adoption, making herself available to Kathy, Robin, and Dan should they need therapeutic support during the process of returning the child.

Edward Thompson, the attorney who had been retained for Kathy by the adoptive parents, had reassured her that she could change her mind and reclaim the child any time within a 30-day revocation period. What he hadn't told Kathy was that the state's 30-day statute of revocation would pit her against the adoptive parents, forcing Kathy to prove her fitness as a mother and that her mothering would be in the child's "best interests." In spite of this daunting news shared by the adoption counselor, Kathy called Robin and Dan and asked to have her baby back.

Robin and Dan were stunned. An adoption that had seemed so idyllic was crumbling around them. Robin had even breast-fed Parker by using a supplemental feeder especially designed for adoptive nursing. A bottle of formula hung suspended between Robin's breasts, while tiny tubes attached to the bottle and taped to her nipples allowed the baby to suckle and receive formula from Robin's otherwise empty breasts. Robin had slept with, rocked, and nursed Parker for five days, held him immediately after birth, and become desperately attached to the baby, only to have him now torn out of her arms. With broken hearts, Robin and Dan packed Parker's belongings and handed the baby back to Kathy a few hours after her phone call.

After Kathy left with the baby, the couple called Edward Thompson, the attorney, and told him that they would be returning to their own state after this shattering experience. Thompson told the couple that they could recover the baby since the state's adoption laws required birth parents reclaiming their surrendered children within thirty days to prove that such a reclamation was in the child's best interests. Kathy would have to prove she was a more fit parent than Robin and Dan, he said. Robin and Dan would have an excellent chance of winning in a contested adoption, because they could show that Parker's mother was unfit. What kind of a mother would give her own baby away, after all? What kind of a mother would leave her children with an abusive husband? Thompson told the couple to get the baby back and reassured them that they would win any contest over the child.

Kathy took little Parker home and renamed her child, calling him "William" after her paternal grandfather. In spite of the medication she had taken to reduce her breast milk, Kathy was still producing it. Baby William eagerly swallowed the mother's milk that Kathy offered from her own breasts. Kathy's tears flowed as she held her six-day-old son, crying, "I will never let you go again, my baby, I'll *never* let you go."

Eight hours after bringing William home, at almost midnight, a sharp knock was heard at the door. Kathy got up with the sleeping baby in her arms to face the county sheriff and a police officer who demanded to have the baby back and stated that they had a court order from the judge who had taken Kathy's consent to the adoption. Kathy was to return the baby to Robin and Dan and appear at a hearing the next morning to prove her fitness to raise her own child. Though they did not produce the court order, the sheriff took the baby while the assisting officer restrained Kathy. Kathy would not see her baby boy again.

After a sleepless night, Kathy frantically called her attorney, Edward Thompson, early the next morning. "They came and took my baby out of my arms!" she sobbed, "I have to get him back! You have to help me get him back!" Thompson curtly told Kathy that she had never been his client, and hung up the telephone. When she and a friend went to court that morning to reclaim baby William, Kathy was shocked to see Edward Thompson representing the adoptive couple. Kathy stood alone, having been abandoned by the adoptive parents who promised her ongoing contact with her baby in an open adoption, by the attorney who had been so solicitous and considerate during the last weeks of her pregnancy, and by the judge who had seemed so kindly to her on the day of her surrender. As soon as Kathy requested services from the professionals who had claimed to have her best interests at heart, she found herself alone.

Kathy was unable to reclaim her child. The court found that married, educated, highly salaried Dan and Robin would be better parents to the baby than Kathy, an unemployed, single parent. Kathy's history of poor choices in partners, first with her husband and then with Carl, proved to the court that Kathy would likewise be likely to make poor choices for her baby boy. Dan and Robin even used the stories Kathy had told them about her childhood abuse to prove that Kathy would be highly unlikely to be a good parent to Parker. After much heart searching, in fact, Dan and Robin had concluded that giving Parker back to Kathy could never be in his best interests. They decided they were the best possible parents for Parker. The court agreed, giving Dan and Robin custody of the baby and allowing them to return to their home state several thousand miles away to complete the adoption. Dan and Robin, formerly so concerned and devoted to Kathy, cut off all communications with the mother who had been promised regular contact, photographs, and visits with her child.

Six months after her child was adopted, Kathy received a bill for "services rendered in the adoption of Baby Boy Tucker" from Edward Thompson, the very attorney who claimed that she had never been his client.

* * *

Susan and Alan Miller were veteran special needs adoptive parents, having adopted three children with special needs in addition to parenting two children born to them. Over their 15-year foster- and adoptive-parenting career, Susan had led several foster- and adoptive-parent support groups as a volunteer and often helped other adoptive parents apply for adoption assistance payments (AAP) and medical assistance for their disabled adopted children.

When the adoption agency that had placed the Millers' third child in the family called for help with a child needing emergency placement, Susan's heart soared. For several weeks beforehand she and Alan had been talking about adopting again. Their oldest children were driving and one was preparing to graduate from high school. When Alan heard that their agency had called, he said, "This is no coincidence, Susy—this kid is meant for us." The agency, with offices in the Millers' home state and a neighboring state, needed a home for a four-year-old legal resident alien Vietnamese girl whose first adoption had failed in the neighboring state.

A social worker, Diana Reese, told Susan and Alan that the child's history included several breaks in attachment, and that she had lived for two years in a Vietnamese orphanage. She also had cerebral palsy, and the combination of her emotional and physical needs had exhausted her original adoptive parents, who had called the agency and asked for the child's removal four months after her placement. The little girl's name was Emma. Diana Reese described Emma as a "happy, determined, and challenged kid who needs a lot of stability and support."

When Alan and Susan told their social worker that they would accept Emma, they felt prepared, confident, and sure that they would be able to successfully advocate for Emma within the bureacracies established for the support, education, and service of children like her. The Millers also knew that they would need adoption and medical assistance in order to support Emma's special needs. Their state statutes specifically provided state-paid adoption assistance payments, monthly cash support payments, and medical assistance to children in private agency custody whose special needs made them difficult to place in adoptive families. Susan had advocated for her own children and those of scores of other adoptive couples successfully in winning AAP, and felt confident that they could help Emma because of their state's policy and legal adoption support provisions for such children. "It will be the usual drill," Susan told Diana Reese, "with the subsidy administrator turning us down several times and us appealing." Sometimes Susan felt that the Department of Social Services (DSS) adoption assistance program ought to be called the "adoption resistance program," state administrators seemed so reluctant to approve any child's application for help.

On March 3, Susan and Alan signed an Adoptive Placement Agreement stating that they would accept Emma upon arrival into their home for the purpose of adoption. Emma and her new family were prepared for the placement through visits and an exchange of information, and Emma and the Miller family alike were cautiously optimistic about the match.

Emma was placed with the Millers on April 15. She had all the anticipated problems associated with attachment problems and loss, with the challenges of having a physical disability besides. Even so, Susan, Alan, and their other children found Emma delightful. Their oldest son, Mark, a Korean-born adoptee said that Emma "reminds me of what's great about being adopted—you finally get to belong somewhere." Also a veteran of Korean foster homes and an orphanage, Mark was preparing to enter college to prepare for a career in nursing.

Susan applied for Medicaid on Emma's behalf, and Emma qualified based on her resources (or lack of them) as a foster child. The Millers enrolled Emma in special education classes and settled in for the long haul, knowing that their commitment to Emma would have to pass whatever tests Emma gave them, and feeling sure that they would eventually win her over.

The required six-month postplacement period flew by, and the Millers prepared to legalize Emma's adoption. As part of the preliminaries to finalization, they applied for adoption assistance payments to their state Department of Social Services. Following DSS written instructions, they completed an AAP application form and submitted accompanying documentation of Emma's special needs and legal status, including a medical assistance application, county court order showing state-licensed agency custody of the child, and the income information about Emma's other families. Because no other documents were required by DSS, the Millers considered their application complete and mailed it in early October. They estimated that they should be able to go to court to finalize Emma's adoption by Thanksgiving. Excited about becoming a "real Miller," Emma asked her mom for a new dress to wear for the occasion.

But eight weeks passed and the Millers still had received no response from DSS. Susan wrote a letter to the state adoption subsidy administrator asking why, when the adoption subsidy eligibility committee met every Tuesday of every month, so much time had elapsed without a decision on Emma's application. A few days later, the Millers received a letter from the state's adoption unit, stating that "based upon a change in statute . . . it is the responsibility of the agency with custody to negotiate the potential contract with the adoptive family and to submit the application with necessary evidence to DSS for determination of eligibility." In other words, they wanted Susan and Alan's social worker, who had never before completed a subsidy application, to submit the very same materials on their behalf. "Anything to keep a wall up between adoptive parents and the agency," Susan fumed.

"Calm down, honey," Alan said, patting his wife's back, "you know you've seen this a hundred times. They're not picking on you; they do this to all the adoptive parents."

"Well, that doesn't make it right!" Susan snapped, "If they spent as much time helping families as they spend finding reasons to turn them away, we'd have a lot fewer kids in foster care in this state!"

Besides requiring the Millers to route their application through their agency, DSS also requested additional documentation not required by law or their written policies, including a copy of the Adoptive Placement Agreement the Millers had signed with their adoption agency. DSS rejected the Miller's application and asked their adoption agency to resubmit all the required forms and documentation.

The Millers were upset by the denial, but determined to see the application through. Having successfully advocated for adoption assistance for other foreign-born or transracially adopted children in their state, Susan and Alan had witnessed what they believed to be institutionalized racism within DSS. Adoptive parents of foreign-born or transracially-adopted, private agency-placed children were, it seemed to them, routinely denied the benefits to which they were legally entitled, having to fight for them through a lengthy administrative appeals process, while state custody children received them summarily.

Susan visited the law library to check on any changes in adoption statutes for their state in order to discover whether a new statute did, in fact, require adoption agencies rather than adoptive parents to apply for assistance on behalf of special needs adopted children. The only changes made to their state subsidy statutes that year had been those allowing children in Indian tribal custody to receive state-paid adoption assistance payments. With further research, Susan learned that state and federal statutes and policies all supported adoptive parents applying for AAP on behalf of their children and, in fact, required that all such contracts be between the state and the adoptive parents, not the placing adoption agency. The placing adoption agency could, at best, only be a third party assistant to negotiating the contract.

Susan reported her findings to Alan later that night over a cup of hot tea, "Can you believe they actually lied to us and to the agency?!"

Alan shook his head, "It's almost like they just don't want to have to deal with adoptive parents. What is wrong with them?"

"It's simple," Susan replied. "They're the experts and they have the power. When we come in as experts on our own kids and start interpreting the law in favor of our kids, we're stepping on their toes. They have to do what they can to keep their power."

"And its' at the kid's expense!" Alan exclaimed.

Susan shrugged her shoulders. "Yeah, usually it is," she said, "but that's OK. The law is on our side, and we're on Emma's side. It's going to work out."

Through past encounters with DSS, the Millers knew that their experience in applying for assistance exceeded that of their agency. They suspected that DSS hoped to deny the application based on incomplete information submitted by the inexperienced agency. Their suspicions were further aroused when they discovered that adoptive parents at other agencies had submitted their own applications successfully. All of the successful parents had been adopting same-race, domestically-born children, though.

Susan and Alan believed that DSS was discriminating against Emma because of her foreign birth.

Susan wrote the state's adoption program administrator and explained that her research had indicated that no statutory change had occurred requiring the agency, rather than the adoptive parents, to apply for assistance for the child. She challenged the program administrator, a master's level social worker (MSW) to send her a copy of any new statute that would support the DSS denial of the application on this basis. She concluded by showing that DSS written policies and instructions for subsidy application did not require copies of any placement agreement, and wrote that she and Alan would, therefore, not comply with the DSS request for the document because it appeared to be discriminatory.

Two months passed before the Millers heard from DSS again. The subsidy review committee had met and denied Emma's application for adoption subsidy on the basis that she had entered the Miller's home on April 15 of that year under an Adoption Placement Agreement dated March 3. The state's adoption program supervisor cited a DSS policy requiring that the child be a resident of the state "at the time of placement," and concluded that since Emma had lived in another state when the Adoption Placement Agreement was signed, she had not been a state resident and was thus ineligible for state-paid adoption subsidy. The program supervisor notified the Millers of their right to appeal the DSS decision, but did not respond to Susan's earlier questions.

Susan and Alan and their agency had refused to provide the Adoption Placement Agreement to DSS, yet the department had somehow obtained it. Their letter of denial clearly stated that they had obtained the Adoption Placement Agreement "from DSS records available for review." When Susan asked DSS what records they had accessed in order to obtain the placement agreement and who had accessed the file, the supervisor said that they had accessed Emma's confidential Medicaid file in the Miller's county of residence, "according to DSS policy." The department would not tell the Millers who had accessed the file. When Susan asked for a copy of the written policy giving DSS the right to access her child's confidential medical files without the written consent of the custodial agency or adoptive parents, she received no response. The Medicaid application she had signed, in fact, cited statutes expressly prohibiting access to the confidential information without consent. Susan and Alan began to suspect that DSS had violated state statutes and their own written policies in accessing such confidential information. They asked one another if the department's interest in denying some disabled children the benefits to which they were entitled by statute was so strong that they would break the law or lie in order to achieve such denials.

The Millers appealed the Subsidy Review Committee's decision and asked for a Fair Hearing on the basis that Emma's date of placement was April 15, the same day on which Emma had become a resident of the state. They also requested information from the state's civil rights office and considered filing a discrimination lawsuit against DSS on Emma's behalf. The Millers knew that obtaining the AAP and permanent Medicaid coverage for Emma was essential to her legal adoption and the family's well-being. Without the financial "safety net" offered through these programs, the Millers would face ongoing financial stress and possible bankruptcy trying to meet Emma's medical, physical, and emotional needs. Alan and Susan decided to pursue the appeal to the state level and to file a lawsuit against the state if they could not prevail through the state's administrative hearings process.

After several months had passed and Emma's adoption remained unfinalized, the Millers attended a Fair Hearing at their county DSS office. Emma's eligibility for AAP hinged on the definition of "adoptive placement." In their denial, the AAP committee had cited a DSS policy requiring that the child be a resident of the state "at the time of placement" and concluded that since Emma had lived in another state when the Adoption Placement Agreement was signed, she was not qualified for state-paid AAP.

The Millers' state volunteer AAP expert, Toni Wayman, attended the hearing with them, having been trained by the North American Council on Adoptable Children to help special needs adoptive parents access adoption assistance. Their state's adoption subsidy supervisor, Mabel Baird, appeared to defend the department's denial of Emma's application for AAP, finally admitting in her written summary that she had accessed Emma's confidential medical assistance file in that county, stating that it was DSS "policy" that allowed her to do so. When asked to produce the written policy supporting such a breach of confidentiality, the supervisor was unable to do so.

"They can't cite the written policy because it doesn't exist," Toni commented during a break.

"How can they do this?!" Susan fumed. "I mean, just lie about the facts and the law. Why doesn't anyone do anything about this?"

Toni laughed wryly, "Because by the time DSS is finished putting them through the AAP wringer, they're so exhausted they don't have the spirit to go back and say, 'So now what about those lies you put in writing?' They're so glad to be done with the fight."

"We can identify," Alan replied, "because all we really want to do is be parents. We never wanted to become our own best lawyers!"

"Didn't they tell you about that in adoptive parent training classes, Alan?" Toni chuckled. "Tell me what?" Alan asked. "That all special needs adoptive parents have to become lawyers—it's a prerequisite to being good parents!"

When the hearing resumed, the focus of the testimony centered on what "time of adoptive placement" meant. DSS claimed that their definition of "adoptive placement" as a process rather than a single event was one upheld by the Child Welfare League of America and the Council for Accreditation Standards. The Millers contended that the "date of adoptive placement" was the date on which the child was physically placed into the adoptive family's home, a definition upheld by DSS written policies and commonly accepted in adoption work.

Fortunately, before the hearing and with Toni Wayman's help, the Millers had done their homework. They had checked with the Child Welfare League of America and the Council for Accreditation Standards and learned that neither body had adopted a formal definition of "time of adoptive placement," even though the state's subsidy program administrator—who also held a national office within an organization of national adoption program administrators—claimed otherwise.

The Millers spent thousands of hours and dollars preparing for their appeal, submitting 52 pages of evidence and 21 appendixes as part of their written and oral testimony. They cited federal, state, and case law supporting their case and proving that DSS had applied their policies arbitrarily.

Two months after the Fair Hearing, the Millers received a notice from the appeals judge that their denial had been overturned. A few weeks later, they received a form letter and an adoption assistance contract from Mabel Baird, the very administrator who had denied their application twice and influenced the state's subsidy review committee to deny it.

Ironically, the form letter began with the following salutation, "Dear Adoptive Parents: Congratulations on the adoption of your child!" Emma's legal adoption had been delayed by nearly one year. Had the application been denied completely, Emma would have remained with the Millers indefinitely as a foster child, or replaced into another family as a foster child—at a much higher emotional expense to the child, not to mention the financial expense to the state.

* * *

In 1980, some 19 years after being adopted by Morton and Elsa Shafran, Robert Shafran enrolled in Sullivan County Community College in Loch

Sheldrake, New York. Bob found the students at the community college unusually friendly, acting as if they already knew him. Another student, Michael Domnitz, then a sophomore, told Bob that there was a remarkable similarity between him and another student who had attended Sullivan College the semester before. Domnitz asked Bob if he happened to be adopted.

"Yes, I am," Bob answered.

"Is your birthday July 12?" Domnitz asked.

"Yes, it is," Bob told him. Domnitz then took Bob Shafran to his apartment and showed him photos of Eddy Galland, a young man who had attended the college the previous semester. The two looked identical. Reeling from the discovery of another person who could have been a mirror image of himself, Bob realized that he must have a twin brother. The two must have been separated at birth. Bob called Eddy Galland's home and told him, "You won't believe this, but I think you're my twin brother."

The brothers reunited, believing themselves to be identical twins separated after their birth at Long Island Jewish Hospital—Hillside Medical Center on July 12, 1961. They had been placed by Louise Wise Services of Manhattan. The story of their separation and reunion was carried, along with a photograph of Bob and Eddy, in area newspapers. Soon after the story came out, David Kellerman, a Queens College student, called Eddy Galland's mother, saying, "I think I'm the third."

David, Eddy, and Bob, it turned out, were identical triplets, occurring only 21 times in every million births. When their birth mother decided to relinquish her infant sons for adoption, Louise Wise Services separated the triplets on the advice of psychiatrist Dr. Viola Bernard, who told the adoption agency that the brothers would better develop their own personalities if they were separated and raised apart.

Within weeks of the triplets' births, Louise Wise Services had placed each brother in separate adoptive families. Each family had previously adopted a daughter from the agency. Each daughter was two years old when the parents adopted one of the triplets. None of the adoptive parents were told that the child they adopted was one of identical triplets, and none of the families was offered the opportunity to raise the brothers together. Furthermore, each adoptive family was told that the son they adopted was already part of a scientific study of child development. The study would involve regular home visits and evaluations by psychologists.

Psychologist Dorothy Krugman, still a consultant for Louise Wise Services in 1997, visited the Kellerman home and studied David for several years. Krugman was later replaced by another psychologist, Christa Balzert. David's development was charted and his behavior studied until he was 13 years old. Robert Shafran, residing in Scarsdale with his parents, and Eddy Galland, living in New Hyde Park with his parents Elliot and Annette, were also studied and told similar stories by the Louise Wise agency and the psychologists who visited them until they were 12 to 13 years old.

Nearly 20 years after they adopted their sons, the adoptive parents learned the truth: the visiting psychologists were conducting more than a mere child development study. The same researchers, under the direction of Dr. Peter Neubauer, visited each home with full knowledge that their subjects, Bobby, Eddy, and David, were identical triplets and that the brothers lived in the same area. The psychologists, conducting research partially funded by the National Institute of Mental Health, had gone from the Shafran to the Galland to the Kellerman home, all in the interest of studying separated twins and triplets adopted by unrelated families. Other twins placed through Louise Wise Services—about a dozen or so sets—were also studied, unbeknownst to them or their parents. Several other adoption agencies also participated in the study of separated and adopted twins and triplets (Saul, 1997). The goal of the study was to glean information useful to the environment versus heredity debate: which had more influence, nature or nurture?

The brothers and their adoptive parents expressed outrage over the actions of the adoption agency and the researchers. Bob Shafran and David Kellerman felt that they had been torn apart and robbed of a lifetime together when they could have been raised in the same family. Their brother, Eddy Galland, cannot comment on the impact of their separation or the covert research: Eddy committed suicide in 1995.

Eddy Galland was not the only separated twin or triplet to commit suicide. In 1952 Louise Wise also separated fraternal twin sisters, raised in Long Island, New York and in New Jersey. When the twins were almost thirty years old, the New Jersey twin found her long-lost sister and, within months of the reunion, committed suicide (Saul, 1997). As with the Kellerman, Galland, and Shafran families, the adoptive parents of the sisters were never told that the child they adopted was a twin.

What rationale or justification did Louise Wise Services offer for their actions, and for supporting the research study of separated twins and triplets? According to an attorney for Louise Wise Services, Nancy-Ledy-Gurren, the brothers' birth mother gave consent to separating the triplets and commented that the separation of the brothers was thought to be in the best interests of the children (Saul, 1997).

Dr. Peter Neubauer, the director of the study, also justified his actions. Neubauer said that the triplets had not been separated for research purposes and that his work was an important contribution to the field of psychology (Saul, 1997). Neubauer (1990) repeatedly alluded to the research in his book about the genetics of personality, *Nature's Thumbprint*. Writing about the ethics of conducting this research without giving informed consent to the research subjects, Saul (1997) comments: "Despite the controversy surrounding it, the study apparently violated no rules requiring informed consent for human experimentation. No such rules governing behavioral studies were in place at the time, and there were no laws prohibiting the separation of twins" (p. 2).

The lack of formalized ethical rules requiring that Dr. Neubauer and his researchers give their subjects informed consent does not mean that these professionals were unaware of the impact of the research. Having undertaken the research with "great curiosity," Neubauer and his colleagues found themselves surprised by the likenesses between the identical twins reared apart (1990, p. 5). In fact, Neubauer wrote: "Identical twins reared separately showed a likeness in the timing and pattern of development and maturation that was truly surprising, as well as a likeness in some of the foundations of temperament and behavior, from sensitivity to activity to emotional response" (p. 6).

An example of such surprising similarities between twins reared apart was found in the case of identical twin sisters separated as infants and raised by different adoptive parents. Researchers asked the adoptive mothers of the two-year-old twins a number of questions about the girls' eating habits. The first adoptive mother reported that her daughter was doing well except for some unusual eating habits: "The girl is impossible. Won't touch anything I give her. No mashed potatoes, no bananas. Nothing without cinnamon. Everything has to have cinnamon on it. I'm really at my wit's end with her about this. We fight at every meal. She wants cinnamon on everything!" (Neubauer, 1990, p. 20).

The second adoptive mother, raising the identical twin sister, reported no eating problems whatsoever for her daughter, commenting that, "Ellen eats well. As a matter of fact, as long as I put cinnamon on her food, she'll eat anything" (Neubauer, 1990, p. 2).

Neubauer seemed to be aware of the impact of this information. The first adoptive mother found fault with her daughter, and possibly herself, over the child's insistence on having cinnamon on everything. In fact, Neubauer noted that, had the researchers been unaware that the children were identical twins with a "predisposed taste for cinnamon," they too "might . . . assume, as did the first mother, that her daughter was challenging her over the issue of food" (p. 21). Continuing with his analysis, Neubauer wrote:

If these preferences are genetically coded, then what at first seems to be the child's rebelliousness can now be seen as a natural predilection, which a parent may still insist on changing but whose origin is no longer either their own or their children's "fault." The underlying root is heredity. Often only the existence of an identical twin can reveal such endowed characteristics. (pp. 21–22)

From reading Neubauer's book it seems clear that the adoptive parents of separated twins and triplets were never told that they were raising a twin or triplet, much less about the similar behaviors of the monozygotic siblings. The mothers of the girls who liked cinnamon were, for example, left to carry on with their children as best as they could, even though the first mother, who perceived her child's craving for cinnamon as a problem, might have been relieved from finding fault with herself or her daughter had she known that the craving was probably hereditary. Neubauer and his colleagues, guardians of information that might have helped the adoptive mother and the adoptee, did nothing to help. Instead, in the name of their helping profession, they used the information to further their own professional goals.

* * *

All of these are true stories, although the identities of most of the people involved have been concealed. There are thousands of similar examples of what is wrong with America's adoption system, illustrating what the lack of applied ethical standards in adoption does to children and their parents and raising many questions about what we are doing, who is accountable for what we are doing, and whose interests we are serving.

Who is responsible for the lifelong heartache of Kathy Tucker, for her increasing symptoms of what Merry Bloch Jones called "birth mother syndrome" (Jones, 1993)? Was it the adoptive parents who promised to have a relationship with, and then abandoned, their child's birth mother? Was it Kathy herself, a birth mother who reclaimed the child she promised to give up? Might it have been Edward Thompson, the adoption attorney who served both the adoptive and birth parents in a situation rife with conflicting interests? Could it have been the judge who came to Kathy Tucker's hospital room to take the consent to adoption from a mother under the influence of narcotics? Was it the hospital administrator and staff who allowed such a consent to be taken without legal counsel or even a court reporter being present? Or perhaps it was the adoption counselor whose job was to counsel the birth mother, but whose fee was to be paid by the adoptive parents.

At whose feet should the traumatization and sexual abuse of little Amanda Hall be laid? The abandonment Eric and Anthony feel after losing their third set of parents in five years? Who is responsible for the disillusionment of adoptive parents like the Halls and the Millers, betrayed by social workers and bureaucrats who administer state programs and engage in child placement like minor deities rather than as public servants?

Who is responsible for Eddy Galland's suicide? Would Eddy have committed suicide had he not been adopted? Would he still be alive had he been raised with his brothers in an adoptive family? Had the researchers studying Eddy and his brothers given them what is now known as informed consent, would the outcomes for these brothers have been any different, their childhoods any happier, their adult selves more successful or complete?

Without ethical standards defining who the client is and how that client should be served, by which professionals and for what purposes, the answers to these questions are elusive. It is answers to these questions that I hope to offer through the pages of this book, challenging adoption professionals to clarify the standards whereby they serve their clients, and the consumers of adoption services to demand such clarification and insist on the ethical practice of adoption.

Chapter 2

Values in Adoption

Our minds are possessed by three mysteries: where we came from, where we are going, and since we are not alone, but members of a countless family, how should we live with one another.

—Edward Muir

Mary Benet wrote that "the moral views of every society have influenced its practice of adoption more heavily than have pragmatic considerations" (1976, p. 13). Certainly this is true of American adoption practice, supported by societal values of providing permanent families for children deprived of them and the protection of abused, neglected, or abandoned children. Coexisting with these values, and not always peacefully, are the values of blood relatedness and the preservation and support of the biological family, along with the values of identity, self-determination, and of knowing as much about one's own history as others know. In writing about value issues in contemporary adoption, Dukette observed that "values often clash with personal interests or with other values, and adoption is full of conflicting values" (1984, p. 234). How are adoption professionals, agencies, and the recipients of adoption services to understand and make ethical decisions in such a complex area, especially when the interests of those involved may be at odds? The answer lies in defining the values undergirding adoption practice and identifying the ethical codes and standards that embody them.

Dolgoff and Skolnik defined ethics as "values in operation, the guidelines for transforming values into action" (1992, p. 100). For the purposes of this book, I define *values* as those ideals regarded as desirable in adoption practice, and *ethics* as the formal, professional rules of right and wrong conduct. Values might thus be seen as the skeletal system supporting the flesh and blood of our ethical codes. *Standards* are commonly accepted, but not necessarily formally or professionally adopted rules of right and wrong conduct in a field.

Adoption professionals have been unable to translate ethical principles into behavior, a failure at the root of many of the problems with adoption services in the United States (Conrad & Joseph, 1991). This chapter examines the historical antecedents of current adoption values, reviewing the philosophical, historical, social, and psychological literature about adoption and its values from ancient to contemporary times.

HISTORICAL ANTECEDENTS OF CURRENT VALUES IN ADOPTION

That values are of fundamental importance in adoption is a view that has been established in the earliest literature regarding adoption. Some of the earliest values supporting the nurturing and care of orphaned children include preventing and punishing child abuse and neglect and providing permanent families for children who had been orphaned or abandoned. Maintaining familial ties, providing heirs, and regarding the state as the protector of society also provided a framework for the treatment of children in antiquity.

In primitive societies, adoption of orphaned children preserved the precious resource necessary to the tribe's survival. Ancient records, legends, and myths are "replete with references to adoption" (Sorosky et al., 1989, p. 25). Whether seen as a way of insuring the continuity of the family or as a way of dealing with children whose biological parents are unable to provide for them, "adoption is a powerful experience that touches upon universal human themes of abandonment, parenthood, sexuality, identity, and the sense of belonging" (Reitz & Watson, 1992, p. 3). "In mythology and folklore," write Reitz and Watson,

> adoption is often presented as a way to rescue a child from parents who are unable to protect the child from harm (e.g., Moses) or from parents who would themselves harm the child (e.g., Oedipus). A common theme of these early stories is that although the adoption enables a child to be reared in safety, it does not forestall the need for the adopted child to work out a destiny in the context of his or her origins. (1992, p. 3)

ANCIENT HISTORY OF VALUES IN ADOPTION AND CHILD WELFARE

Biblical Accounts of Adoption

As Reitz and Watson point out, one of the best-known examples of adoption can be found in the Hebrew chronicle of Moses, the Hebrew who as an infant was drawn out of the Nile River and adopted by the daughter of Pharaoh.

According to the Biblical account, the Egyptians oppressed the captive Hebrews by telling the Hebrew people to throw their newborn sons into the Nile but to allow their infant daughters to live. When Moses was born, his mother hid him for three months until she could hide him no longer. She then made a waterproof basket and put him into it, placing the basket among the reeds by the bank of the Nile River, and sent his older sister Miriam to watch over him.

Pharaoh's daughter, coming to bathe, found Moses in the basket and pitied him, having recognized him as "one of the Hebrews' children" (Exodus 2:6). Moses' sister Miriam then asked Pharaoh's daughter if she could go and fetch a wet nurse for Moses to nurse the child.

Pharaoh's daughter agreed, and Moses' original mother, Jochebed, took Moses and nursed him until he was weaned around age two or three years (Unger's Bible Dictionary, 1978). At that time Moses was returned to Pharaoh's daughter, "and he became her son" (Exodus 2:10).

Moses grew up as a member of Pharaoh's household, though he knew that he was a Hebrew by birth. In fact, Moses frequented the work sites where the Hebrew slaves performed hard labor for the Egyptians. One day during a visit to such a site, he saw an Egyptian beating a Hebrew, "one of his brethren" (Exodus 2:11). Angry over the mistreatment, Moses killed the Egyptian and buried him in the sand. The following day, Moses saw two Hebrews fighting and pleaded with them to stop. One said to Moses, "Who made you a judge over us? Are you intending to kill me as you killed the Egyptian?" (Exodus 2:14). The matter became known to Pharaoh, Moses's adoptive grandfather, who sought to have Moses executed for the murder of the Egyptian. Moses fled to the wilderness of Midian, where at Mount Horeb he encountered the God of the Hebrews in the burning bush. The Bible comments that Moses, at one time or another, was rejected by both his birth and adoptive families (Acts 7:27–29, 35, 39). When God met Moses at Horeb, though, He spoke to him, saying, "I am the God of your father, the God of Abraham, the God of Isaac, and the God of Jacob" (Exodus 3:6). The Biblical account refers to Moses's "fathers" as those related to him by blood, not by adoption. In the New Testament, the book of Hebrews underscores the importance of Moses's spiritual inheritance by telling the reader that "Moses, when he had grown up, refused to be called the son of Pharaoh's daughter; choosing rather to endure ill-treatment with the people of God, than to enjoy the passing pleasures of sin; considering the reproach of Christ greater riches than the treasures of Egypt; for he was looking to the reward" (Hebrews 11:23–29).

Other passages of the Bible, such as Exodus 6, trace Moses's genealogy through his biological, not adoptive, family. There is no clear evidence that ancient Israelite law supported the institution of legal adoption. Moses was adopted by Pharaoh's daughter under Egyptian law, while in another Biblical account of adoption, Mordecai's adoption of the future queen, Esther, reflected Persian customs rather than Israeli law (Esther 2:7).

Talmudic rabbis relied upon these two references to adoption to support their teaching that an orphan brought up in one's household was, according to Scripture, to be treated as a child born to the family. Talmudic law does not recognize legal adoption. Today, although nothing prevents Jewish families from legally adopting, adopted children can be treated differently than biological children under certain religious laws (Jacobs, 1995).

Eastern Adoption Practices

Other ancient references to legal adoption can be found in the Code of Hammurabi (1700 B.C.), a Babylonian law. The Hammurabic Code had a tremendous influence on all the Near Eastern countries and addressed some aspects of adoption law. Based on older collections of Sumerian and Akkadian laws, the Code stated that biological fathers and mothers could not demand their child back once he was given up for adoption. If the child offended his adoptive parents, however, he could be returned to the biological family. In the Babylonian culture,

> the meaning of the blood tie was so strong that the only acceptable method of initiating non-relatives was to make them artificially blood relatives by adoption. Adoption into the group, therefore, meant complete severance from one's original family or group, with the promise of allegiance and total loyalty to the new family. To seek one's origins or to question one's true identity was seen then, as now, as dangerous, ungrateful, and disloyal. (Sorosky et al., 1989, p. 26)

In China and Japan, adoption was intertwined with a highly ritualistic system of ancestor worship and the preservation of the genealogical line (Benet, 1976). In China as recently as a century ago, custom allowed a male without heirs to claim the firstborn child of any of his younger brothers because to die without a son was considered one of life's greatest misfortunes.

In India, adoption was a well-established custom, with adoptee-adoptive parent matching on traits of caste, kinship degree, and social level. In the Indian system of adoption, the adoptee was to be as much as possible like the biological child would have been. Twelve different types of adoption were described in Hindu law, but the foundational motive of all was to provide heirs for a family. Modern Hindu adoption law, as a result of past colonial rule, is an admixture of Eastern and Western philosophy. Adoption was also widely practiced in Oceania, where it served as an exchange function to preserve coalitions between kinship groups.

Early Islamic teachings considered adoptive ties equal in every way to those between blood relatives. Muhammad himself adopted a freed slave, Zaid, and raised him as his son, teaching by precept and example the equal standing of children born and adopted into a family.

Islamic teaching changed after Muhammad's adopted son grew up and married a beautiful woman, Zeinab. One day Muhammad caught a glimpse of his partially-clad daughter-in-law and was captivated. He demanded that Zaid divorce Zeinab so that Muhammad could marry her himself, in direct defiance of his own ban on a father's marriage to the wife of a son. Following the shocked reactions of the community, Muhammad had a revelation that "it was a mistake by Muslims to consider adoption as creating the same ties as blood kin" (Brooks, 1995, p. 83). The post-revelation teachings of the Koran are that Muslims are to declare the true parentage of any adopted children. "God, the revelation disclosed, had arranged Muhammad's marriage with Zeinab to disclose to Muslims the error of their previous beliefs" (Ibid., p. 83).

Adoption in Greece and Rome

Ancient historical and philosophical works refer to the obligations of society toward children, particularly to those who, deprived of parental care, needed the protection of the state. Plato urged the guardians of orphans to regard them as a supreme and sacred trust, requiring individuals who defrauded orphans to pay damages twice as high as those normally paid to children with living parents. Aristotle later wrote that since infanticide was forbidden by ordinance, birth control should be practiced by all citizens, and if a child was conceived in spite of contraception, an abortion "should be procured before the embryo has acquired life and sensation" (Aristotle). Aristotle also wrote that "no cripple shall be reared," recommending instead that deformed or handicapped children should be abandoned. The values underlying the approach of the Greek city-state to children in special circumstances was clearly that the needs of families and individuals were secondary to the mandates of the state. Should the citizens become too numerous or, due to incapacity, require resources of the state without showing any promise of contributing to their own keep, their numbers should be reduced. Thus, although children had some sentimental value and healthy children were regarded as the future of the citizen-state, the Greece of Plato and Aristotle subjected the value of the individual child to the value of maintaining a well-functioning state.

The Roman conquests of most of Europe, Asia Minor, and North Africa had a profound effect on the laws of these societies, including adoption law. The Romans established complete adoption statutes for the first time in history (Sorosky et al., 1989). Roman law established two types of adoption: *patria potestas*, which applied to children, and *arrogation*, which applied to people who had no family or who were adults. As with Babylonian law and primitive customs, continuity of the adopter's family was the primary purpose in both cases. Adoption was typically accompanied by religious rituals symbolizing the severance of old family ties. The adoption of a child or children by barren couples was most acceptable, while adult adoption was considered unnatural and unsafe. The Roman Empire, like many primitive societies, regarded the family as the foundational societal unit. The family head, who demanded complete loyalty, controlled the rights of the individual. The rights of individuals, however, were subject not only to the needs of the family, but also to the needs and requirements of the larger society. By the time of Justinian (527–565 A.D.), ruler of the Eastern Roman Empire, the individual was considered much more a member of society than a member of his family, with an accompanying shift of allegiance and loyalty. Justinian's code of law, reflecting this difference, indicated that an adoptee could and usually did retain the right of inheritance from his birth father. Interestingly, in many U.S. states today, adoptees can also inherit property from birth parents whose parental rights have been terminated.

In the first century A.D., the Emperor Narva established colonies for poor families to abate the drowning and abandonment of infants, largely due to the value the state put on its youngest citizens. The increase of the Roman empire required an ever growing supply of soldiers and pioneers, resulting in the utilitarian value of children "not for their own sake or for any moral reason, but again for the interests of the state" (Doxiadis, 1989, p. 14).

The expansion of Christianity had a profound effect on the values related to the treatment of orphans. The interests of the state became subject to the interests of the individual human being created in the image of God. Children came to be regarded as valuable for their own sake, perhaps based on biblical admonitions such as that of the Apostle James, "This is pure and undefiled religion in the sight of our God and father, to visit orphans and widows in their distress" (James 1:27).

Through laws that respected both the value of caring for children deprived of parental care and the value of blood ties, in 452 A. D. the Synod of Arles provided for the shelter of abandoned infants in any church for a minimum of ten days while officials searched for the biological parents. During the fifth century in the Byzantine Empire, St. Basil founded the first orphan asylum for abandoned infants; and historical works are replete with references to numerous foundling asylums established for the care of abandoned children during that time. In the West, Archbishop Datheus established the first foundling asylum in the year 787 A.D. Nurses at the orphanage breast-fed infant foundlings, and children were fed and clothed until they were eight years old.

Adoption in Europe

Not long after the collapse of the Roman Empire in 476 A.D., formal adoption in western Europe virtually ceased to exist, although the value of protecting children deprived of parental care continued to find expression across political boundaries and through subsequent centuries.

One of the earliest medieval foundling asylums was the *Ospedale degli Innocenti* in Florence, established in the 1420s to care for orphaned or abandoned children (Gies & Gies, 1989). Renaissance architecture was said to be initiated with Brunelleschi's radical design of the asylum, but there were not enough institutions of its kind to house the children needing shelter, food, and protection (Goldthwaite, 1972). Because adoption was seldom practiced in the Middle Ages and the Renaissance orphaned and abandoned children struggled to survive. Older children cared for their younger siblings, and impoverished parents sold their daughters as household help to the affluent (Gies & Gies, 1989).

In the sixteenth and seventeenth centuries acts of parliament in France demanded that nobles who found abandoned infants on their property be required to bring up the foundlings as their own, but few complied (Doxiadis, 1989). Napoleonic codes defined standards for adoptive parents and supported the termination of parental rights and permanency of adoptive ties, upholding the value of providing permanent families for children whose parents could not raise them (Cole & Donley, 1990).

Although Napoleon established adoption-specific codes in France, the adoption laws of most European countries, Australia, New Zealand, Canada, and the United States have their origins in Roman tradition and law.

On the North American continent, adoption among Native American tribes developed concurrently on an informal basis, uninfluenced by European traditions. Among the Choctaws, for example, informal adoption of orphans was common and adopted children shared equally in the inheritance of the adoptive parents. Laws (1995) wrote that some adoptees even received better legacies than the biological children of their parents.

Prior to industrialization, adoption in European and Nordic countries was likewise practiced on an informal basis. Among the noble and wealthy farmers, children were sent away at an early age for training or work in homes of country-dwelling strangers, a practice similar to the apprenticeship arrangements undertaken in England and, later, in the colonies (Kristinsdottir, 1991).

In England during the rule of James I, British statutes for binding out (or apprenticing) children were used for sending them to America. The apprenticing of poor children to the Virginia Company began as early as 1620. A record of 1627 reads, "There are many ships going to Virginia, with them 1400 or 1500 children which they have gathered up in diverse places" (Sorosky et al., 1989, p. 30).

Indentured servanthood was the only way that poor and dependent children in Europe and the United Kingdom had of securing homes. Authorities routinely bound out young orphaned or destitute children during their minority to households in the community where, under formal contract, a child earned his room and board through productive labor. When the child became 18 or 20 years old, he left with some money, cattle, clothes, and a new Bible. The apprenticeship system "gave children secure, surrogate families and delayed the need for legal adoption laws" (Sorosky et al., 1989, p. 30).

While many children who had families were apprenticed or indentured, children whose parents or families could not care for them were sent to foundling homes, which developed concurrently with urbanization and industrialization. Many orphans died in such homes. Those who survived were used as inexpensive industrial laborers when they were 12 to 14 years old; others were placed on "orphan trains" and taken to the countryside "where farmers and their wives would choose healthy-looking children and adopt them to use as farm hands" (Rosenberg, 1992, p. 9).

Increasing industrialization interrupted the indenturing of children in England and Europe, which had been the basis of informal adoption there. England, with a legal system based on common law, was one of the last countries to codify adoption. In 1741, charitable workers in London, England, established the country's first foundling home for the many foundlings who were abandoned daily in the streets. Children were valued as heirs or as workers and contributors to the family's upkeep. Poor, abandoned, and orphaned children, though they came to be protected, were still valued only as indentured servants or apprentices. Adoption was created by a 1926 statute in Great Britain. Even then, the laws did little to define adoption-specific values. To the contrary, the history of adoption since before colonial times demonstrates an overriding concern for the needs and interests of adults rather than children. Any benefit to children "was a secondary gain" (Cole & Donley, 1990, p. 274).

HISTORY OF VALUES IN AMERICAN ADOPTION

Colonial America

The Puritans brought apprenticeship to America, where it became the model for early adoption practices. By 1648, the Massachusetts Bay Colony had passed laws giving the colony the right to remove unruly, incorrigible children from their parents and place them in another home. During the same period Connecticut dispensed the death penalty "for a rebellious son and for any child who should smite or curse his parents," though the courts tended to prefer placing the child with another family to executing him (Sorosky et al., 1989, p. 30). When both parents died, dependent children were given to relatives, according to the will of the deceased parent. If no relatives able or willing to take the orphan existed, he was apprenticed or "bound out," or, if there was one nearby, sent to an asylum. The first orphan asylum in the United States was founded by Ursuline nuns in 1729 to shelter and nourish children who had been orphaned in a massacre at Natchez, Mississippi (Weisman, 1994). Orphanages remained relatively scarce in America until after the Civil War.

In early America orphans were in great demand because of the shortage of labor, and "it was said that America could absorb all the orphans of England, thus ridding the mother country of its dependents" (Sorosky et al., 1989, p. 30). Consideration of the needs or welfare of the child was not of concern during this era.

Visitors to the United States from England were impressed by "how easily and frankly children are adopted, . . . how pleasantly the scheme goes on, and how little of the wormwood of domestic jealousies or the fretting prickle of neighbor's criticisms interfered with it" (Sorosky et al., 1989, p. 31).

The reality of adoption in the United States during the time was more corrupt than it appeared to the casual observer. "Thousands of children were sent by the so-called children's societies to uninvestigated, available homes all over the prairies. Newspapers carried ads for children wanted for adoption, and parents either sold or gave them away" (Sorosky et al., 1989, p. 31). The earliest adoption statutes in the United States, based on English law, came about because of the need to control the wholesale distribution of children to homes where they were used as cheap labor.

According to Laws (1995), on the American frontier another means of obtaining children was through abduction or reciprocal kidnappings, which evolved into a type of adoption practiced both by Native Americans and by European settlers. Native American children kidnapped by European-Americans and European-American children kidnapped by Native American tribes suffered trauma and grief that was largely ignored by the kidnappers-cum-adoptive parents. Prior to colonization, Native American tribes generally regarded their children as valuable resources and adoption as a means of safeguarding these human resources. Among the Blackfoot Indians, for example, widows and grandmothers adopted orphaned children, a benefit to the child because he gained an experienced parent, and a benefit to the adoptive mother because the child could help her in her old age.

Sir William Phips, an early governor of Massachusetts, was the first person to adopt a child in the original 13 colonies. Like other early American adoptions, the Phips adoption was formalized through a special legislative bill granting the adoption of the specific child.

Establishment of Legal Adoption and Growth of Child Welfare

As in England, adoption in the United States is a statutory creation. Massachusetts enacted America's first adoption laws in 1851. Until then, adoptions had been undertaken informally, established by special legislative acts, as with the Phips adoption, or through the filing of a deed to the child in much the same way that property was acquired. Usually, the purpose of adoption was to provide an heir to a family, rather than providing families for children who needed them.

During the mid-1800s, humane societies developed nationally, promoting values that were hotly debated at annual conferences and in the literature (Anderson, 1989). Humane societies served both animals and children, demonstrating the relative value of children at the time.

The protection of children deprived of parental care fell largely to private charitable organizations during the early and mid-1800s. One such charitable organization, the New York Children's Aid Society, which was founded by Charles Loring Brace, sent needy children to rural Midwest "free family homes" on what became known as "orphan trains" for foster care beginning in 1854. By 1859, 20,000 to 24,000 children had been placed throughout the Midwest in this manner (Cole & Donley, 1990). Such arrangements had no written contracts, and legal guardianship was retained by the society or the birth parents. Philanthropists and opportunists alike removed orphaned and needy children from urban areas to the countryside to teach them agricultural skills, to reform those in need of reform, and to provide inexpensive farm hands for rural families (Platt, 1969).

Detractors of Brace's methods, most notably the Catholic church and press, depicted his system of child placement "as a slave trade in which Irish youth were auctioned to the highest bidder in midwestern town squares" (Sutton, 1990, p. 1375). The Catholic community developed its own child protection system through a network of institutions designed to separate Catholic children from the Protestants. The Irish were the first to provide institutions for their children, followed by the German, Polish, and Italian immigrants who created institutions for their orphaned children.

Over time and with the rise of industrialization, the countryside remained a common site of children's foster placements in America and in other countries (Kristinsdottir, 1991). The children who were thus removed usually came from orphanages or almshouses, were poor, between 12 and 14 years old, and often were moved without consent or through force. Some have suggested that the goal of these removals was evident: to clear the cities of the poorest children for the comfort of the upper class and emerging middle class.

Rapid industrialization after the 1860s provided new occupations for poor children. By 1870 approximately one out of every eight children was employed. There is no record of any significant demand for adoptable infants in the late 1870s and 1880s, and unwanted babies were more likely to die than be adopted. The infant mortality rate in foundling asylums was between 85 percent and 90 percent. The only profitable undertaking involving infants was the "business of getting rid of other people's [unwelcome] babies" (Zelizer, 1985, p. 170). Individuals who came to be known as "baby farmers" agreed to board unwanted, and usually illegitimate, children for around ten dollars a month. The only children in great demand by adoptive or foster parents during this period were typically older than ten and male, with three times more boys placed than girls (Rosenberg, 1992). The citizenry of the time, much like the Greeks and Romans, showed more concern for the needs and interests of adults than of children. Though orphans and poor children were sheltered, fed, and, hopefully, emotionally nurtured by foster and adoptive families, this benefit was secondary to providing useful children for families who needed them.

Even purportedly reputable child placing agencies profited from the market conditions of the time. One national organization that placed children in free foster homes, the Children's Home Society, charged parents $50 to take their child, $100 if the baby was illegitimate and thus harder to place (Zelizer, 1985).

In the 1870s, child welfare workers launched a crusade against the monetary approach to child care and in support of homes that would take children based on charitable motivations. Baby farms in particular were criticized as little more than "baby-killing" concerns based on a mercenary approach to adoption (Zelizer, 1985, p. 176). The infant mortality rates at unlicensed baby farms was not much different from those at licensed or approved foundling homes or almshouses, however. The term "adoption" came into use during this time and referred to general child placement with both relatives and nonrelatives. Many states still had no legally binding adoption provisions.

Reforms during this era focused on the removal of children from adult institutions such as jails but also focused on children remanded to almshouses, where orphans as well as the indigent, the insane, the elderly, petty criminals, and homeless children were housed (Sutton, 1990; Weisman, 1994). The National Conference of Charities and Correction passed a resolution in 1876 calling for the withdrawal of children from almshouses. By the turn of the century, 12 states had enacted legislation mandating such removals. Because the states did not provide for the establishment of alternatives to the almshouses, however, removed children were usually sent to other public or private institutions, including independent baby farms.

In 1910, an investigation of New Hampshire baby farms confirmed that the foster care and adoption of children were more matters of profit than love in the state. Baby farmers during that decade made as much as $10,000 a year through the boarding and sale of infants (Zelizer, 1985).

Private charities organized to provide child welfare services including foster care and adoption. The largest and most influential of the private charities was the National Conference of Catholic Charities (Catholic Charities USA), founded in 1910. Thomas Mulry, the "unofficial Catholic ambassador to the charity organization movement" (Sutton, 1990, p. 1377), pronounced family preservation or reunification the primary goal of Catholic charities and proposed that local, private agencies were best able to accomplish this goal.

Other clergymen, social workers, or child welfare advocates, however, united in "spreading the new gospel of adoption," describing a man's biological children as priceless treasures, a value that was "almost equally true of those children that come into our homes by adoption" (Zelizer, 1985, p. 178).

The Sentimental Value of Children

The labor value of children in the United States began to disappear as their new sentimental value became increasingly monetized and commercialized. By the turn of the century, the professional position on adoption in the United States had evolved from a monetary to a sentimental practice, to "a search for child love and not child labor" (Zelizer, 1985, p. 170). Among foster and adoptive parents, however, the needs of adults rather than those of dependent children continued to be paramount. Child placement workers found that young girls came to be in particular demand among foster and adoptive parents due to "an acute servant problem" and that "generous people who sought to adopt children for the children's sakes were few and far between" (Zelizer, 1985, p. 179).

In spite of their reform and advocacy roles in child welfare, some workers at adoption agencies continued to believe that the foster child or adoptees as laborers role could be combined with the new emphasis on the best interests of the child and on sentimental adoption. For example, John N. Foster, superintendent of Michigan's State Public Schools, distinguished between "kind-hearted, well-meaning people . . . desiring a child to help mind the baby, run errands, prepare vegetables," from families who took a child, "simply with reference to its commercial value" (Zelizer, 1985, p. 181).

The trend in child welfare and adoption, however, was clearly in the direction of a more romantic and less utilitarian view of abandoned and orphaned children. Although the practice of utilizing foster and adopted children in working homes persisted into the 1920s and 1930s, it occurred mostly in street trades or rural areas, and then as exceptions. The Great Depression also temporarily restored the need for child labor in some households, including middle-class biological families.

Evolution of Child Welfare Standards

In 1912 the United States Children's Bureau was established as the first public child welfare agency in America. Since that time, professional agency adoptions and independent, non-agency adoptions have continued to function on parallel and often competitive courses in the United States. At the 1915 National Conference of Charities and Correction, Carl Carstens, the general agent of the Massachusetts Society for the Prevention of

Cruelty to Children, called for development of public programs of child welfare and cooperation among progressive children's societies with one goal being the development of standards addressing child placement. In 1916, Congress passed the first federal child labor law. A few years later, during the 1919 White House Conference on Child Welfare Standards, the Committee on Cooperation for Child-Helping Organizations established the Bureau for the Exchange of Information among Child-Helping Agencies, which became the Child Welfare League of America (CWLA) in 1921. Carstens, the first executive director of the CWLA, "considered the league a professional federation and insisted upon qualifying standards for membership" (Anderson, 1989, p. 227).

The Child Welfare League developed standards for child welfare service and child protection before it developed adoption standards. While statutes governing the adoption of children were still evolving, foster care, indentured servanthood, and apprenticeship models of caring for children deprived of parental care, based on the labor value of children, had been established for over a century. The separate functions of child welfare services—child protection, foster care, and adoption—fragmented the practice of child welfare in the United States and made establishing nationally uniform standards much more difficult (Anderson, 1989). Societies such as the American Humane Association and the Child Welfare League of America "jockeyed for ascendancy as the standard-setting federation in child protection," competing, too, with private organizations such as Catholic Charities USA and the Florence Crittenton Association in establishing such standards (Anderson, 1989, p. 240; Sutton, 1990).

The process of developing standards regarding the treatment of children in the labor force, foster care, and adoption resulted in conflict between professionals who specialized in child placement and those, such as doctors and attorneys, who did not (Cole & Donley, 1990; Solinger, 1992). The practice among some doctors and attorneys of selling children subverted professional adoption practice and conflicted with the evolving ideal of sentimental adoption. At loggerheads were the values of providing children for families who wanted or needed them (children as chattel, utilitarian adoption based on adult needs) and those of providing permanent, qualified families for children whose parents could not raise them (adoption in consideration of the child's best interests).

Changing Views of Illegitimacy and the Needs of Children

Although public regulation of adoption increased and licensing standards for foster homes and adoption agencies were developed, baby brokering did not stop. Studies of the time showed that the majority of children adopted in the 1920s were adopted without assistance from social agencies (Zelizer, 1985). Such independent adoptions were often arranged informally by nonprofit adoption facilitators. But in many cases, intermediaries, often doctors or attorneys, built a profitable business by selling babies in the black or gray market that thrived in the 1930s and 1940s.

During the same time, changing philosophical and psychological views led to changes in adoption statutes throughout the country. In 1917 the first law judicially sealing adoption records and the adopted child's original birth certificate was passed in Minnesota; by 1929, five states had sealed records, and by the 1940s, nearly every state had followed suit (Dawson, 1993; Melina & Roszia, 1993). The primary idea behind the sealed records policies was that adopted children should be protected from the embarrassing knowledge that they were immorally conceived and illegitimately begotten (Baer, 1995). The Child Welfare League of America's 1938 adoption standards recommended that "the birth records of an adopted child be so revised as to shield him from unnecessary embarrassment in case of illegitimacy" (CWLA, 1938).

Psychologists and other experts replaced earlier views of unwed mothers as genetically inferior with theories of neurotic young women expressing a need to have revenge against their mothers. Similarly, the illegitimate child, formerly seen as "being tainted by 'bad blood,' " came to be seen "as *tabulae rasae* who should be protected from untoward experiences" (Rosenberg, 1992, p. 9). The closed adoption record would also protect the neurotic birth mother from the deeds of her past, enabling her to forget her illegitimate child and go on to live a productive, reputable life.

Some of today's adoption experts suggest that the practice of judicially sealing adoption records and cutting the adoptee off from all information about his or her past arises out of a peculiarly American mind-set. Giving adoptees and their birth parents a fresh start "occurred in a cultural climate that supported the idea of people making a clean break with their past and starting over. America was settled by outcasts who were unwanted in their homelands, and later immigrants came to America because it was a place where it didn't matter who you were or where you came from" (Lynch, September-October-November, 1997, p. 24).

Although rare in the previous century, legal adoption became increasingly popular in the twentieth century as the "bad blood" theory of adoption fell into disfavor. Psychologists who favored giving adoptees and their birth parents a clean start in life also promoted the idea that environment, not heredity, was the primary shaper of personality. This new attitude caused an increase in the number of adoptions, leading a judge from the

Boston Probate Court to remark in 1919 that "the woods are full of people eager to adopt children—the number appearing to be in the increase" (Zelizer, 1985, p. 190). By 1927, the *New York Times* reported that the new problem in adoption "has become one of finding enough children for childless homes rather than that of finding enough homes for homeless children" (Zelizer, 1985, p. 190).

Legal adoptions increased threefold between 1934 and 1944 in spite of increased regulation and the more demanding process of approving prospective adoptive couples for adoption. The historical ascendancy of institutional care for dependent children came to an end during the 1900s. Adoptive parents began paying as much as $1,000 to adopt the healthy infant who only thirty years earlier had sold for under two dollars.

A romantic and mythologized view of adoption evolved as high-profile public figures such as Minnie Maddern Fiske, Al Jolson, Gracie Allen and George Burns, Mayor La Guardia, Babe Ruth, and Eddie Rickenbacker became adoptive parents. The popular cartoon strip about Little Orphan Annie and her wealthy adoptive father and savior, Daddy Warbucks, reflected society's fairy-tale view of adoption. This sentimentalized view of adoption in turn led to changes in the demographical profile of the typical adoptive parent during the late 1800s and early 1900s. The majority of the adoptive fathers of younger children had higher occupational levels (professional, semiprofessional, and managerial), whereas the adoptive fathers of older, and therefore potentially useful, children were more likely to be skilled, semiskilled, or unskilled laborers or farmers (Zelizer, 1985).

A 1922 study conducted by the New York State Charities Aid Association brought commercialized adoption under public scrutiny through its investigation of newspaper advertisements offering and seeking children for adoption. The study, which revealed a wholesale exchange of children, found that an average of one infant per day was being bought or sold in New York (Zelizer, 1985). Other large city newspapers also commonly ran advertisements offering and seeking children for adoption.

By the 1930s, childless couples were paying large sums of money to purchase a black market baby, providing business opportunities for unscrupulous baby brokers and thieves through agencies like the Tennessee Children's Home Society (Austin, 1993). Infant adoption became quite popular during this time, the greatest appeal being for blonde-haired, blue-eyed little girls, a demand that outstripped the demand for boys two to one. Jewish parents, who called for three-year-old boys more often than little girls, were the exception (Zelizer, 1985).

Control of Unwed Mothers

The increased demand for adoptable infants and toddlers paralleled developments in social welfare policy that served to keep unwed mothers and their infants together through mandated breast-feeding or laws prohibiting the separation of mother and child in some states, while other laws punished unwed mothers by denying them Aid to Dependent Children (Cole & Donley, 1990). Although eventually all the states passed legislation giving unwed mothers the right to receive Aid to Dependent Children, in the late 1940s and early 1950s, laws were passed in several states that established investigative units charged with discovering unwed mothers who dated men so that their welfare eligibility would be rescinded (Sutton, 1990). As late as 1960, southern states were purging "thousands of clients from the AFDC rolls simply on the grounds that in these cases women had a child outside of marriage" (Lawrence-Webb, 1997, p. 13).

The social control of unwed mothers increased in the early 1950s and 1960s as states moved to deny welfare aid to unwed mothers who had more than one illegitimate child. Nineteen states denied Aid to Dependent Children to such unwed mothers, and twelve more states (California, Connecticut, Delaware, Georgia, Illinois, Iowa, Maryland, Ohio, Tennessee, Mississippi, North Carolina, and Virginia) enacted or presented legislation "mandating imprisonment or sterilization of women who had more than one illegitimate child" (Solinger, 1992, pp. 22–23). The Aid to Families with Dependent Children (AFDC) program "emphasized the morality and worthiness of its recipients as part of the means test for determining eligibility for assistance," regarding out-of-wedlock pregnancies and "illegitimate" children as "prima facia evidence of promiscuity" on the part of the unwed mothers (Lawrence-Webb, 1997, p. 13).

Interestingly, the call for welfare reform in the late 1990s has also seen several states consider legislation disallowing welfare assistance to mothers who have more than one child outside marriage. Lawrence-Webb commented on this development, writing:

> The current policies in welfare reform are not new; they are just past discriminatory policies cloaked in the language of today. The importance of understanding the origin of past policies embedded in current rhetoric is necessary in terms of preventing past practices of mass expulsions of children from the welfare rolls without any means of support and the reestablishment of discriminatory practices that would deny assistance to those most in need—children. (1997, p. 25)

Caucasian and African American single mothers were treated differently under the law in the pre-*Roe v. Wade* era following World War II, a fact documented by historian Rickie Solinger:

[Black unwed mothers] were viewed as socially unproductive breeders, constrainable only by punitive, legal sanctions. Proponents of school segregation, restrictive public housing, exclusionary welfare policies, and enforced sterilization or birth control all used the issue of relatively high rates of Black illegitimacy to support their campaigns. White unwed mothers in contrast were viewed as socially productive breeders whose babies, unfortunately conceived out of wedlock, could offer infertile couples their only chance to construct proper families. (1992, p. 24)

The Caucasian single mother was expected to pay for violating norms against premarital sex and conception. Her pregnancy, according to experts, was a neurotic symptom. Experts also agreed that only the most seriously disturbed unwed mothers kept their babies rather than giving them up to middle-class Caucasian couples for adoption (Solinger, 1992). While 90 percent of African American single mothers kept their babies between 1945 and 1965, over 90 percent of Caucasian unwed mothers in maternity homes relinquished their babies for adoption. The view that giving up her infant for adoption was the only path to psychological redemption for the Caucasian single mother was promoted by officials and professionals employed by the United States Children's Bureau, Florence Crittenton Association of America, the Salvation Army, and Catholic Charities, as well as by psychologists, psychiatrists, and clergy.

The social mandate of giving up children for adoption paralleled an increase of infertility among Caucasian couples of childbearing age and an increased demand for adoptable healthy, Caucasian infants (Zelizer, 1985; Silber & Speedlin, 1983). At the same time, African American women received the mandate to keep and raise their illegitimate children, a mandate so strong that an African American unwed mother who tried to give her baby up for adoption could be charged with desertion. In a paper presented at the National Conference on Social Welfare in 1953, Caucasian, unmarried mothers were referred to as "breeding machines, a means to an end. As individuals . . . they are overlooked, and popular support tends to concentrate upon securing babies for quick adoptions" (Solinger, 1992, p. 28).

Solinger (1992) reported that by the mid 1950s, one in ten of all marriages were involuntarily childless and couples approved to adopt waited one to three years to obtain a child. Ninety thousand children per year were being placed for adoption, an 80 percent increase since 1944. There was no federal law prohibiting commercial placement or independent adoption of a child across state lines, and 34 states had no laws against selling children within the state. Private charitable organizations such as the Salvation Army, which in earlier times had undertaken the task of assisting single mothers in raising their children, found that adoption agencies increasingly usurped their role, intent on serving infertile couples whose only aim was to secure adoptable infants.

The Maturing of Adoption Practice

In 1955, a big year in adoption history, international adoption originated through congressional action and a national conference on adoption sponsored by the Child Welfare League of America set the stage for reforms in practice that reflected an orientation toward the "best interests of the child" (Cole & Donley, 1990; Laws, 1994). At the same time, the federal government charged Senator Estes Kafauver, chair of the Subcommittee to Investigate Juvenile Delinquency, with the investigation of black market interstate baby selling, along with other matters. One of the goals of the subcommittee was to propose federal legislation that would control or eliminate the black market in adoption. The special counsel of the subcommittee, Ernest Mitler, voiced another legislative goal as well, contending that a good child welfare law would assure the appropriateness of the adoptive home, "a criterion that could not, by definition, be met in homes provided by unmarried mothers" (U.S. Congress, 1956, in Solinger, 1992, p. 166).

The CWLA underscored this value in its 1960 standards, stating that

> in our society, parenthood without marriage is a deviation from the accepted cultural pattern of bearing and raising children. It represents a specific form of social dysfunctioning which is a problem in itself and which in turn creates social and emotional problems for parent and child. . . . It is generally accepted in our society that children should be reared in families created through marriage. The legal family is the approved social institution to ensure sound rearing and development of children. (pp. 1–2)

The federal government and the CWLA with its member agencies worked concurrently to define ethical and practice standards in adoption through legislative and professional means as a way of supporting the transition from a market economy in children, based on adult needs, to one that valued children and was based on their needs. The CWLA developed its first standards for adoption practice in 1959, based on a national survey of adoption agencies about their practices and after analyzing the results and convening a national conference on adoption (CWLA, 1959; CWLA 1988).

The best interests of the child as a primary value in child welfare was more fully defined some 20 years later, when Goldstein, Freud, and Solnit (1973) published their seminal work on the subject. From its inception, however, the Child Welfare League of America asserted that the purpose of adoption service should "not be . . . to find children for families, and it should not be expected to provide help for many of the problems associated with childlessness" (CWLA, 1988, p. 10). This child-centered focus has been clear in CWLA standards from the very beginning.

Other adoption and child welfare agencies such as Catholic Charities and the National Association of Social Workers also began to develop standards of practice in child placement during the 1960s and 1970s for the purpose of providing services based on increased knowledge and professionalization in the adoption field. Kadushin summarized these practice guidelines but characterized them as resulting from practice wisdom, social values and philosophy, and "a modest amount of empirical research" (1984, p. 4).

The United States Children's Bureau also proposed standards of care and service to children in the United States, particularly those who were dependent, neglected, or deprived. The National Council for Adoption (NCFA) ad hoc Committee on Ethical Standards in Adoption established principles of practice in infant adoptions, commenting that "many in the field are concerned about the unprofessional and unethical practices in both [independent and agency] systems and have expressed a desire to set basic standards for good adoption practices to protect the parties in an adoption" (NCFA, 1991, p. 1).

Infant adoption reached its zenith during the 1950s and early 1960s in the United States. During the 20 years spanning 1945 to 1965, there were 200 licensed maternity homes in 44 states in America. Two-thirds of these homes were Florence Crittenton Association, Catholic Charities, and Salvation Army homes. Approximately 80 percent of maternity home residents gave up their babies for adoption, amounting to 20,000 adoptions annually or approximately 400,000 adoptions during this time period (Solinger, 1992).

In 1970, 80 percent of unmarried mothers gave up their illegitimate infants for adoption; only 4 percent of unmarried mothers did so in 1983 (Rosenberg, 1992). This dramatic change in the availability of adoptable infants resulted largely from the social and sexual revolution of the 1960s, the increased use of more effective methods of birth control, and the availability of legal abortion beginning with *Roe v. Wade.*

International Adoption

International adoption was virtually unknown in the United States before World War II. Between 1935 and 1948, fewer than 14 children per year "under 16 years of age, unaccompanied by parent" immigrated to the United States (Adamec and Pierce, 1991, p. 168). Of these, it is unclear how many actually entered the country for the purpose of adoption.

War creates casualties, many of them living. To address the needs of orphans left in the wake of World War II, Congress enacted the Displaced Persons Act in 1948, allowing 3,000 sponsored orphans to enter the United States. While sponsors did not have to promise to adopt these displaced orphans, they did have to provide proper care for them. Following the Korean War, American servicemen—including some who had fathered Korean-American children while stationed in Korea—expressed interest in adopting Korean orphans. Beginning in 1953, Congress annually allowed up to 500 orphans who would be adopted by servicemen or employees of the federal government to enter the country.

Unfortunately, many more than 500 Korean orphans a year needed families, and there was little hope that these children could be helped unless the restrictions Congress had imposed could be lifted. In 1955, an Oregon couple concerned about the plights of these Korean American orphans set out to adopt some of them. Though it took an act of Congress, Harry and Bertha Holt eventually adopted eight Korean children and in 1956 founded the Holt Adoption Agency, the nation's oldest and largest international adoption agency. Through the auspices of their agency, the Holts encouraged other Americans to adopt Korean orphans, laying the foundation for international adoptions in the United States.

Prior to the advocacy work of the Holts, orphan immigration for the purposes of adoption was limited. Between 1953 and 1956, the Refugee Relief Act allowed only 4,000 orphan visas for children entering the United States for adoption. The numerical limits on orphan visas were removed by Congress in 1957, but "Congress perceived the need and desire to adopt orphans from other countries as a short-term situation" (Adamec and Pierce, 1991, p. 169). Immigration of orphans for the purpose of adoption was normalized through the Immigration and Nationality Act in 1961, which established a lasting legal means of international adoption.

The adoptive families created in the years following the Korean War sought out one another for support and education in the transracial and transcultural adoption experience. In 1967, a decade after the Holts had founded their agency, adoptive mother Betty Kramer founded what became the largest international adoption support group in the United States, Parents of Korean and Korean-American Children (Laws, 1995). In 1968 the group, by then communicating with international adopters nationwide, changed its name to OURS (Organization for a United Response) and began publishing a magazine called *OURS Magazine*. Although the majority of international adopters continued to adopt from Korea, many Vietnamese children were also adopted in the post-Vietnam War era. As other countries began to allow their children to be adopted by American (and other) parents, OURS continued to evolve and restructure, and in 1989 became Adoptive Families of America (AFA) (Laws, 1995). The magazine published by Adoptive Families of America, *Adoptive Families*, is the country's most widely circulated adoption-specific publication today.

Since 1985, approximately ten thousand children born in other countries have been adopted by Americans every year (Joint Council on International Children's Services [JCICS], 1997–1998). During the 40 years after Harry and Bertha Holt adopted their Korean-born children, more Korean children were adopted in the United States than children from all other countries combined. With the opening of Eastern Europe and China to adoption in the 1990s, the tide of international adoption turned. In 1997, Russian and Chinese orphans were adopted more often than children from all other countries combined (*Adoptive Families*, December 1997).

Like other facets of adoption in the United States, international adoption has had its problems. Baran and Lifton, writing about the changes in international adoption since the Korean and Vietnam wars, commented that "international adoption has shifted from the rescue of war orphans to the legal or (in some cases) illegal trafficking in children" (1997, p. 72). Adoption facilitators eager for financial gain have used coercive and illegal means of obtaining adoptable infants for American couples. Some facilitators in foreign countries such as Guatemala have gone so far as to have nonrelated women pose as surrendering birth mothers of stolen infants. Reputable agencies have had to resort to DNA testing and other means of proving that infants have been relinquished for adoption legally.

Adoption and Minority Race Americans

When we talk about adoption and race in this country, generally we are talking about one of two types of adoption: in-race, culturally self-determined adoption and out-of-race, culturally imposed adoption. When Americans who are ethnic minorities have adopted children or given children for adoption, they have historically done it without much oversight or interest by the dominant culture. Thus, adoption among ethnic minorities in the United States has been informal, accomplished through close-knit groups of relatives, friends, and neighbors rather than through the institutional means imposed by the dominant Anglo culture. Minority races in America have taken care of their own and have seldom wanted, much less invited, intrusion into their traditional ways of providing for their neglected and orphaned children.

When the dominant Anglo culture has imposed its values onto minority groups we have done it through the laws we have written and the institutions we have staffed, largely without minority group member consent or counsel. As a result, transracial adoption—the adoption of a child of one race by parents of another race—has, in practice, meant the adoption of children of color by Caucasian parents. African American, Hispanic, Asian, and Native American adoption activists have agreed that the American child welfare system has historically not served most children very well, but particularly has failed children of color (Babb and Laws, 1997; *Families for Kids of Color*).

Adoption and Native Americans

When Christopher Columbus kidnapped a Taino Indian child in 1492, making him an interpreter and later adopting him, it may well have been the first transracial adoption on North American soil. Columbus baptized the child into the Christian faith and named him Diego, justifying "the forced adoption through a belief that he was saving Diego's immortal soul. Ironically, this same type of arrogance continued well into the 1970s. . . . Indian babies were routinely removed from Indian reservations not by American Indians, but by Caucasian adoptive parents, many of whom believed the baby would be 'better off' away from the Native American culture" (Babb & Laws, 1997, p. 165).

In the late 1970s and 1980s, one of the unfortunate results of the decline in adoptable Caucasian infants and the increased demand for them was that public and private child welfare and adoption agencies increased their efforts to place Native American children in need of temporary care or adoption with nontribal adoptive parents. In addition, Indian children in other away-from-home living situations, such as boarding schools, were prevented from practicing tribal traditions, stripping them of much of their cultural identities. Considering this practice a threat to the continuation of their tribes, Native Americans worked together to encourage the passage of Public Law 95–608, the Indian Child Welfare Act (ICWA), passed in 1978 by Congress.

ICWA established nationwide procedures for the handling of Indian child placements and authorized the establishment of child and family service programs for Native American children (Couch, n.d., p. 1). Among the adoption standards were requirements that preferences be given first to an adoptable child's extended family, then to tribal members of the child's tribe, and then to other Native American families. Tribes have the option of allowing non-Indians to adopt Indian children.

Adoption and Hispanic Americans

Hispanic peoples lived in this country two hundred years before Europeans colonized what would become America. The child welfare and adoption systems that developed in this country have treated Hispanic children in much the same way that children of other minority races have been treated because of institutionalized racism and a lack of cultural competence among child welfare workers in providing services to Hispanic children and their parents.

The cultural needs of Hispanic children who came into temporary and long-term foster care were largely overlooked until the late 1970s. Before then, adoption was largely accomplished informally by Latino families, as was the case among most other minority races in the United States. In 1978 in New York, although they comprised 25 percent of the foster care population, Hispanic children were "systematically placed along color lines in foster care and adoptive homes. The practice was to place dark skinned Latino children with African American families and lighter skinned children with White families" (Montalvo, 1994, p. 1). The cultural needs of Hispanic children were hardly considered until 1979, when New York's Council on Adoptable Children (COAC) developed the first Hispanic Adoption Program in the United States. Three years later, in 1982, the Committee for Hispanic Children and Families (CHCF) was organized by Latino professionals as an advocacy group for Latino families (Montalvo, 1994). In spite of the organization of these and other Hispanic advocacy groups, adoptable Hispanic children continue to be underserved in the United States.

Adoption and African Americans

As with other minority groups in America, adoption among African Americans has traditionally been an informal process through which relatives or friends of children deprived of parental care took such children into their homes and loved them as their own. Although modern-day African Americans can adopt children formally through our child welfare institutions, informal adoption continues to be prevalent in the African American community.

Prior to World War II, formal, institutionalized adoption services were not available to African Americans or to African American children. The Social Security Act of 1935 and later civil rights acts opened formalized adoption to more African Americans (Jackson-White et al., 1997). At the same time, legislation such as Public Law 87–31 (which provided financial incentives for states to place children into protective care), policy rulings related to Aid to Families with Dependent Children (AFDC) (such as the Flemming Rule), and the 1962 Public Service Amendments resulted in an increased number of African American children entering the child welfare system. This, combined with culturally insensitive treatment of African American families, contributed to a disproportionate number of African American children entering that system and becoming available for adoption (Lawrence-Webb, 1997).

Lawrence-Webb (1997) provides an excellent analysis of the historical process leading to our present-day problem of large numbers of African American children lingering in foster care in the United States. Between 1955 and 1959, African American families were systematically denied AFDC benefits based on their race and, sometimes, on the presence of children born outside marriage in the home. Other race parents in similar circumstances were also denied AFDC benefits when their homes were declared unsuitable. Then, in the early 1960s, African American families were denied AFDC benefits when substitute fathers or other nonrelated men lived in the home, there were one or more illegitimate children in the family, or the mother was dating or cohabiting and unmarried. When the single parent made application for AFDC, her request was investigated and if the home was found to be unsuitable or immoral, AFDC benefits were denied.

Between 1950 and 1960 several states, including Florida, Louisiana, and Mississippi, expelled large numbers of children, particularly African American children, from AFDC rolls under arbitrary "home suitability" rules. The expulsions were clearly racially motivated: in Florida, over 90 percent of the children expelled were African American. This created a large number of poverty-stricken parents, whose children were then declared neglected because of a lack of adequate resources.

In response to these expulsions, Arthur Flemming, then Secretary of the U.S. Department of Health, Education and Welfare, made a landmark administrative decision called the Flemming Rule. The Flemming Rule "declared that if a state believed a particular home was 'unsuitable,' that state had to (1) provide due process protections for the family, and (2) provide service interventions to families that were deemed to be 'unsuitable.' States could no longer simply apply a label of 'unsuitable,' expel the family from the AFDC rolls, and ignore the family" (Lawrence-Webb, 1997, p. 12).

Unfortunately, the Flemming Rule, intended to protect children, came to be used "in an oppressive manner that proved to be detrimental to the very children whom he was attempting to protect" (Lawrence-Webb, 1997, p. 23). After the Flemming Rule was instituted, when AFDC investigators entered the applicant's home and found it to be unsuitable, state intervention was mandatory. Culturally insensitive, unprofessional, and often racist services were offered, failed, and then the home situation declared neglectful (Lawrence-Webb, 1997; McRoy, Oglesby, & Grape, 1997). Federal policy and law under Public Law 87-31 required court intervention for the protection of neglected children, and African American and other parents declared unsuitable or unfit found themselves "locked into the Caucasian child welfare system," which consequently "began to experience an increase in the number of protective service, foster care, and adoption cases" (Lawrence-Webb, 1997, p. 21).

During the post-Flemming Rule era (1963–1965), parents were denied AFDC benefits when an unrelated father figure was present in the home or when a caseworker declared the home unsuitable, neglectful, or abusive. The numbers of African American children and other children of color in foster care began to grow, until in 1963, half the children in public agency foster care were African American or Native American, while in private agencies the proportion approached 60 percent (Jeter, 1963). Of all children in foster care in 1963, 81 percent had unmarried or divorced parents (Jeter, 1963).

Over the next decade, more children of color, particularly African American children, entered the child welfare system—so many that "some observers began to describe this decade as the 'browning' of child welfare in America" (Brissett-Chapman, 1997, p. 49). African American children represent 15 percent of the U.S. child population, but 40 percent of all American foster children who are free for adoption. A number of reasons for the disproportionate number of African American children entering and remaining in the child welfare system were identified by McRoy, Oglesby, and Grape (1997), including:

- More African American children (44%) live in poverty, the "greatest predictor of the removal of children of any age from their biological parents and placement in out-of-home care" (McRoy et al., 1997, p. 87).

- Protective service workers do not understand cultural and child-rearing differences among African Americans, perceive and report different practices as neglectful or abusive, and remove the child from the family.

- Once they enter the child welfare system, African American children remain in care longer and receive fewer services.

- African American parents receive fewer contacts from their social workers than do their Caucasian counterparts.

- Case workers are less likely to arrange visits between African American families and their children in care than for Caucasian parents and their children.

The increase of adoptable Native American and African American children in the child welfare system and the demand for adoptable infants and children by Caucasian adopters, combined with a growing acceptance of transracial adoption due to social changes, created a rise in the number of transracial adoptions in the country. In addition, the problems traditional public and private agencies have in recruiting same-race adoptive families for children of color have resulted in more transracial placements (McRoy et al., 1997).

Calling the practice of placing African American children into Caucasian families genocide, in 1972 the National Association of Black Social Workers (NABSW) initiated efforts to put an end to the practice (Baran & Lifton, 1995). The NABSW said that increased culturally aware efforts would result in more same-race adoptions in the African American community, a belief supported by the experiences of specialized minority adoption programs (McRoy et al., 1997; Jackson-White et al., 1997).

In spite of the proven efficacy of specialized minority adoption programs and agencies, the trend in state and federal policy and law is to support, rather than restrict, transracial placements. The Multiethnic Placement Act (MEPA), signed into law in 1994 as Public Law 103-382, prohibits denial of adoption based only on race, but allows for the consideration of cultural or ethnic factors when other factors are also considered. Most experts agree that the legislation will probably only affect a small percentage of all adoptions of African American children, and then mostly those by Caucasian foster parents. One untoward result of MEPA is that workers will now be "challenged to find ways to justify the placement of African American children with African American families and to justify the use of specialized minority programs, due to the restrictive laws limiting consideration of race" (McRoy et al., 1997, p. 101).

The law of supply and demand can nowhere be more clearly seen than in the area of transracial adoption. Transracial adoptions have always involved the flow of minority race children into majority race adoptive families; the minority race parent adopting a majority race child is unusual, indeed. In spite of federal laws fobidding race matching in the placements of children of color, McRoy, Oglesby, and Grape point out that race matching has been, and continues to be, "standard practice in the placement of Caucasian children," ostensibly because there are many Caucasian prospective adoptive parents and few adoptable Caucasian children.

The Adoption Reform Movement

Social scientists and geneticists came to new understandings of the roles of genetics and heredity at the same time that Alex Haley's 1976 book, *Roots*, captured the imagination of a nation increasingly interested in discovering and preserving its family bonds and ethnic heritages (Melina & Roszia, 1993). The work of scientists such as John Bowlby and Elisabeth Kübler-Ross regarding death and dying and how children experience loss affected the way people thought about early loss in the lives of children, including the loss of the mother. At the same time, adoptees such as Jean Paton, Florence Fisher, and Betty Jean Lifton began to tell their tales as adult adoptees who longed for a connection to their birth families. The searches of such adoptees for their original parents were nearly always hindered by sealed adoption records and amended birth certificates standard in American adoption practice since the 1940s. Many adoptees questioned this practice and formed groups to provide support and information for others in search and to promote changes and reform in adoption laws, including the opening of the adoptee's sealed original birth certificate and adoption records. The International Soundex Reunion Registry (ISRR) was established by Emma Mae Vilardi in Carson City, Nevada as a no-cost, voluntary reunion registry for those separated by adoption and searching for one another.

By the mid-1970s, groups such as Adoptees Liberty Movement Association (ALMA), Orphan Voyage, the American Adoption Congress (AAC), and Concerned United Birthparents (CUB) had been founded by adoptees and birth parents who were working to inform the public about the effects of adoption and the violation of their civil and human rights through the sealing of the adoptee's original birth certificate. Such groups found that their efforts to inform the public about their goals and struggles were often hindered by the laws and social mores viewing adoptees as perpetual children and birth parents, particularly mothers, as shadowy figures separated through secrecy and shame, by an "invisible barrier . . . from the bulk of humanity" (Jones, 1993, p. xiii). Such views hindered adoptees and birth parents not only legally, but also sometimes socially. In 1979, AAC founders Margaret Lawrence and Jean Paton wrote

Organizing into . . . a political force is difficult for any people, but perhaps more so for adoptees who are considered to be perpetual children and are conditioned to see themselves as their caretakers see them. One real effect of the adoption experience is an inhibited individual initiative. Like the powerless child, we wait for the sanction and direction of others. We are too well taught to respect authority and to look to it for direction. And so the adoption movement limps on with only a few doing real, productive work while the majority wait for sanction to do anything at all. While there is a tendency among all people to "let George do it," we have seen that this is the monumental stumbling block in the path of adoption reforms. (M. Lawrence & J. Paton, personal communication to AAC Board of Directors, December 1979)

In her master's thesis, Janine Baer (1995) wrote about the consequences of secrecy and sealed records in adoption, consequences that provided impetus for the adoption reform movement. Baer enumerated the results in "the order in which they could appear within the cycle of an adoption," listing baby selling, concealment of the child's adoption by the adoptive parents, emotional effects on birth parents of not knowing what happened to their relinquished children, adoptee struggles with identity, impact of unknown genetic and medical information on the adoptee, development of the adoption search industry, and genetic research problems for historians, genealogists, and the children and descendants of adoptees (p. 74).

In the 20 years following its establishment, the adoption reform movement has matured. The late 1990s saw local, regional and national adoption reform groups spearheading legislation and participating in lawsuits that increased access to the original, sealed birth certificate for adult adoptees. An adoptee activist group, Bastard Nation, was founded in 1996 as a one-issue, no-compromise organization advocating adult adoptee access to the original birth certificate as a civil right. But in spite of progress in the open records movement, in 1996 Orphan Voyage and AAC founder Jean Paton had this to say about adoption reform since the late 1970s:

> I am sure, by now, that it is the voice of the adopted person that is missing in the public picture, and this is largely due to their inner conflict of loyalties, and the resultant fear of action which could be interpreted as disloyalty to their adoptive parents. Even I, for all my courage, waited until both adoptive parents were deceased before making my search, and I was fortunate to get the records while they were still open, and to see from that how it can be. Thus at the age of almost fifty I knew who I was for sure, and was able for this reason (and other reasons) to continue in the work. . . . Thus, according to the above analysis, we must somehow give courage to the adopted person, and along with that educate society about what the sealed records destroy. (J. Paton, personal correspondence, January 9, 1996)

Special Needs Adoption

As adoptees grew up and expressed an adult need to know their roots, many American children continued to wait to be adopted, particularly those who were older, of minority race, needed to be adopted with siblings, or who had handicaps. Formerly labeled "unadoptable," such children came to be regarded as merely "hard to place" as the availability of healthy Caucasian infants declined dramatically and prospective adoptive parents increasingly turned to nontraditional forms of adoption, such as special needs adoption, transracial adoption, or international adoption in order to satisfy their desires to parent. Advocacy on behalf of the growing number of children in America's foster care system led to legislation such as the Adoption Opportunities Act (Public Law 95–266), which removed obstacles to special needs adoption and established regional Adoption Resource Centers, and the Adoption Assistance and Child Welfare Act of 1980 (Public Law 96–272), which provided the legal and financial incentives necessary to compel states to place waiting children. The act, through the establishment of adoption assistance payments, offered foster parents and prospective adoptive parents the means with which to raise children with special needs.

The experiences of large transracial and transcultural adoptive families popularized in books and films such as *Nineteen Steps Up the Mountain* (Blank, 1976) and *The Family Nobody Wanted* (Doss, 1954) brought such nontraditional types of adoption into the public eye, with the effect of increasing both the acceptability and popularity of such adoptions. Adoption groups such as the North American Council on Adoptable Children (NACAC), founded by Peter and Joyce Forsythe, Adopt a Special Kid (AASK), founded by Bob and Dorothy DeBolt, and Adoptive Families of America (AFA), founded by Betty Kramer, were also founded in the 1960s and 1970s. Barbara Eck Menning, who authored a book about infertility, founded a support group for infertile couples called Resolve and brought into the public consciousness the fact that infertile couples experience grief that can have a serious and long-lasting influence on infertile adopters if left unresolved. Meanwhile, a citizen's foster care review committee pilot project in Michigan grew into the nationwide Court-Appointed Special Advocate (CASA) program through an Edna McConnel Clark Foundation grant to the National Council of Juvenile Court Judges (Babb & Laws, 1997). The photolisting of adoptable children originated through the efforts of Michigan newspapers and Spaulding for Children, the nation's first special needs adoption agency.

The establishment of many of these groups and their resultant influence on state and private sector adoption agencies

> was the result of changes in a system that had historically seen its role as one that would approve of adoptive applicants and thus control adoption, to a view of the system and the applicants as collaborators, one that gave agencies the role of educators and parents that of pupils. Children came to be seen as those who were the most needy, and professionals began to advocate for the right of children to have parents, rather than the right of parents to have children. (Babb & Laws, 1997, pp. 13–14)

The Origins of Open Adoption

During the 1970s and early 1980s, agencies in Wisconsin, Texas, California, and Michigan, based on requests from adoptive and birth parents, began to allow more open contact between birth and adoptive parents and their adopted children, which came to be known as "open adoption" (Rosenberg, 1992). A popular book of the time, *Dear Birthmother: Thank You for Our Baby*, reproduced letters that had been exchanged between birth and adoptive mothers in open adoptions and lent the credibility of experienced social workers, along with agency support, to the new adoption specialty (Silber & Speedlin, 1983).

Author and social worker Jim Gritter credits Catholic Social Services of Green Bay, Wisconsin, as the first American agency to formally implement open adoption practice (personal communication, November 6, 1997). Under the leadership of Marge Gilling, Catholic Social Services of Green Bay began practicing open adoption in 1974 in response to the increasing numbers of adoptees who returned to the agency as adults, seeking information about their original families. Professionals at the agency reasoned that promoting a more open exchange of information between birth and adoptive families might prevent, or at least mitigate, future secrecy-based frustration among adoptees (J. Gritter, personal communication, November 6, 1997).

The move toward more openness in adoption occurred in a society that had changed markedly since adoption records had been sealed in the early 1900s. The birth parents and adoptees who founded the adoption reform movement spoke out about the pain, loss, and anger they felt over having had their pasts judicially taken from them. The sexual revolution of the 1960s and 1970s resulted in the unstigmatized increase of abortion and unwed motherhood. Unwed mothers had choices, and the declining numbers who planned adoption for their babies wanted to know how their children were doing in their adoptive families. Likewise, adoptive parents found themselves frustrated over living with the ghosts of their adopted children's birth parents. They wanted facts, not fables—something only open adoption could offer.

Some suggest, too, that the most important contributor to the rise in open adoption was the declining number of adoptable infants available for adoption. Sharon Kaplan Roszia, open adoption practice pioneer, has said:

Faced with waits of up to ten years at agencies, prospective parents looked at ways to circumvent the agency process and were willing to give up confidentiality if necessary. Birthmothers gradually learned that babies for adoption were needed so desperately that they could have more control than ever before over the adoption process. And what many birthmothers wanted was to choose the people who would be raising their children, to meet them, and to stay in touch with them. Agencies that didn't respond to the changes birthparents wanted soon found that birthparents were turning instead to attorneys and doctors, as well as to direct advertisements by prospective adopters. These agencies realized that if they were to continue to offer adoption services, they would have to offer the same kind of control and openness that other agencies, independent facilitators, and adoptive parents themselves were offering. (Lynch, September-October-November 1997, p. 24)

Today, open adoption and what is called open adoption (but is actually something less than open) has become a standard option at many adoption agencies in the United States, and is particularly popular in attorney-facilitated (private) adoptions. Although open adoption arrangements are not legally binding in most states, the increase in the acceptance of open adoption indicates that it is an option preferable to many birth and adoptive parents as a type of adoption with the potential to truly serve the adoptee.

Jim Gritter (1997) identifies a number of different types of open adoption, or adoptions that are inaccurately referred to as "open" adoptions. He identifies three important values of open, cooperative adoption as pioneered by Sharon Kaplan Roszia—child-centeredness, flexibility, and cooperation—and then describes the particular type of open adoption he favors, *values-based open adoption*. The values underlying this type of open adoption are honor for the adoptee, candor, free choice, honoring the pain in adoption, covenant keeping, transformation, adaptability, and building relationships.

Adoption as an Industry

Concomitant with the increase of special needs and transracial adoptions and the development of open adoption were increases in infertility and abortion rates and a decrease in the number of adoptable infants. Recent estimates have indicated that 10 to 20 percent of couples in their thirties are infertile, and that as many as 60 couples wait to adopt each healthy infant (Silber & Speedlen, 1983; Mason & Silberberg, 1993). The dearth of healthy adoptable infants resulted from a number of social factors, including increased infertility rates, postponed childbearing among women, the use and effectiveness of contraception and abortion, and the acceptance of unwed motherhood in modern society. At the same time, the number of older adoptable children who have been neglected or abused has continued to increase over the past 30 years. In spite of the increasing number of special needs children awaiting adoption in America's child care system, the demand for such children has remained relatively small. Most prospective adoptive parents seek healthy infants or toddlers (Courtney, 1997).

According to some, the "adoption industry" takes advantage of the demand for adoptable infants, but does not create the demand (Zelizer, 1985; Babb, 1996). Others have concluded that adoption has historically been a service designed to meet the needs of adoptive parents, although it has been "described as an act of kindness intended to save children from harmful environments" (Reitz & Watson, 1992, p. 3). Few have been willing to examine the "dynamics of supply and demand in the adoption 'market,' " (Courtney, 1977, p. 792). Fewer still have attempted to dispel the myths and traditions in American adoption practice that so often meet adult needs at the expense of children. Though entering a new century, America's piecemeal adoption system continues to be driven by the demands of the majority of prospective adopters, usually infertile Caucasians who see adoption "as a second-best alternative to biological parenthood, and as a last resort," relatively few of whom "are willing to adopt a child with physical, mental, or emotional difficulties" or to adopt transracially, particularly African American children (Courtney, 1997, p. 755). Harvard law professor Elizabeth Bartholet (1993) explains why: "Prospective adopters with money can escape all but minimal screening. They can also exercise extensive choice among the children available for adoption, and it is they who are most likely to end up adopting the healthy infants who are most in demand" (p. 73).

The idea that the source of our adoption practices might be found through simply following the money trail is unpleasant, but the arguments in favor of a utility-driven mechanism are strong. The ethical implications of such an approach to adoption are more closely examined and discussed in the final chapter of this book.

Adoption and Mental Health

Mental health professionals historically have "paid little attention to adoption" (Brodzinsky & Schechter, 1990, p. ix). Research and theoretical work related to maternal deprivation, institutionalization, and early childhood experiences first awakened the mental health community to an interest in adoption as a field ripe for research (Bowlby, 1951; Schechter, 1960). Bowlby's work had a profound effect on the mental health and adoption theories of the day and inspired an emphasis on early placement, changed the focus from heredity and genetic determinism to concerns with the external and internal environments of the human being, and changed the focus from evaluating the child to evaluating the adoptive parents (Babb, 1994). A good deal of discussion and research ensued in the mental health community that examined the over-representation of adoptees in mental health settings as well as numerous studies of the clinical symptoms of adoptees both inside and outside clinical settings (Borgotta & Fanshel, 1965; Brinich & Brinich, 1982; Deutsch et al., 1982; Schechter, 1960; Simon & Senturia, 1966; Brodzinsky et al., 1984; Hoopes, 1982; Sigvaardson et al., 1984; Brodzinsky & Schechter, 1990).

In 1964, H. David Kirk, an adoptive father, published his sociological analysis of adoptive kinship in his book *Shared Fate*, the first theoretical approach to the issue. Kirk's work had a profound affect on the way professionals thought about adoption, for it offered a theoretical basis from which to view adoption, normalized the adjustment problems that many adoptees and adoptive parents faced when building a family through adoption, and fostered increased honesty and openness in adoption. Prior to Kirk's work, adoptive parents were often advised by professionals to take the adoptee home and love him or her "as if" the adoptee was the adoptive parents' own child, and many adoptive parents kept the fact of the adoption a well-guarded secret. *Shared Fate* had the effect of promoting more telling of the adoption story and disclosure of additional background information about the adopted child (Baran & Pannor, 1990; Brodzinsky & Schechter, 1990).

Kirk's theory was the first to question the ethics and practice of the professional promotion of secrecy within the adoptive family. Child development experts, psychiatrists, and other experts of the time promoted a complete break between the adopted child and his or her biological parents, asserting that having an attachment to only a single set of parents was necessary to the healthy development of the child, and that the biological mother "needed to achieve as unambiguous a separation from the child as possible" (Dukette, 1984, p. 236; Baran & Pannor, 1990).

The research of Bowlby and others surrounding maternal deprivation and the effects of foster care found that the absence of continuity of caretakers in the life of a child had profound negative effects (Bowlby, 1951; Rutter, Quinton, & Liddle, 1983; Triseliotis & Hill, 1990; Kristinsdottir, 1991). Even so, child placement continued to prosper although its theoretical underpinnings had "not been analyzed profoundly" (Kristinsdottir, 1991).

During the 1960s and 1970s, the changing nature of the family, the civil rights movement, a focus on the rights of oppressed minorities, and shifts in social values all contributed to new policies, standards, and values in adoption (Dukette, 1984; Brodzinsky & Schechter, 1990). Contemporary adoption standards are examined in Chapter 3.

CONTEMPORARY ADOPTION STANDARDS

Foundational Values in Child Welfare and Adoption

A number of authors have identified foundational values in child welfare and adoption, or means of making values-based decisions in adoption work. At times vague and ambiguous, some of these so-called ethical codes or standards of practice appear to be ill-conceived and based on practice traditions rather than research or a firm foundational understanding of ethics. In this section, an overview will be given of the major values and practice standards identified by others, followed by increasingly detailed explorations of values in American adoption practice. The research on ethics and the ethical codes influencing American adoption practice will be more closely scrutinized in later chapters.

Sachdev (1984) identified the following guidelines for adoption practice as set forth by various national and international organizations such as the CWLA and the United Nations:

1. Adoption is always a substitution for the biological home and should not be considered as an option until it becomes clear that the child's own family will not be able to raise the child; the best place for the child is with his own family, in his own community, and in his own country. The value of blood ties or blood relatedness underlies this standard.

2. If a child's family cannot raise him or her, the first efforts should be made to find an adoptive home in the child's own racial, national, ethnic, and religious community, underscoring what Dukette (1984) called the "value of identity." Closely tied to the value of blood relatedness, such an approach esteems the adoptee's racial, cultural, and national origins.

3. The primary purpose of adoption is to provide a permanent family for the child, and the child's welfare, needs, and interests are the basic antecedents of good adoption practice—*the best interest of the child* standard, based upon the belief that all human beings, including children, have innate worth and dignity.

4. When a child cannot be raised in his or her own family, adoption is the best alternative, an expression of the value of providing permanent families for children whose parents cannot raise them (also an expression of the value people place on families, as compared with that of institutions).

5. Every child who needs adoption should receive the service, and receive the service as soon as possible.

6. Everyone who is party to an adoption should be given the opportunity to make informed, thoughtful decisions regarding the alternatives to adoption and help in implementing the alternative of choice. If adoption is chosen, assistance should be provided in understanding the implications of adoption, the anticipated problems, and the necessary preparation. The values of integrity and respect are fundamental to this standard: integrity, in facilitating adoptions and offering assistance with a commitment to presenting information both positive and negative about adoption, which provides an accurate picture of the service and its alternatives; respect, in recognizing each person's right to what social work calls the ethic of self-determination—to autonomous decision making.

7. Some delays—between the decision to surrender the child and the actual legal surrender, and between the placement of the child for adoption and the legal finalization of the adoption—should be introduced so as to allow for informed, thoughtful decision making. Again Sachdev (1984) emphasizes the primary value of exercising professional authority ethically in adoption by providing clients with the information and time they need to consider their options and make informed decisions.

8. Adoption severs the relationship between the biological parents and the adoptee, and that confidentiality regarding the identities of the biological parents and the adoptive parents should be safeguarded. Implicit to this guideline are the values of confidentiality and privacy.

9. Adoption is a life-long process and not a one-time event. Dukette, commenting on traditional American adoption practice, which forces a complete break with the adoptee's genetic past, wrote that adoption triad members "are striving to complete a broken circle, a completion that does not deny adoptive ties but weaves them into a complete life experience, with a beginning as well as a future" (p. 242). Viewing adoption as a life-long process respects the value of blood ties and identity, but also recognizes the rights of others to self-determination, autonomy, and tolerance. A system based on respect would acknowledge the adopted child's need for protection and security, and the adoptive family's

desire for cohesion, at the same time making allowances for the needs of adult adoptees to know their identities, and of relatives separated by adoption to locate and establish relationships with one another if they choose to do so.

10. The community has a concern in adoption: the right to intervene in family life in order to protect children who are abused, neglected, or otherwise deprived of adequate parental care.

11. In implementing "this concern [of the community in adoption], some attention needs to be given to developing a trained professional cadre of social workers with a specialized knowledge of and skill in adoption practice" (Sachdev, 1984, p. 6), again reflecting the value of protecting children, as well as the value of professional integrity.

Among postindustrialized nations, only the United States and some provinces of Canada uphold the eighth principle, that of confidentiality, by judicially sealing identifying information about the adoptee's birth parents and original family identity. Other countries observe confidentiality by allowing the adult adoptee, and sometimes birth and adoptive parents, access to the identifying information (sometimes referred to as open records), while not making the same information available to the general public. In this way, confidentiality of adoption records is respected in much the same way that medical records are safeguarded in the United States. Such records can be released to professional service providers and to those to whom the records pertain, thus supporting the ethic of confidentiality while also respecting that of client self-determination.

Vitillo (1991) also identified some of the foundational values in child welfare and adoption by examining the adoption standards embraced by the United Nations Convention on the Rights of the Child in its 1985 *Declaration on Social and Legal Principles relating to the Protection and Welfare of Children, with Special Reference to Foster Placement and Adoption Nationally and Internationally*. The standards, adopted by the U.N. General Assembly on December 3, 1986, are:

1. Priority should be given for a child to be cared for by his or her own parents and support for the family should be provided by governments.

2. Intercountry adoption should be considered only when adoption in the child's own country fails.

3. Biological parents and the child should be involved in the decision to place internationally.

4. Children in intercountry placements should receive special protections.

5. Countries should enact measures to combat child abduction and illicit placement.

6. Placements resulting in "improper financial gain for those involved" should be condemned.

Sachdev (1984) and Vitillo (1991), in recounting the standards established by American and international child welfare organizations and the United Nations, underscored the values from which such standards arise. As Doxiadis wrote, "Each culture is sensitive to the special needs of children" (1989, p. 13). The standards identified by Vitillo, like those enumerated by Sachdev, spring from the following values:

- The value of protecting children who are abused, neglected, or abandoned because of the innate worth and dignity of human beings, including children.

- The value of blood ties and identity; the latter includes knowing as much about one's own past as others know, respecting and maintaining when possible a person's racial, cultural, national, and religious identity.

- The value of family, expressed by providing permanent families for children whose original parents cannot raise them.

- The value of professional integrity, including honesty, loyalty, and trustworthiness.

- The value of respect of humanity, including recognition of each person's right to autonomy, self-determination, privacy, and tolerance.

- The value of citizenship, including upholding laws that give responsibility to professionals and institutions to act as agents of society, punishing those who mistreat children (including those who use children for personal or financial gain), and respecting the legal processes of nations.

Some of these same values can be seen in Cole and Donley's (1990) list of standards underlying adoption practice. These include raising children in nurturing families, the family of origin when possible; providing an adoptive family in a timely manner when birth parents cannot raise a child; regarding adoption as a lifelong process; enabling birth and adoptive parents to choose the type and extent of pre- and post-adoption contact; giving adoptees all the information about their birth, original families, genetic and social histories, placements, and reasons for being adopted, even if adoptive parents disagree with disclosure; making the same information available to the adoptive parents of infants and young children; and preparing adoptive parents for competent parenthood rather than scrutinizing them.

Gritter (1997) admitted that adoption professionals have shirked their duty of discussing quality in adoption, and recommended eight foundational values specific to values-based open adoption:

1. Quality adoption focuses on the needs of the child.
2. Quality adoption shines with candor; it volunteers information that is not sought.
3. Quality adoption results from true choice and is thus completely endorsed by its participants.
4. Quality adoption acknowledges the pain inherent in adoption.
5. Quality adoption is covenental, honoring the commitments it makes.
6. Quality adoption transforms its participants.
7. Quality adoption is flexible and adaptable.
8. Quality adoption recognizes those related by adoption as part of an interdependent kinship system.

Finally, the Joint Council on International Children's Services Ethics Committee issued recommended standards of practice to member agencies based on the following values (B. McDermott, Chair of JCICS Ethics Committee, personal communication, March 4, 1998):

- The value of children and respect for their needs for permanency in a loving family.
- The value of international adoption as a child welfare service focusing on the best interests of the child.
- The values of integrity, honesty, and service.

- The value of continued professional excellence through improved knowledge and understanding.

- The value of abiding by laws and regulations governing adoption in spirit and form.

- The value of disclosing accurate, comprehensive, and objective information as often as possible to everyone involved in an adoption.

The JCICS adopted revised Standards of Practice in 1998 that established standards for education, preparation, and adoption home study of adoptive parents, placement services, postadoption services, finances, humanitarian aid, interagency relationships, and professional conduct.

THE VALUES UNDERLYING AMERICAN ADOPTION PRACTICE

The Value of Helping the Helpless Child

We have seen that, from antiquity, the nurture and care of orphaned children has been valued in all societies worldwide. Plato and Aristotle considered orphans worthy of special care and protection. The state was, particularly in Greek and Roman times, seen as the protector of society. As such, the state had an interest in the protection of orphans. Early societies recognized that orphans had been deprived of humankind's most important natural protection, that provided by parents. This value has continued to be fundamental in adoption and child placement up to modern times.

Much evidence of humankind's continuing concern for the helpless can be seen in the laws and social programs of all countries, particularly those related to adoption. The value of protecting children who are abused, neglected, or abandoned is expressed through the power of states to intervene in family life, the responsibility of helping professions to act as agents of society, and the punishment of parents (and others) who abandon or mistreat children. Americans, like citizens of other countries, acknowledge that society has an interest in the care and protection of children deprived of parental support and nurturing. We also agree that as citizens of the world, we have obligations to orphaned children worldwide and should express our obligations through our orphan immigration laws by allowing and encouraging international adoptions.

The Value of Human Relatedness in the Context of Families

The value of human relationships in the context of the family includes the value of blood ties and of providing permanent families for children whose parents cannot raise them. Early societies valued maintaining family ties and considered the provision of heirs through adoption as one means of underscoring the value of families. From early times tribes, governments, and nations have provided permanent families for children whose parents cannot raise them, a reflection of the value a society places on children and on the continuation of society. The gain of providing children for families who want them has come to be regarded as only a secondary gain of adoption (Dukette, 1984).

Adages such as "blood is thicker than water" and "the hand that rocks the cradle rules the world" are common expressions of the value placed on the nurturing family, and especially of blood ties. Dukette (1984) called this the value of identity, expressed through standards of giving birth parents every chance to raise their own children and of providing timely and permanent adoptive placements for the children of those parents who cannot or will not raise them. Practice and policy related to family preservation and kinship placement and adoption also illustrate the importance we place on the family. Our valuation of the family is so high that we forbid the state from interfering with it until parents are criminally convicted of violating their obligation to act in the best interests of their children.

Dukette (1984) also pointed out that the value of families has been expressed in traditional American adoption by the erroneous establishment in practice as well as law, of adoptive parents as the *only* parents, which has led to the secrecy and judicially sealed adoption records that continue to be part of our standard adoption practice. Bartholet (1993) concurred, suggesting that the sealed original birth certificate belies a uniquely American fear that any connection of the adoptee to his or her birth family presents a threat to the integrity of the adoptive family:

> The sealed record system stands in significant contrast to the manner in which our society structures other complex family relationships. . . . The legal system ordinarily makes no attempt to write out of existence, by sealing records or other such mechanisms, the various parental figures who walk out of their children's lives, such as the divorced parent who relinquishes custody. It is only in regulating adoptive families—families formed in the absence of any blood link—that the government feels that it has to seal records so as to figuratively destroy the existence of the family that *is* linked by blood. (p. 55)

Other developments, such as the passage of legislation encouraging the adoption of waiting children in this and other countries, also uphold the value of finding permanent families for children and continue to influence child welfare practice. The development of values-based open adoption and its commitment to relationships among adoption kinship system members has also been an expression of our value of human relatedness in the context of families (Gritter, 1997).

The Value of Human Beings, Including Children, as Having Innate Worth and Dignity

Values arising out of this primary one include the recognition of each person's right to autonomy, self-determination, justice, beneficence, privacy and tolerance, the respect of the uniqueness of each person, and the consideration of humans as alive and growing toward increasing levels of satisfaction in life. Other beliefs related to this value are that all people, regardless of their situations in life, have common needs (food, shelter, safety, education, health care, and recreation) and mutual responsibilities to one another and to their society (Poppendieck, 1992).

With the rise of Christianity came an increased conviction of the worth of children among Christian nations. Rather than being viewed merely as the building blocks of the family or society (i.e., valuable only insofar as they served a purpose), children more and more often came to be viewed as inherently valuable, even if not particularly useful. The care of the early churches for orphans through orphan asylums in Eastern and Western Christendom illustrated the growing concern of societies for children. This concern continued to manifest itself through the ongoing improvement of institutional care for needy children, bringing us into the modern era.

The Value of Expertise and Science, as Expressed Through Professional Behavior

Societies governing child welfare services and child protection emerged in the United States during the early 1900s. More and more, child welfare, child protection, and adoption became the concern of people with experience—for example, experts or professionals in these areas. Ideas about professional behavior and preferred approaches to dealing with people provided the impetus for the growing professionalization of child welfare. The values included client self-determination (whenever possible), integrity among professionals, and the improvement of professional competence in child protection and adoption. These values are expressed in modern social work's principles of propriety (high standards of personal conduct as a social worker), competence and professional development, service to others, integrity, and scholarship and research (NASW, 1996).

The expressed concern about professional behavior and establishment of the helping professions (other than medicine, which has been a profession since ancient times) as bona fide professions was preceded by the commitment of child protection workers to achieving desired outcomes for children. Workers and societies first sought to meet the basic needs of children for food, shelter, safety, education, health care, and recreation. The development of helping professions such as social work came later, once child advocates saw that they had made some headway in protecting children and serving them according to their needs. Poppendieck (1992) noted that social work has always been more successful at achieving desired outcomes for people than it has been at achieving social justice or broad-based recognition of the discipline as a profession.

The development of child placement standards by various societies in the 1960s and 1970s underscored the confidence of professionals and society that their services were valuable. By 1973, Goldstein, Freud, and Solnit had developed their work on the best interests of the child, firmly establishing the value of providing child-centered, informed services for children. Much of this work has focused on rectifying some of the power imbalances experienced by children in societies governed by adults.

Part II

Explorations

Chapter 3

Ethical Inquiry

Only if we develop a coherent perspective can we have any assurance
that we will act with moral integrity and with the seriousness required
by our power over others' lives.

—Margaret Rhodes

PHILOSOPHY AND ETHICS

An exploration of ethics in any field would be incomplete without an overview of its philosophical underpinnings. In this chapter, we will examine
the philosophical frameworks out of which our ethical assumptions arise,
review the research into ethics in psychology and social work, and discuss
the conflicting values and ethical challenges experienced by adoption specialists.

The word *ethics* is derived from the Greek word *ethos*, meaning "character," and from the Latin word *mores*, meaning "customs." Thus, ethics historically can be seen as the expression of society's customs of right and
good. A person who conforms to the law or to a formally-adopted code of
ethics could be said to be operating ethically. Custom and law in a society
do not always describe what is truly ethical, however. The law may permit
actions that are unethical, while disallowing actions that are ethical. For
example, the U.S. Supreme Court's *Dred Scott* decision declared slaves to
be property, not citizens, a decision that was unethical but still legal (60
U.S. 393, 19 How. 393, 15 L. Ed. 691). A law or standard defining certain

actions as legal does not, therefore, mean the action is ethical. Similarly, in American adoption practice at one time adoption records were legally open to the parties to each adoption (birth parents, adoptive parents, and the adoptee); today in most states, all such records are closed to the parties except under certain circumstances. At one time, it was permissible to withhold critical medical and psychiatric information about adopted children from their adoptive parents; today agencies and professionals who withhold such information wrongfully can be sued. Many times laws arise out of philosophical assumptions that have not been thoroughly examined. Instead, they can arise out of the social and political climate of a culture.

In her book about ethics and social work practice, Margaret Rhodes (1991) shows that all social work arises from ethical and political assumptions, whether or not social workers realize and acknowledge these assumptions. Ethical and political assumptions are likewise foundational to adoption practice, whether or not adoption is practiced by professionals or by lay facilitators. Implicit in every transaction involving adoption are ideas about what is right and wrong, what is best for people—particularly children—and what sort of society or government controls are desirable and should be promoted.

One standard in American adoption is that of the "best interests of the child." Although the best interest of the child standard is spoken and written about as though it were a universal standard that could be applied to each child at risk of losing his or her family of origin, no such standard actually exists. In America, the best interests of children are defined by legislatures, courts, agencies, adoption specialists, child welfare agencies, parents, and others involved with the lives of children. Because they are so loosely defined by people and circumstances and not by clearly written and universally understood and applied standards, the best interests of American children are actually defined by individuals making ethical and political assumptions. Because our adoption practice grows out of such assumptions, adoption practitioners ought to examine their own beliefs and values along with the political and ethical structures of the agencies and organizations in which they work.

Unfortunately, professionals are ill prepared to understand, much less apply, ethical decision making in adoption practice (Conrad & Joseph, 1991). Unless professionals working in adoption organize, educate, and regulate themselves—or become government regulated, as in other countries—adoption services will continue to be provided by practitioners with widely divergent views, beliefs, practices, and results. Adoption clients will continue to receive inconsistent services provided by specialists who cannot prove that they are competent in adoption or that they are ethical practitioners. The results of such a sloppy approach to permanency planning for children can be disastrous. American citizens have more assurance of quality control when they buy a table lamp or receive a flu shot than they have when planning the adoption of a child.

Attorneys and judges fare somewhat better when arguing for or making decisions on behalf of children, because federal and state laws offer some guidelines about what actions serve children's best interests. For instance, the Adoption Assistance and Child Welfare Act of 1980 (Public Law 96–272) made ongoing federal financial support available to certain children adopted with special needs, indicating that requiring adoptive parents to bear the financial burdens of special needs adoption by themselves could not serve the best interests of waiting children. The Multiethnic Placement Act of 1994 (Public Law 103–382) prohibited delays in permanency planning for children based on racial matching alone, suggesting that an adoptive family of another race serves the needs of the waiting child better than would waiting months or years in foster care for a same-race family. Additional federal and state laws speak to other ways of serving children's best interests.

The best interests guidelines offered by statutes and case law are sadly inadequate for modern adoption practice. They do not tell us who is truly qualified to dissolve and create families, who should adopt, who is adoptable, and whose interests we are serving in American adoption. In spite of increased adoption legislation and regulation of agencies, the number of legal orphans has increased in the United States. Before we can address these and other practical issues and attempt to solve some of our problems, we first must have a philosophical framework, set before us like Israel's stones of memorial, signposts showing where we have been and giving us perspective on where we are going.

Rhodes provides an excellent study of the various philosophical frameworks out of which our ethical and political assumptions arise, writing that "only if we develop a coherent perspective can we have any assurance that we will act with moral integrity and with the seriousness required by our power over others' lives" (1991, p. 23). Drawing from her training in philosophy and social work, Rhodes presents seven basic ways of thinking about human relationships and responsibilities: utilitarianism, duty-based Kantianism, rights-based theories, Marxist-based ethicial frameworks, intuitionist ethical theories, virtue-based frameworks, and nformed relativism (also called limited objectivity). These philosophical frameworks and two others (ethics of care and causuistry) and those underlying the suggested ethical standards in following chapters are briefly discussed here to assist the reader in understanding the assumptions underlying adoption practice in the United States. No single philosophical theory explains all, or even most, of what we do when we practice adoption in the United States; instead, these theories are parts of the collective whole of our philosophical heritage. We can begin to understand the ethical assumptions we make after we understand their theoretical underpinnings.

Utilitarianism

Utilitarianism promotes the ultimate well-being of society as a whole through promoting the good of individuals within the society. Arising as a way to address the injustices of eighteenth- and nineteenth-century European and English societies, utilitarianism sought to provide a moral basis for decision making based on rational deliberation rather than religion or social order. Utility can be defined in terms of pleasure, happiness, ideals, or interests as defined by proponents of utilitarianism such as Jeremy Bentham, John Stuart Mill, G. E. Moore, or R. B. Perry. One could say that the goal of utilitarianism is the greatest happiness for the greatest number.

Utilitarianism views all people's welfare as being on an equal basis, with one person's happiness being as important as the next person's. According to this viewpoint, writes Rhodes, "Altruism is viewed as mutual self-interest: in the long run, promoting our own interests will also promote those of others" (1991, p. 27). Unfortunately, utilitarianism assumes that the greatest good for the greatest number of people in a society can be defined and agreed upon. In reality, consensus about the greatest good often (if not usually) cannot be achieved, particularly in a multicultural society like ours. Sometimes even when consensus appears to be reached it may not, in fact, promote the greatest good or may promote the good of the majority at the expense of a minority. Congressional acts supporting special needs adoptions could be viewed as utilitarian, since society is served when children with special needs are adopted. A utilitarian approach to adoption can also be seen in some adoption research studies, comparing, for example, open and closed adoption. When researchers attempt to sum up the overall happiness and pain for triad members and evaluate their satisfaction without defining it, they rely on utilitarian approaches.

Kantianism

Kantianism postulates that each human being is rational and, as a rational being, has fundamental worth. Its originator, Immanuel Kant, believed that people can use reason to develop a consistent set of timeless, irrefutable moral principles. Kant's arguments in favor of his ethical system are summarized in his categorical imperative, "Act only on that maxim whereby thou canst at the same time will that it would become a universal law" (Pojman, 1995, p. 253). In other words, if an action is right for all people, then it is moral.

His second formulation of the categorical imperative is that people should always act so as to treat humanity, whether in their own person or in that of others, as an end and not a means. In other words, people should not be coerced, manipulated, or used as a means of achieving good for society at large. Kantians, in contradiction to utilitarians, believe that altruism is a duty owed to other people who are suffering, whether or not an act of goodness is in our own best interest. Kantian ethics also view morality as being universal and consistent, and morals as never conflicting with one another.

Rights-based Theories

Rights-based theories have been promoted by individuals such as Rosseau and Locke, whose ideas are reflected in the Declaration of Independence, and more recently by John Rawls, Joel Feinberg, Ronald Dworkin, and Alan Gweirth. Rights-based theorists, unlike utilitarians and Kantians, assume that agreement about what is right or good cannot be achieved in society. The freedoms and interests (or good) of individuals must be balanced against those of others, and the "good society is one which protects the rational autonomy of every individual through maximizing the extent of individual freedom consistent with justice for all" (Rhodes, 1991, p. 33). While rights-based theorists do not assume, with utilitarians, that one person's happiness is as important as the next person's or that the greatest good for the greatest number of people in a society can be defined and agreed upon, they do believe that people are basically rational creatures and that one person's rationality is equal to the next person's. In addition, rights-based theorists believe that natural rights exist and can readily be identified. Those who disagree say that "natural rights no more exist than do unicorns and witches," and, like Alasdair MacIntyre, say that the mistake of rights-based theorists is to derive rights from needs and to make political and social assumptions without proving them (Pojman, 1995, p. 715).

America's practice of using sealed adoption records to balance the adult adoptee's right to have her original birth records against the rights of birth and adoptive parents could be seen as arising out of rights-based theories. Also rooted in a rights-based approach is our traditional (and often times legal) view of children as having only interests and not rights because we formulate rights in terms of autonomy, which children cannot possess.

Intuitionist Ethical Theories

Intuitionism is the theory that the good or the right thing to do can be known directly through human intuition rather than rationally. Intuitionist ethical theories are personal, feelings-based, and subjective. They rely upon the individual's duty to do the right thing based on what he or she feels, under the circumstances, to be right. Intuitionists, disagreeing with Kantians and agreeing with the moral objectivist view, believe that moral principles are not absolutes, but rather that presumptive moral duties can and should be overcome by more binding moral duties. Much of American adoption practice relies upon intuitional ethics, since, in the absence of universal ethical or practice standards, practitioners are often left to follow self- or agency-devised ideas about duty and morality.

Virtue-based Frameworks

Virtue-based ethical systems have been promoted by philosophers such as Plato, Aristotle, Bernard Mayo, Walter Schaller, and Alasdair MacIntyre. Instead of defining ethics through actions or duties, virtue-based ethical frameworks emphasize character. Duty-based ethical theorists ask, "What should I do?" Virtue-based theorists ask, "What sort of person should I become?"

Our Judeo-Christian traditions are rooted in a virtue-based framework defining what it means to be righteous or good. Virtues are qualities such as trustworthiness, honesty, fidelity, respect, personal and civic responsibility, justice, fairness, caring, compassion, and generosity (Josephson, 1993). Although in America the virtue-based approach to ethics is often couched in Judeo-Christian terminology, many believe that core ethical values "transcend religious and socio-economic differences" (MacIntyre, 1995; Josephson, 1993, p. 1). Thus, people who reject Judaism or Christianity can nevertheless embrace what virtue-based theorists believe are timeless principles, such as the "Rule of Reciprocity," or doing unto others as one would be done by. Josephson, in fact, shows that Confucius, Aristotle, Mahabharata, and Jesus promoted the Rule of Reciprocity, calling it the "most basic and useful ethical theory" (p. 29).

Rhodes concludes that a virtues-based framework is inadequate for social work, arguing that such theories "reflect different concepts of human excellence and human society, and the social and political assumptions are not always made explicit" (1991, p. 42).

Relativism

The two main types of relativism are cultural and ethical. Cultural relativism, a descriptive thesis, states that moral beliefs across cultures are widely divergent. Ethical relativism, a normative thesis, holds that there are no universally valid moral principles, but that all moral principles are valid relative to cultural or individual choice. *Subjectivism*, one form of ethical relativism, assumes that morality is a personal decision. *Conventionalism*, another form of ethical relativism, proposes that an act or principle is moral only if it is allowed by one's society or culture. An example of cultural relativism is our acceptance and tacit approval of the abandonment and subsequent adoption of Chinese children, at the same time that child abandonment is denounced as illegal and therefore wrong in the United States.

Informed Relativism

Informed relativism allows an ongoing openness to comprehending approaches and perspectives different from one's own, leading to an enlarged understanding and reevaluation of one's own opinions. This attempt to understand the perspective of another by entering into that person's way of thinking "involves a constant reevaluation of one's own position in light of other people's experiences" (Rhodes, 1991, p. 50). One of the strengths of relativism is in its recognition of ways we are apt to misunderstand others because of imposing our value system without trying to understand theirs.

The Ethics of Care

Arising from feminist writings, the ethics of care theory concentrates on character traits that are especially important in intimate relationships: friendship, compassion, empathy, love, loyalty, and so on. The ethics of care differs from traditional theories in that it encourages consideration of attachment rather than the detachment characteristic of some philosophical approaches. The ethics of care could be particularly helpful in the context of open adoptions, kinship care, and postadoption family therapy, for example, because it encourages recognition and support of family relationships.

Casuistry

Casuistry relates to "practical decision making about particular cases in which the judgments cannot simply be brought under general norms such

as principles and rules" (Beauchamp & Walters, 1994, p. 20). Casuists believe that the idea of a unified ethical theory is only a dream, because moral
decisions are decisions that arise out of character traits such as wisdom and
common sense. Rather than demanding rigid adherence to a particular
moral theory, casuists encourage decision makers to consider moral theories but not to rely upon them exclusively. Rather, people should make decisions based on moral rules, standards, circumstances, information, and
experience.

PHILOSOPHICAL BASIS OF ADOPTION ETHICS

Just as practitioners and researchers have been able to identify the
shared ethical values of the helping professions, so have philosophers
agreed that a general, normative moral theory will contain principles of
right and wrong (Schmeiser, 1992; Beauchamp & Walters, 1994). This
book is built upon the foundational belief that shared moral rules can be
identified and agreed upon, and that they include what Beauchamp and
Walters (1994) call *major ethical principles*. These major ethical principles
include respect for autonomy, beneficence, and justice.

Respect for Autonomy

Respect for autonomy is what is meant when we talk about self-
determination, self-mastery, freedom of choice, voluntariness, privacy, and
accepting responsibility for one's own choices. Closely related to respect
for autonomy are tolerance of the beliefs of others, acceptance of individual
differences (and rejection of prejudices), and exercising authority in such a
way that it gives those subject to one's authority the information they need
to make informed choices. Beauchamp and Walters point out that many
conflicts in moral theory arise from the failure of experts or those in authority to disclose information to those who need it, concluding that "the burden of moral justification [for nondisclosure] rests on those who would
restrict or prevent a person's exercise of autonomy" (1994, p. 23).

Truthfulness, nondeception, honesty in communication, and honesty in
conduct are required by this moral principle, since people are unable to exercise self-determination and make informed choices without accurate,
complete, and truthful information.

Respecting the autonomy of others naturally conflicts at times when exercising such respect violates the other major principles of beneficence and
justice. Adoption practice is full of moral dilemmas and competing interests, as we shall see in later chapters.

Beneficence

Beneficence is among the oldest of foundational values, if not the oldest, expressed as those actions which do no harm and express kindness, generosity, compassion, or reciprocity. Frankena (1973) expressed the elements of beneficence through four characteristics:

1. One should not inflict harm or evil upon others;
2. One ought to prevent harm or evil;
3. One ought to eliminate harm or evil; and
4. One ought to do good or advance good.

A beneficent person weighs and balances the benefits of an action against its potential (or actual) harm, its benefits against other benefits, and its harms against other harms. The principle of beneficence will be more closely examined in the context of adoption practice in later chapters.

Justice

Beauchamp and Walters describe the principle of justice thus:

A person has been treated justly if treated according to what is fair, due, or owed.... Any denial of a good, service, or piece of information to which a person has a right or entitlement based in justice is an injustice. It is also an injustice to place an undue burden on the exercise of a right; for example, to make a piece of information owed to a person unreasonably difficult to obtain. (1994, p. 26)

There are a variety of principles related to justice, among them the concept of equality (people equal in certain respects under consideration ought to be treated alike), fairness, impartiality, equity, being willing to admit error, and distributive justice.

Prima Facie *Duties*

A *prima facie* duty, as opposed to an actual duty, is one that should be acted upon unless it conflicts with another duty. *Prima facie* duties are always right and should be observed, as long as a competing and more compelling duty does not conflict with its observance. *Prima facie* duties are those such as fidelity, loyalty (avoiding conflicting interests, safeguarding confidential information), gratitude, pursuit of excellence (self-improvement), and diligence. There are no foundational principles upholding the *prima facie* duties identified by Ross (1930); rather, they are said to reflect our moral customs and beliefs. They nevertheless figure prominently in much of the practice of adoption services and will be discussed more thoroughly in later chapters.

Integrity

Before we examine the research into ethics and ethical decision making in social work and psychology, some attention should be given to the important principle of integrity. The word "integrity" has been used popularly and perhaps overused, even becoming the title of a best-selling book (Carter, 1996). While it most often seems to be used to refer to truth telling, Stephen Carter defines integrity as

1. Discerning what is right and what is wrong;
2. Acting on what you have discerned, even at personal cost; and
3. Saying openly that you are acting on your understanding of right and wrong. (p. 7)

Related to integrity are principles of steadfastness, promise keeping, and courage. Integrity refers to moral wholeness, the kind of wholeness and purpose that produces consistency between principle and practice, between words and actions—it means practicing what you preach, not expecting others to "do as I say, but not as I do." The person of integrity bases decisions and actions on moral rules and is willing to elevate principle over self-interest. Failure and mistakes are not rationalized away. The person of integrity considers the commitments he or she makes and avoids unwise or unclear commitments.

Sometimes, the word "integrity" is used when people actually mean virtue. Integrity is a particular and somewhat broad kind of virtue, virtue being a general goodness or conformance to moral rules. People who are virtuous exercise all of the values we have discussed—integrity, beneficence, justice, and respect for others—because they are concerned about people besides themselves. Although those subscribing to an ethic of care would say that caring is not a strictly defined virtue and thus should not be included among a group of virtues, others would disagree (Beauchamp & Walters, 1994). For the purposes of this discussion, virtue means a general goodness and conformance to moral rules, while integrity describes one's duties of steadfastness, promise keeping, courage, and moral wholeness. In

Chapter 6, integrity will be discussed in the context of the specific definitions of integrity used by several professions.

Because the duties arising from integrity cannot apply to all people at all times in all situations, they might also be considered *prima facie* duties. For example, the adoptive parents who promise the older adopted child that they are his "forever family" may later dissolve the adoption because the child's undisclosed emotional problems cause behaviors that are damaging to others in the family. The parents' duty of promise-keeping conflicts with the parents' duty of protecting their other children. In one such case, a brother adopted along with his younger sister was found to be sexually abusing the girl. The anguished adoptive parents eventually dissolved his adoption, having learned the hard way that promises of a "forever family" sometimes cannot be kept. Most experts now advise adoptive parents not to make such promises.

In spite of the limitations of an ethic of integrity, it remains a foundational value and one that will permeate the remainder of this book.

ETHICAL INQUIRY IN PSYCHOLOGY AND SOCIAL WORK

The desire to create an ethical discourse in any field of practice has been seen as a sign of the professional's desire to better serve the interests of clients (Pine, 1987; Kristinsdottir, 1991). Adoption of and adherence to a code of ethics is the cornerstone of a profession and differentiates between professional and quasi- or semi-professional practice (Greenwood, 1957; Etzioni, 1969; Poppendieck, 1992). Among the professions, ethics are the formal, professional rules of right and wrong conduct.

Ethical inquiry has only been reflected in the professional literature of psychology and social work for a scant 20 years (Rhodes, 1991). In addition, there has been a great deal of debate and disagreement regarding ethics in the practice of child welfare in general, and adoption in particular. The professions have no clear criteria or means of applying ethical decision making in adoption, nor any way of determining when an action promotes or detracts from the best interest of a child (Pine, 1987; Walden, Wolock, & Demone, 1990; Amadio, 1991; Fein & Maluccio, 1992; Sachdev, 1992; Melton & Flood, 1994).

Some of the ethics areas that have proved to be challenging for professionals at best, and problematic at worst, are conflict of interest, identifying the client, disclosure of information, responsibility to clients, and maintaining and improving professional competence (Babb, 1998). These areas are examined in the following sections.

Conflict of Interest

A number of researchers have identified conflict of interest as particularly problematic in planned infant adoptions when professionals or agencies served more than one party to an adoption (Voss, 1985; Valentine, Conway, & Randolph, 1988). Legal professionals have considered the issue of possible conflicts of interest as they serve both birth and adoptive parents in independent infant adoptions (Silverman, 1989; Amlung, 1990). Social workers and psychologists who specialize in adoption have also examined conflict of interest (Dukette, 1984; Amadio, 1991; Sachdev, 1992; Babb, 1996).

Professionals who practice adoption are not the only parties susceptible to conflicting interests or values. The needs of waiting adoptive parents who want to adopt healthy infants and toddlers conflict with the needs of waiting children who have special needs, and combine with a market economy in children to produce situations in which agencies and adoption facilitators can "sell" the waiting child to naive or desperate prospective adoptive parents (Valentine, Conway, & Randolph, 1988; Babb & Laws, 1997).

Margaret Rhodes (1991) has pointed out that, while the social workers' code of ethics spells out the responsibilities of social workers to their clients, it also requires social workers to promote societal welfare—obligations that can, and often do, conflict. Thus, the public or private adoption agency social worker may well find herself confronted with the conflicting claims of agency, client, and society, and no clear guidance from her ethical code.

Identifying the Client

Professionals have not been able to agree about whether the birth mother, the birth father, the adoptee, the adoptive parents, or a combination of these were the client(s) in an adoption, particularly in infant adoptions (Babb, 1996). Valentine, Conway, & Randolph (1988) found that professionals saw themselves as child advocates rather than advocates for either set of parents, a view that obscured the "potentially devastating consequences for adoptive parents and families" of adoption disruption (p. 136). Voss, writing for Catholic Charities agencies in the United States, considered the unborn child of the pregnant woman the client, calling unborn children "the most oppressed sub-group in contemporary American society" (1985, p. 40). Dukette (1984) likewise, having found adoption to be full of conflicting values and interests, settled upon the best interests of the child as the guiding principle in adoption because the child is the "most dependent party" (p. 234). A more detailed discussion of the best interests of the child standard has been undertaken in Chapter 5, while identifying the client is discussed in more depth in Chapter 6.

Disclosure of Information

The professional's duty to disclose accurate and complete information has been discussed in the professional literature more than any other ethical value other than confidentiality. In international adoptions, the duty of adoption agencies to disclose medical information has been discussed (Campbell, 1988; Hostetter et al., 1989), as have the ethical problems of kidnapping, child selling, coercion of birth parents, and abusive adoptive parents in unregulated international adoptions (Vitillo, 1991; Fieweger, 1991). The need for full disclosure of background and medical information has likewise been described as it relates to domestic adoption of infants and older children (Feigelman & Silverman, 1986; Rosenthal & Groze, 1992).

Wrongful Adoption

Attorneys have examined their roles in nonagency infant adoptions (Davie, 1984; Silverman, 1989), and a new tort of "wrongful adoption" has been established (Amadio, 1989). Courts have begun to recognize that adoption agencies have a duty to obtain and disclose health and background information about children placed for adoption, and adoption agencies have been ordered to pay monetary damages for failing to carry out this duty (DeWoody, 1993). Failure to accurately or fully disclose background, health, and behavioral information about adoptable children has been particularly problematic in special needs and older child adoptions (Rosenthal & Groze, 1992; Babb, 1996).

DeWoody (1993) identified four areas in which an adoption agency could be legally liable for monetary damages: (1) intentional misrepresentation of the health or background of the adoptee; (2) deliberate concealment of health or background information; (3) negligent disclosure of information, or giving information that later proves to be inaccurate; (4) negligent withholding of information, or sharing information, but failing to disclose some information so that adoptive parents are misled.

Sealed Records

Another aspect of disclosure is the common American practice of judicially sealing the adoptee's original birth certificate and adoption file and allowing their disclosure to the adoptee only by court order. The issue of adoptee-accessible adoption records versus sealed adoption records is rife with ethical, legal, and theoretical conflicts (Gonyo & Watson, 1988; Cole & Donley, 1990; Rumpf, 1993). The development and perpetuation of judicially sealed adoption records in the United States was said by some to result from myths and tradition more than from ethical principles or sound professional practice (Feigelman & Silverman, 1986; Baran & Pannor, 1990; Watson, 1992). Dukette (1984) pointed out that the freedom of information movement during the U.S. civil rights era was initiated by people who considered their civil rights violated when others had information they themselves were barred from having. Bastard Nation, an adoptee rights organization, similarly maintains that the adoptee's access to the original birth certificate is a civil right, since all nonadopted Americans have access to accurate records of their own birth. Although numerous psychological arguments have been advanced in favor of giving the adult adoptee access to his or her original birth certificate, many adoptees are not motivated by psychological or emotional needs or interested in searching for their birth parents; they simply seek the dignity afforded by equal rights.

The issue of unsealing the original birth certificate and some adoption records for adult adoptees has been seen by others as an ethical one, since giving adoptees equal access to their birth records relieves power imbalances, allowing adult adoptees to more equally share power in society with birth and adoptive parents (Dukette, 1984; Babb, 1996). That closed adoptions present more problems for adoptees in search of their biological, and even psychological, selves was evident in the literature (Feigelman & Silverman, 1986; Watson, 1992; Sachdev, 1992; Gonyo & Watson, 1988; Sorich & Siebert, 1982; Baran & Pannor, 1990). Sachdev (1992) described the motivation of adoptees to search thus:

> What propelled adoptees . . . was their compelling need to attain a more cohesive identity. Because they had been cut off from their past they felt a void, a missing link, a discontinuity in life. By knowing that they belong to their genetic roots and that they look like someone related to them by blood, they hoped to experience the life they had lost by separation. Behind the overlay of informational need lay the emotional pain, hurt, and frustration of the loss of years. (pp. 58–59)

As a result of research on adoptee identity development and search behavior, researchers urged agencies to revise policies and practices to reflect current social changes and research findings in adoption (Sachdev, 1992; Gonyo & Watson, 1988). Sachdev (1992) contended that agencies promoted sealed adoption records in adoption based on the assumption that they provide safeguards against unwanted intrusion by the triad members, and that contacts between them would be problematic. He challenged these claims by showing that secrecy in adoption "hardly serves the interest of the participants in adoption; instead it promotes fears and misconceptions about each others' motives" (p. 66).

A few authors noted that adoption agencies are often ignorant regarding the laws surrounding confidentiality and disclosure of adoption information. DeWoody (1993) recommended that adoption agencies be able to answer the following questions: (1) Is disclosure of health and background information mandated by the state in which the agency operates? (2) If mandated, does the mandate apply to all adoptions? (3) What is the extent of the agency's duty to investigate, collect, update, and disclose health and background information? (4) What information must be collected and disclosed?

Open Adoption

Open adoption, the pre- and post-placement process whereby birth parents and adoptive parents have personal contact with one another, also involves disclosure of information. In open adoption, however, generally the clients assume control of the flow of information rather than the professional maintaining such control. Rhodes discusses the implications of secrecy and control of information by describing two of Bok's hypothetical societies, one in which we cannot keep anything secret but others can, and the other in which we have the secrets of others but they cannot have ours (Rhodes, 1991). About the contrast between these two imaginary societies, Rhodes comments:

> Their contrast reveals clearly how much power resides in knowing secrets, particularly if it is not reciprocal. More disturbing, the two societies resemble the relationship between social worker and client to an uncomfortable extent. Confidentiality in casework is almost always one-sided. The social worker encourages the client to reveal personal matters and is taught not to reveal anything about her own personal life and little about her personal opinions. Usually the social worker has other kinds of power over the client as well—the power to give money, take away children, combat bureacracies—power conferred on her by her agency. And there are often class or racial differences, which may increase the client's sense of powerlessness. (p. 67)

In adoption practice, the danger of using the professional ethics of disclosure of information and confidentiality as cloaks for the professional's control of adoptions and the persons who are party to them is great. When professionals possess and control information and secrets that are not given to adoption clients, the risk that the imbalance of power inherent in the professional-client relationship will be abused increases. The inequality resulting from such one-sided confidentiality is, writes Rhodes, "an inequality that is easily abused—it can lead to perpetuating dependency, to ignoring clients' demands, or to unjust manipulation of clients" (1991, p. 74).

Open adoption, by facilitating face-to-face contact between birth and adoptive families, replaces the one-sided confidentiality characteristics of traditional or closed adoptions with a more equitable arrangement whereby parties to an adoption can decide what, and how much, information they will disclose to one another. The adoption professional becomes a facilitator rather than a controller, and the risk that the professional's personal or political biases will become part of the adoption process diminishes as the probability that the birth and adoptive families will be able to imprint the adoption with their own values increases.

Open adoption has, for the past 15 to 20 years, offered an alternative to the American tradition of secrecy in adoption (Silber & Speedlin, 1983; Melina & Roszia, 1993). In spite of the evidence of the efficacy of open adoption, open adoption agreements have been legally protected in only a few states, and the open exchange of information between birth and adoptive families has actually been prohibited in most states, although many allow for mutually agreed-upon exchanges of information (Babb, 1994; Silberberg, 1996). Even when states protect open adoption agreements by making them enforceable, these agreements usually have no effect on the adoptee's later access to the judicially sealed original birth certificate. Most adoptees who have ongoing face-to-face contact with their birth parents and who have complete identifying information about their families of origin still do not have unfettered access to the original birth certificate after the adoption has been finalized. The original birth certificates of adoptees in open adoptions are still sealed and an amended birth certificate issued in most states. Thus, while open adoption gives birth and adoptive families access to one another, it does nothing to address the right of the adult adoptee to have access to his own birth certificate.

Etter (1993) found that 98.2 percent of participants in open adoptions showed high levels of compliance with adoption agreements and 93.8 percent expressed satisfaction with their open adoptions. Berry (1991) likewise found that the majority of adoptive families in 1,396 open adoptions were comfortable with ongoing contact with the birth parent(s) of their adopted child, a finding echoed by the birth and adoptive parents in the review of open adoption surveys undertaken by Gross (1993). Grotevant and his colleagues (1994) found that more openness in adoption resulted in less fear among adoptive parents.

Sorich and Siebert (1982) found that closed adoption intensified loss and inhibited healthy grieving among birth mothers. The research of Blanton and Deschner (1990) contradicted this finding, showing that birth mothers in open adoptions appeared to express more grief than did birth mothers in closed adoptions.

Responsibility to Clients

The needs of each party to an adoption to receive professional services, including postplacement and postadoption services, have been established (Deykin, Patti, & Ryan, 1988; Blanton & Deschner, 1990; Watson, 1992; Rosenthal & Groze, 1992).

Adoptive Parents

In their study of failed adoptions, Valentine, Conway, and Randolph (1988) found that the overwhelming majority of adoptive families whose adoptions failed were not offered and did not receive any postdisruption contact or counseling from either their adoption agencies or their adoption workers to help them with the loss of their adopted children and the accompanying grief. The authors found that professionals "stretched" families too far in placing children with special needs and in giving the adoptive parents children with characteristics that the adoptive parents had stated they could not accept.

Adoptive families in the study had been given inaccurate or incomplete information upon which they based their adoption decisions. Many families felt social workers "sold" them children and that they were persuaded by professionals to take these children against their better judgment. Few of the families studied were prepared for special needs adoptions, and nearly all felt that the adoption professionals' involvement in their placements only intensified the stresses of adoption. The authors concluded that adoption professionals and adoption agencies should develop empathy with adoptive parents and become family advocates rather than being child advocates alone (Valentine et al., 1988).

Birth Parents

While some writers showed how professionals "sell" children to prospective adoptive parents (Valentine, Conway, & Randolph, 1988; Babb & Laws, 1997), others described how professionals sold adoption to expectant mothers by telling them that "their baby would be better off with people who [could] take 'proper' care of a child and that the best thing for them to do would be to place their child for adoption and go on with their lives" (Brodzinsky, 1990, p. 309). In infant adoptions, relinquishing mothers in particular have suffered as a result of inadequate (or nonexistent) pre- and post-surrender counseling. Brodzinsky noted that "when counseling does occur, it is often compromised by conflicts of interest, limited understand-ing, and lingering social stigmata associated with out-of-wedlock preg-nancy" (p. 309). Personal narratives such as Schaefer's *The Other Mother* (1991), Riben's *Shedding Light on the Dark Side of Adoption* (1988), or Jones's *Birthmothers* (1993) underscore the failure of many professionals to serve birth parents ethically or even competently.

One responsibility professionals have to their clients is that of informed consent—giving clients complete information about the risks of treatment or intervention, and of the extent and nature of the services to be provided (Dolgoff & Skolnik, 1992; Kugelman, 1992). There is agreement among many professions that informed consent to a treatment or service can only occur when a person receives complete disclosure about it, if the client un-derstands the disclosure, if the client acts voluntarily and is competent to act, and if the client consents to the treatment or service (Beauchamp & Walters, 1994). Thus, a birth parent could be said to give informed consent to adoption service when he or she understands the possible short- and long-term results of relinquishing parental rights to a child, when the par-ent is acting from volition rather than compulsion, is competent to choose, and agrees to have his or her parental rights terminated.

Research on the postadoption experiences of birth mothers has indi-cated that grief is central to the experience of giving up a child for adop-tion, and that the grief of placing a child for adoption has more profound and debilitating effects than the grief of losing a child to death or miscar-riage (Blanton & Deschner, 1990; Brodzinsky, 1990; Sorosky et al., 1989). Some suggested that professionals who tell their pregnant clients otherwise or who embrace the myth that birth mothers will be able to forget the child and go on with their lives violate this ethical principle (Sorosky et al., 1989; Brodzinsky, 1990; Baran & Pannor, 1990; Babb, 1994).

Adult Adoptees

Schechter and Bertocci (1990) wrote about the dearth of postplacement services and professional support for adult adoptees originally placed through independent means or in agency adoptions, particularly through public agencies. They concluded that "the need for these services beyond the placement should compel the provision of adequate legislation, fund-ing, and staffing, with expansion of research efforts at all levels" (p. 87).

Rosenberg and Groze discussed the problems created by secrecy and denial in adoption practice, writing about the difficulty in becoming "an autonomous person with an integrated sense of self when society hides the information about one's biological heritage in sealed records" (1997, p. 529). They recommended that laws be changed to give adult adoptees access to their original birth certificates, with retroactive access.

While much in the literature examined the legal, psychological, and political implications of adoption practice for adoptees, there was little to be found about ethical implications, even though so much about adoption practice is to be undertaken in the best interests of the (adopted) child. Kevin McCarty, adoptive father and administrator of the Adoption Web Ring (a group of over 300 adoption-related websites), writes that child advocacy groups persuade the state to do "all kinds of things 'in the best interests of the child,' a sentimental appeal that encourages paternalism" (personal communication, April 25, 1998). McCarty suggests that adoption advocates should be concerned about the best interests of the *person*, a person being someone who begins life as a child, then becomes an adult and remains so for the majority of his or her lifetime.

Postadoption Services

Spencer (1987) proposed a model for a postadoption service center where the professional staff would: (1) keep up with social changes as they apply to adoption; (2) share background information with parties to an adoption; (3) offer intermediary services for the exchange of nonidentifying information; (4) assist with searches; (5) offer counseling for individuals and families; (6) offer illustrations and explanations of functional family relationships; (7) give transracial and transcultural adoptive families an understanding of the culture or ethnic group from which the adoptee came; (8) assist transracial adoptive families with coping as a mixed family; (9) help children understand why adoption was planned for them; (10) assist transracially adopted individuals with identity issues related to transracial adoption and adoption; (11) provide for more openness; and (12) offer counseling to those in private adoptions or relative adoptions.

Maintaining and Improving Professional Competence

Researchers have recognized the value of obtaining, maintaining, and improving professional competence in adoption practice. Sachdev called for the development of a core group of professionally trained social workers who possess a "specialized knowledge of and skill in adoption practice" (1984, p. 6). In addition to calling for professional education in ethics, researchers recommended mastery among practitioners, expertise from the normative specialties of moral philosophy, theology, and law, and proficiency from the social sciences of psychology, sociology, and social work (Rest, 1988; Conrad & Joseph, 1991; Kugelman, 1992).

In their research on certification for child protective workers in Texas, Birmingham, Berry, and Bussey found that "over the past decade the number of trained social workers involved in child welfare services has fallen while the need for trained, highly specialized staff members has risen" (1996, p. 728). They wrote that only 28 percent of American child welfare workers in 1987 had undergraduate or graduate social work degrees, and that many states hire workers with degrees in other disciplines and some require no degrees at all. They concluded that "the child welfare service system has been deprofessionalized," but found that most Texas child welfare supervisors supported efforts to professionalize child welfare services through certification (p. 728).

Criticizing a systemic lack of professionalization in America's child welfare system, Brown and Bailey-Etta described it as "no system at all" (1997, p. 68). Fein noted that "the lack of federal leadership in promoting professional standards of practice and effective policy initiatives has permitted 50 separate state 'systems' " (1991, p. 576), while Everett referred to our law governing American adoptions as a "patchwork of federal and state initiatives designed to support the principle of permanence" (1995, p. 377).

ETHICAL (IN)COMPETENCIES

A handful of researchers have studied ethical problem solving in various social work settings, including those involving adoption, and discovered that ethical dilemmas are common (Conrad & Joseph, 1991; Poppendieck, 1992; Dolgoff & Skolnik, 1992; Kugelman, 1992). Researchers also found that social workers, including those handling adoption-related dilemmas, rely upon rules more readily than principles, fail to systematically use the National Association of Social Workers (NASW) Code of Ethics, are usually unable to define ethical dilemmas in "value and ethical terms," and tend to have a non-theoretical, lay perspective with regard to ethics (Conrad & Joseph, 1991, p. 12; Kugelman, 1992). Silverman and Weitzman wrote that adoption, involving some of the most sensitive, fragile, and complex aspects of all human services, has historically "been more completely in the hands of lay persons than any other area of social welfare" (1986, p. 2).

Moreover, Conrad and Joseph (1991) studied master's level social workers who were field instructors in the discipline and learned that only 2 percent could identify the central ethical dilemmas in their case studies. Likewise, only 2 percent of the social workers based their interventions on ethical issues that had been correctly defined. Instead, they resolved ethical dilemmas using lay philosophies, technical practice methods or techniques, organizational rules, administrative power, or personal experiences— a finding supported by other research (Kugelman, 1992; Conrad & Joseph, 1991; Thomasma & Pisaneschi, 1977).

Joseph (1983) found that ethical competencies can improve social work practice and strengthen client confidence. Kugelman (1992) found that those social workers who were motivated by ethical principles persevered in advocating for the best interests of the client, whereas the majority of the social workers who were not informed by ethics failed to fully advocate for the client. The author concluded that the lack of ethical decision making had "clearly negative" consequences "in respect to quality of services delivered in the field" (p. 76).

Pine identified ethical issues as "inherent in all aspects of child welfare practice," but noted that they are "rarely sorted out and dealt with systematically" (1987, p. 315) and that, in child welfare practice, decisions were often made without regard to ethical concerns. Rest (1988) concurred, finding that education in ethics was poorly delivered and received in American professional schools. Researchers stated that ethical functioning in professional situations required special education and preparation, but found that this rarely occurred (Dukette, 1984; Pine, 1987; Rest, 1988). The reasons for this educational failure included lack of institutional time, training, and supports; the concept that competent practice is based on clinical, not ethical, competence; an overemphasis on the need for value-free practice; and the idea that ethics is the purview of the philosopher, not the practitioner.

The literature reflected a paucity of models and standards for ethical decision making and professional competence in the field of child welfare. One report characterized the failure of child welfare to develop and apply scientific and ethical knowledge as system-wide, stating: "The field needs scholars who are committed to work in the area, knowledgeable about previous findings (including relevant research in other disciplines), thoughtful and creative in developing theories and hypotheses, and expert in overcoming the various legal, ethical, and methodological hurdles that they face" (Melton & Flood, 1994, p. 21).

Chapter 4

Ethical Codes Influencing Adoption Practice

> We cannot escape these ethical questions. We must focus on them if
> we want to act well toward others and act with personal integrity.
> —Margaret Rhodes

ETHICAL CODES OF CONDUCT INFLUENCING
ADOPTION PRACTICE: A RESEARCH STUDY

This chapter is an overview of the author's research studying the procedures established by licensed adoption agencies and adoption-related organizations in the implementation and application of professional ethics in
adoption practice (Babb, 1996). This survey analyzed adoption practice
standards for licensed child-placing agencies and the codes of ethics, values, or standards adopted by professional, child welfare, and adoption-
related organizations in the practice of adoption. Fifty state licensors of
adoption agencies and 23 professional and child welfare associations and
adoption-related organizations were surveyed.

The statutes governing adoption in the 50 states were not studied because statutes often do not codify or express ethical professional behavior
and sometimes even conflict with ethical behavior. For example, 70 percent to 90 percent of adoptees want access to identifying information regarding their biological parents, and professionals have often agreed on the
need to give adult adoptees their original birth certificates—yet in only
a few states in the Union (Alaska, Kansas, and Tennessee [at the time of
this printing Oregon was still in the courts deciding its legality]) may adop-

tees receive their original birth certificate without first petitioning a court. An ethical dilemma in working with adult adoptees in search is thus presented, for example, to the social worker who must practice under the law and yet who is also prompted by the NASW code of ethics to first consider the best interests of the client. An ethical dilemma is likewise experienced by attorneys who practice in closed records states but who understand the importance of adult adoptee access to the original birth certificate.

METHODOLOGY

In her research of the ethical codes of the professions, Schmeiser (1992) identified 13 major areas of ethical conduct: the professional's role in society; integrity; client-employee relations, objectivity and independence; diligence and due care; confidentiality; fees; form of practice; advertising and solicitation; consulting, advising, and evaluation; contractual relationships; communication; and supervision. Her research found a high degree of commonality among the ethical codes of the professions and a popular operational definition of ethics that promoted "the same type of ethical standards" although they were applied to "very different types of work" (p. 7).

Schmeiser studied the codes of ethics in the professions of accounting, advertising, architecture, banking, engineering, financial planning, human resource management, insurance, journalism, real estate, dentistry, medicine, mental health, nursing, social work, and law. Of these, the professions most often involved with adoption were social work, law, medicine, nursing, and mental health—including psychology, counseling, and marriage and family therapy. These five professions shared the following ethical standards:

1. The professional's role in society (uphold law, maintain professionalism, improve profession, assure product safety and quality, maintain public interest).

2. Client/employee relations (responsibility to client, type of client, no discrimination).

3. Integrity (unfair tactics, undue influence, violations of law, fraudulent practice, honesty/fairness, misconduct, misrepresentation).

4. Diligence/due care (competence, improvement of knowledge, impairment, obligations, maintenance of competence).

5. Confidentiality (authorized disclosures).

6. Communication (warning of adverse consequences, disclosures).

Of the five professions commonly involved in adoption (social work, mental health, nursing, law, and medicine), all but one shared these additional ethical standards:

1. Objectivity/independence (conflict of interest, adverse positions). (Except medicine.)
2. Fees (type of fee, commissions, maintaining client property). (Except nursing.)
3. Consulting services/advising/evaluating (opinion founded on adequate knowledge, objective and truthful reports, not financed by interested parties, referrals, expert testimony). (Except nursing.)
4. Contractual relationships (professional should represent the client's interest). (Except nursing.)

Adoption-specific items reflecting the ethical standards of the foregoing 10 categories were included in the instrument used in this research. The respondents were asked to complete a 53 item questionnaire of adoption-specific items corresponding to Schmeiser's (1992) 10 ethical categories common to the professions most often involved with adoption, and return it within two weeks. A cover letter explained the purpose of the study and offered instructions about how to complete and return the questionnaire. A follow-up questionnaire was mailed after the completed questionnaire had not been received. Respondents were asked to return the second questionnaire within one week.

SAMPLE

The National Council for Adoption (NCFA) declined participation in the research and stated that the NCFA had no positions on the ethical standards asked about in the survey and would not respond unless guaranteed confidentiality. The Institute for Black Parenting failed to return the survey after a second written contract and two telephone calls. Of the 75 organizations surveyed, 73 returned completed questionnaires for a return rate of 97 percent.

The final population consisted of the 50 state licensors of adoption agencies and 22 professional, adoption-related, or child welfare associations. The 22 associations and organizations surveyed were: Academy of Adoption Professionals, Adopt a Special Kid, Adoption Exchange Association, Adoptive Families of America, American Academy of Adoption Attorneys, American Academy of Pediatrics, American Adoption

Congress, American Association of Open Adoption Agencies, Catholic Charities USA, Children Awaiting Parents, Child Welfare League of America, Concerned United Birthparents, Council for Equal Rights in Adoption, International Concerns Committee for Children, National Adoption Center, National Association of Black Social Workers, National Association of Social Workers, National Resource Center for Special Needs Adoption, North American Council on Adoptable Children, National Council of Juvenile and Family Court Judges, Native American Child and Family Resource Center, and Rocky Mountain Adoption Exchange. Surveys for the now defunct Academy of Adoption Professionals were completed by separate organizers representing different constituencies for a total of 23 respondents.

Public state adoption licensors represented the largest proportion of respondents, 68.5 percent. Child welfare and professional associations each represented 9.6 percent of the respondents, while adoption-related organizations were 12.3 percent of the survey population (Table 4.1).

Table 4.1
Frequency and Percentage Distribution of the Types of Organizations

Type of Organization	N (N=73)	Percent (100)
Public State Adoption Licensor	50	68.5
Child Welfare Association	7	9.6
Professional Association	7	9.6
Adoption-related Organization	9	12.3

Of the adoption-related organizations, groups with membership divided among the adoption triad comprised 33 percent, while adoptive parent groups and adoption professional groups amounted to 22 percent of the adoption-related organizations each. Table 4.2 describes the membership of the adoption-related organizations in more detail.

PRELIMINARY ANALYSIS

Once the frequency data had been tabulated, a second level of data analysis was undertaken in which the chi-square statistic was used to identify patterns of significant differences between groups. To this end, the population was further divided into the following categories: State licensors, groups with over 50 percent birth parent membership, groups with

Table 4.2
Frequency and Percentage Distribution of Membership Types Among
Adoption-Related Organizations

Type of Membership	N (N=9)	Percent (100)
Over 50% birth parents	1	11.1
Over 50% adoptees	0	–
Over 50% adoptive parents	2	22.2
Over 50% adoption professionals	2	22.2
Divided among adoption triad	3	33.3
Association of private agencies	1	11.1

over 50 percent adoptive parent membership, groups with over 50 percent professional membership, groups with membership divided among the triad, associations of private adoption agencies, special needs adoption groups, ethnic minority advocacy or service groups, legal professional associations, and medical associations. Table 4.3 shows the distribution of membership types among the population.

Frequency data were tabulated for various items and summarized through the use of frequency tables. The data were then analyzed using the chi-square statistic, allowing any patterns of ethical behavior or standards established to be identified through the analysis. Main effects and interactions between independent variables were identified and described through factorial analyses, which were used to explore the effects of particular variables and the findings described and analyzed (Babb, 1996).

MAJOR FINDINGS: SHARED THEMES

The research results showed that shared standards for ethical adoption practice could be identified and categorized. Shared standards were found in areas of the adoption professional's role in society, client-employee relations, nondiscrimination, diligence and due care, communication, objectivity/independence, fees, what constitutes the best interest of the child, contractual relationships, and some aspects of confidentiality. The shared standards are described in more detail in the following sections.

Table 4.3
Frequency and Percentage Distribution of Membership Types Among
Total Population

Type of Membership	N (N=73)	Percent (100)
State licensor	50	68.5
SN adoption group	7	9.6
Over 50% helping professionals	5	6.8
Private adoption agencies	3	4.1
Divided among triad	2	2.7
Legal professional association	2	2.7
Over 50% adoptive parents	1	1.4
Ethnic minority service group	1	1.4
Over 50% birth parents	1	1.4
Medical association	1	1.4

The Adoption Professional's Role in Society

This common ethical standard describes the professional's duty to uphold the law, maintain professionalism, improve the profession, assure product (or service delivery) safety and quality, and maintain public interest. Respondents said that adoption practice specifically should be based upon common values or a code of ethics, professional practice principles, and research and clinical findings in adoption.

Client-Employee Relations

Responsibility to Clients

This ethic speaks to the professional's responsibility to the client and the professional's duty to avoid discrimination in any form. Related to the professional's responsibility to the client, one of the most important responsibilities was that of giving information to adoption clients. Respondents said that adoption professionals should always inform birth mothers of their rights to reclaim their surrendered children and that adoptive parents should always receive nonidentifying information about birth families and children's histories prior to finalization of adoptions. They said that birth and adoptive parents should be given nonidentifying social, educational, and medical history information prior to the finalization of adoptions. After adoptions are finalized, adoptees, adoptive parents, and birth parents should be given nonidentifying information about each other.

Nondiscrimination

Although the respondents underscored the adoption professional's duty to observe nondiscrimination, the findings showed that people with mental illness, gay men, and lesbians were more likely to be discriminated against in adoption placement practice. The majority of respondents supported transracial (91.4%) and single parent heterosexual (98.6%) adoption, but fewer respondents supported adoption by gay men or lesbians (69.6%). The majority also supported adoption by the physically handicapped (98.6%) and those with low incomes (98.6%). A lower percentage of respondents agreed with adoption by individuals with mental illness (29.9%), although several commented "it depends on the type of mental illness."

Although the majority of respondents agree with the principle of nondiscrimination in adoption practice, the findings showed that people with mental illness, gay men, and lesbians are more likely to be discriminated against in adoption placement practice. Table 4.4 shows the responses to the question.

Table 4.4
Should Certain Types of Adoption Be Allowed?

Descriptor	n	Response		Percent (100)	M	SD
Transracial	72	yes	66	91.7	1.08	0.28
		no	6	8.3		
Gays	71	yes	50	70.4	1.30	0.46
		no	21	29.6		
Lesbians	71	yes	50	70.4	1.30	0.46
		no	21	29.6		
Single Women	71	yes	70	98.6	1.01	0.12
		no	1	1.4		
Single Men	70	yes	70	98.6	1.01	0.12
		no	1	1.4		
Disabled	71	yes	70	98.6	1.01	0.12
		no	1	1.4		
Low Income	71	yes	70	98.6	1.01	0.12
		no	1	1.4		
Mentally Ill	67	yes	20	29.9	1.70	0.46
		no	47	70.1		

Diligence and Due Care

This ethical standard speaks to the professional's competence, improvement of knowledge, impairment, obligations, and maintenance of competence and also to the professional's duty to have an opinion that is founded on adequate knowledge, to make objective and truthful reports, and to not be financed by interested parties.

The majority of respondents said that adoption-specific training or education should be required of professionals working in adoption. Most said that competence in adoption work could be vouchsafed through generalized education in a helping profession, in-service training, and on-the-job training or experience.

Fewer respondents considered adoption conference attendance, a child welfare course with an adoption unit, or work with lay search and support groups as of value to the adoption worker. The majority of respondents said that adoption-specific training or education should be required of professionals working in adoption, although 19.7 percent disagreed. All of the respondents agreed that adoption professionals should receive continuing education, however.

Communication

This standard requires professionals to warn clients of adverse consequences of actions or services offered and asks professionals to tell clients about their rights, risks, opportunities, and obligations associated with professional service. There was universal agreement that adoption clients should receive accurate and complete disclosure of information about adoption and the adverse consequences of adoption, a finding supported by other research (DeWoody, 1993; Rosenberg & Groze, 1997).

Everyone said that prospective adoptive parents and expectant mothers considering adoption should be given accurate and complete information about adoption; all agreed that birth and adoptive parents should be given accurate and complete information about the types of adoption available; all agreed that birth and adoptive parents should be given information about the possible risks resulting from adoption and that adoption clients should be helped to understand the consequences of decisions they make regarding adoption.

When asked, "Should expectant mothers considering adoption be encouraged to attend a search support group for birth parents and adult adoptees before making an adoption plan?" 66.7 percent answered yes, while 33.3 percent answered no.

Objectivity and Independence

Dual Relationships

Conflict of interest and adverse positions are addressed by this ethic, which asks professionals to avoid relationships that can impair the professional's objectivity or ability to serve the client well. The American Association for Marriage and Family Therapy (AAMFT), for example, requires its members to avoid exploiting the trust and dependency of their clients by making "every effort to avoid dual relationships with clients that could impair professional judgment or increase the risk of exploitation" (1991, p. 1).

Defining the Client

Respondents agreed that adoption professionals should identify who the client is in an adoption (for their own benefit and that of the client) and what relationship the professional will have with each person involved in an adoption. Birth and prospective adoptive parents who are party to the same adoption should be served by separate adoption and legal professionals. Concerned United Birthparents suggested that a code of ethics in adoption should be established that would identify who the client is during each phase of the counseling process when an adoption is a possibility but has not yet occurred.

Conflict of Interest

When a conflict of interest arises between clients, more than half of the respondents said that the professional should withdraw from one or both relationships and refer one client to another professional. Some said that the professional should clarify the relationships and continue to serve both clients and seek consultation with a colleague.

Best Interest of the Child Standard

One standard identified by the research that is unique to work with children is the "best interest of the child." The professions agree that professionals should serve the client and consider the welfare of the client as of paramount importance. The research showed that consideration of the best interest of any child involved in an adoption was a primary concern of those surveyed.

Asked to choose the three most important factors in determining the best interest of the child, respondents identified the desire and ability of birth family members to raise the child, the potential or actual parenting ability of those parents, and the option of being raised with biological relatives as the three most important determinants. Fewer respondents thought that attachment to and time spent with adoptive parents determined the best interest of the child, and fewer than 10 percent thought that comparisons of the emotional or financial resources of the birth and adoptive families should be considered in determining the best interests of the child. These findings supported Dukette's (1984) conclusion that birth parents should be given every opportunity and support to raise their own children, a valuation of biological relatedness shared by the respondents. Table 4.5 shows the responses.

Table 4.5
Determinants of the Best Interest of the Child Standard (N = 64)

Response	Responses (100)	Percent
Desire and ability of birth family to raise child	53	82.8
Potential or actual parenting ability of each parent	49	76.6
Being raised with biological relatives	47	73.4
Attachment to and time spent with adoptive parents	24	37.5
Comparison between emotional resources available to child in birth and adoptive families	5	7.8
Comparison between financial resources available to child in birth and adoptive families	2	3.1

A possible conflict between the value of supporting client self-determination and that of serving the best interests of the child exists in adoption. In infant adoptions, for example, when adoption agencies or professionals serve the expectant parents, prospective adoptive parents, and child, the professional may be unable to identify only one client. This is also true in older child adoptions when the adoption worker serves both the child and the prospective adoptive parents. The needs of one client, such as the child, may be perceived by the professional to conflict with the needs of another client, such as the expectant or birth parent. The interest of the prospective adoptive couple in raising the child can conflict with the interest of the birth parents. The increased value conflicts in adoption require greater professional watchfulness, self-analysis, and peer review, lest personal bias or discrimination occur in adoption practice delivery in spite of the professional's best intentions.

Finally, there is also the issue of money in adoption, for at least two-thirds of all adoption workers are employed in a private or public agency setting, their employment supported through client fees or government funding. As a result, professionals "may find it difficult to separate clients' best interests from their own self-interest in building their practice" (Rhodes, 1992, p. 45).

Fees

This ethic speaks to types of fees charged, commissions, and maintenance of client property. One of the values of several of the helping professions related to fees is to charge the client according to his or her ability to pay.

Adoptive Placement and Service Fees

Most respondents agreed that adoption placement and service fees should not be charged. Instead, children needing the service of adoption should be considered the responsibility of the local, state, and federal governments and service fees for their care and placements charged to the appropriate governmental agencies. If service or placement fees are charged, though, they should be disclosed to the person responsible for paying them prior to an adoptive placement and should be based on the client's ability to pay. Any fees charged for special needs adoptions should be lower than those for the adoptions of children without special needs.

Reasonable Adoption Fees

Many of the participants (28) did not respond when asked, "What is a fair and reasonable adoption fee for the placement of a healthy infant?" It might be assumed that, since the majority (72.7%) said that no adoption service fees should be charged, the question should be left unanswered. Table 4.6 shows the responses to the question. No organization said that more than $10,000 would be a reasonable fee for the adoption of a healthy infant, a surprising finding in a country where well-heeled adoptive parents pay as much as $150,000 to adopt a healthy, Caucasian infant.

Birth Parent Fees

Most of the respondents said that birth parents should pay no fees. A small number said that the birth parent should pay fees when working with a fee-charging adoption agency, commenting that the birth parent is the client, and expecting the adoptive parent(s) to pay the professional's fees presents a conflict of interest to the professional (i.e., the professional or agency will not be paid unless an adoption occurs). During the course of the research, others suggested that, particularly in infant adoptions, adoption counseling fees should be charged to expectant parents based on their ability to pay the same way that counseling fees are charged to clients not involved with adoption. The suggestion that birth parents bear the responsibility for paying their own fees is consistent with the CWLA's standards in adoption service for birth parents (CWLA, 1988).

Adoption Search and Reunion Fees

Most of the participants thought that fees should not be charged for adoption searches, including for agency disclosure of nonidentifying or identifying information. One-fourth of those surveyed thought that it was acceptable for such fees to be charged. Of those who responded with an estimate of a fair and reasonable fee for adoption searches, 81.8 percent answered "under $100," and 18.2 percent said $100 to $500. No one said that an adoption search fee should be over $500.

The responses to questions about adoption search and reunion fees were interesting in light of the increasing encroachment of state agencies into an area that formerly belonged nearly exclusively to lay adoptee and birth parent search groups. During the 1990s, several states passed passive and active reunion registry and confidential intermediary systems as compromises to full adoptee access to the original birth certificate. Some states have also implemented "white-out" provisions which give birth parents the right to have their names removed from the original birth certificate—still an amendment unwanted by most adoptees.

Active reunion registries and confidential intermediary (CI) systems usually involve charging fees to adoptees, birth parents, and adoptive parents searching for one another. Fees can be charged by the state, by the confidential intermediary, and by others involved in the process of uncovering information.

Prior to the advent of state-sanctioned registry and intermediary systems, adoptees and birth parents found one another independently, with the help of lay adoption search groups, or through voluntary private registries such as the International Soundex Reunion Registry in Nevada, which charges no fees for its services.

Adoptees who wanted nonidentifying and identifying information also usually sought information from adoption agency professionals who developed fee schedules and charged adoptees for the scant, often inaccurate, and sometimes untruthful information they released. As adoptees returned to the agencies and attorneys that placed them, adoption facilitators learned that they could continue to charge, and receive, fees for releasing

Table 4.6
Fair and Reasonable Adoption Fee in Healthy Infant Adoption (N = 46)

Response	Responses (100)	Percent
Under $100	27	58.7
$100–$500	4	8.7
$500–$1,500	2	4.3
$1,500–$3,500	3	6.5
$3,500–$7,000	4	8.7
$7,000–$10,000	6	13.0
$10,000–$20,000	–	–

M 2.37; SD 1.92

the much sought-after information, no matter how paltry it was. Baer (1995) pointed out that an entire industry, the adoption search industry, resulted from the sealed adoptee birth record. Legal and illegal means of obtaining adoptee and birth parent information sometimes have significant price tags attached to them, including emotional costs. Bastard Nation's Alfia Wallace has pointed out that, in addition to having to pay for inaccurate or false information about their origins, adoptees have sometimes been "made to feel ashamed for even wanting this information by adoption social workers at agencies" (personal communication, April 26, 1998).

The market economy in children co-existing in the United States with a child-centered, service model of adoption conflict in the area of fees. Public and private agencies compete for the same moneys funding special needs adoptions, while independent practitioners and private agencies compete for a dwindling supply of healthy adoptable infants in a society with ever-increasing demands. When the demand for the product (the child) drives the entire system, professionals, too, succumb to the market economy, either as they work for agencies whose continued existence depends upon completed adoptions, or as they work independently to achieve the same end.

Most respondents (73.1%) commented that though they believed that special needs adoptions, in particular, should either be accomplished with no fees, or at substantially reduced rates, they also recognized that special needs adoptions were more labor intensive for professionals and required much more ongoing postlegal support than healthy infant adoptions. Still, as public and private agencies compete for dwindling government funding, professionals who work in special needs adoption and those who specialize in infant adoption both face the same conflicts: a professional obligation to serve clients to the best of their abilities, and a responsibility to serve the organizations within which they work, which are largely supported by financial means and fees. Ken Watson of the Chicago Child Care Society was one of few professionals who had concrete suggestions regarding the philosophy behind charging fees in adoption and a plan for abolishing adoption fees (1994). The data supported Watson's contention that agencies should find other ways besides charging fees to finance adoption services.

As noted earlier, most of the respondents (92.6%) said that birth parents should pay no fees. Some (7.4%) said the birth parent should pay fees and commented that the birth parent is the client, and expecting the adoptive parent(s) to pay the professional's fees presents a conflict of interest to the professional (i.e., the professional or agency will not be paid unless an adoption occurs).

There was very little research about adoption fees reported in the literature. That only a handful of private adoption agencies in the United States are able to function without charging fees for service, and that adoption is a multimillion dollar industry that is largely unregulated or monitored in this country is a concern to many involved in adoption (Kadushin, 1984; Cole & Donley, 1990; Amadio, 1991; Severson, 1994; Watson, Summer 1994; Babb, 1994). Research regarding how fees are charged, how much money changes hands in adoption in the United States, and how agencies can operate as they would like to operate (i.e., without charging fees) should all be explored through research and theory.

It should be noted that the majority of the survey participants who said that fees for adoption services should not be charged did not derive any income from adoption fees. Some attention should be paid by agencies, policy makers, judges, attorneys, and advocacy groups to how adoption fees are charged and how such fees can be reduced or eliminated altogether, or fee structures and the responsible parties changed so as to avoid conflict of interest.

Contractual Relationships

This ethic says that the professional should represent the client's interest first and foremost at all times. Participants responding to questions in this area believed that professionals or others outside the organization should be consulted when it is in the best interest of the client, and adoption clients should be allowed or encouraged to seek advice, information, or support from other groups even when the philosophy of the group differs from those providing the primary services.

Contested Adoptions

When asked for whom the adoption professional should advocate if an adoption is contested before it is finalized, 90.6 percent said "the child." A few said that the worker should advocate for the birth parent (7.8%) or the prospective adoptive parent (1.6%).

Time for Revocation of Consent to Adoption

Participants were asked how much time birth parents should have to revoke their consent to adoption without cause after signing it during a voluntary placement. Before an adoption is finalized in court, the parental rights of the birth parents must be judicially terminated. Birth parents relinquishing children voluntarily are asked to sign a *Consent to Adoption*, which allows the court, agency, or other adoption facilitator to place the child for adoption. Many states require that the birth parent give a "good cause" or prove fraud or duress prior to having the child returned. This question asked how many hours, days, weeks, or months should be allowed for revocation of the adoption consent (and reclaiming of the child) without the birth parent or parents offering any reason at all.

Four of the organizations did not answer the question. Answers ranged from zero hours after signing a consent to as long as six months. Thirteen respondents (18.8%) said that there should be no period of revocation. The majority (80.8%) said that there should be some period of revocation, ranging from twelve hours to six months, with most respondents stating that the revocation period should be measured in weeks, not months.

There were significant differences between groups surveyed on this issue. State licensors were the most likely to state that no revocation period should occur, while medical and legal professional groups—traditionally more likely to practice adoption independent of a licensed agency—replied that a 12 to 24 hour revocation period was preferable. Birth and adoptive parents, those most personally affected by the question, preferred revocation periods of longer than 24 hours. Research into the motivations for these answers would provide data that could help policy makers with this controversial question.

Changing Policy or Practice

Participating organizations were asked if they had changed any of their policies or practices as a result of employee, client, or membership disagreement with organizational policies. Half of the respondents (50.7%) said yes, and 49.3 percent said no.

Respondents who answered yes were asked to indicate all the areas in which the organization had changed its policies or practices (a total of eight possible responses). The majority of changes in policy or practice related to openness in adoption, followed by participation in adoption search and reunion, family preservation services, policies regarding access to adoption information or records, services to adoptive families, services to adoptees, services to birth families, and political activities. Table 4.7 shows these results.

Confidentiality

Confidentiality requires authorized disclosures, professional respect of the client's privacy, and a mandate to hold in confidence all information obtained in the course of professional service. There was complete agreement that birth and adoptive parents should be told, prior to an adoption, that the adoptee may conduct a search for the birth parents in the future. The majority (62%) said that adult adoptees should be given access to their original birth certificates, supporting the idea that the ethics of confidentiality and client self-determination can be observed without conflict in adoption practice. The value of supporting client self-determination (in the case of the adult adoptee wanting his original birth certificate) and that of observing confidentiality (of the birth parents) are interpreted as con-

Table 4.7
Areas in which Policy or Practice Changed as a Result of Employee, Client, or Membership Disagreement (N = 36)

Response	Responses (100)	Percent
Openness in adoption	21	58.3
Participation in search & reunion	20	55.6
Family preservation services	20	55.6
Access to adoption records	18	50.0
Services to adoptive families	18	50.0
Services to adoptees	17	47.2
Services to birth families	13	36.1
Political activities	12	33.3

flicting only in the United States and some provinces of Canada, which continue to support the sealed record as one aspect of confidentiality. Other nations do not operationalize the confidentiality ethic similarly.

In fact, professionals who do not undertake adoptive placements as their primary function have argued about whether they should edit records. An example is the editing of medical records commonly undertaken by psychiatrists, who keep their medical and counseling charts separately for purposes of confidentiality. Physicians have asked whether the patient's right to confidentiality "includes a power to control information, including a veto over information in their medical record," a question with important parallels to adoption records legislation, contact vetoes, and disclosure vetoes (Beauchamp & Walters, p. 129). Markus and Lockwood conclude the view that

> in general, autonomy should take precedence over what others think might be best for the patient (beneficence), is widely held. It reflects the status of the patient as an adult capable of weighing up the implications of his or her own decisions. Moreover, we think a case can be made out that the patient, in a moral sense, retains a proprietary interest in such personal information as is revealed to the doctor in the course of a consultation. It remains his or her secret, and it should remain for the patient to have the ultimate say as to what that information is put to and to whom it is revealed—always assuming, of course, that no one else's welfare is at stake here. (1994, p. 184)

With reference to the access or prevention of access to the adoptee's original birth certificate and other records related to his or her adoption, adoptees argue that their welfare is, in fact, at stake and therefore the state has no moral right to hide the information. Political groups opposed to birth certificate access for adult adoptees say that birth parents received an implied promise of confidentiality and their names should thus remain confidential. Adoptees and open records activists argue that the information on the original birth certificate, including the names of birth parents, are government documents verifying the facts of an American citizen's birth, and as such, are rightly disclosed to the adult adoptee. In a rebuttal to such arguments, Markus and Lockwood respond with a viewpoint that will be eerily familiar to open adoption records activists: "Even if the records, as physical objects, are government property, it does not follow that this is true also of the information they contain. Personal information disclosed in a consultation should perhaps be seen as effectively 'on trust' to the doctor for the period of treatment, or for the period in which the doctor continues to have the person as a patient" (1994, p. 184).

One of the controversies surrounding the sealed adoption record is about which information is private, personal, and thus confidential, and which information belongs to the state. Most adoptees rightly argue that the birth certificate is an official government document to which all non-adopted Americans have access. They say that it is their civil right to have the same information that others have about themselves. Many philosophers would agree that adult adoptee access to the original birth certificate fulfills the moral duty of justice.

Access to the prospective adopted child's child welfare, medical, social, and other records has also been controversial. For many years, only summaries of information contained in such records were given to adoptive parents. After the tort of wrongful adoption developed, however, child welfare workers and administrators reexamined their ethical duties to adoption service recipients. In a number of states, full disclosure is mandated by law, making it illegal to withhold whatever information the adoption specialist considers "personal" about the child.

Clearly, in some situations what is regarded as morally right is actually dictated by law. Rather than developing their own standards of practice related to disclosure of information, professionals specializing in adoption work have waited for judges and legislatures to tell them what is personal and to be kept confidential under threat of prosecution and what is not personal or confidential and how (and to whom) it may be disclosed. Despite their disagreements in these areas, legal and helping professionals have tended to agree that

> the concept of confidentiality—as used by opponents of access to identifying information—has taken on a role that is virtually unrecognizable from its social work and legal meanings. Through a politicalization process, confidentiality has been transformed from a principle based on the privacy of personal information to a guarantee of secrecy and anonymity that is asserted to be essential to the stability of adoptive relationships, family integrity, and even appropriate reproductive decision-making. (Freundlich, 1997–1998, Winter-Spring, p. 5)

The findings of the research showed that agency licensors, professional groups, child welfare, and adoption organizations in the majority agreed that the professional ethic of confidentiality is not violated by adoptee birth certificate access. The responses are illustrated by Table 4.8.

Table 4.8
Confidentiality and Adoptee Access to Birth Certificates in Adoption

Question	n	Response		Percent (100)	M	SD
Should all adoption records be held in confidence?	68	yes no	39 29	57.4 42.6	1.43	0.50
Should adult adoptees receive their original birth certificate?	69	yes no	43 26	62.3 37.7	1.38	0.49
Should birth parents receive the child's original birth certificate after a consent is signed?	66	yes no	41 25	62.1 37.9	1.38	0.49
Should birth parents have access to the amended birth certificate?	67	yes no	23 44	34.3 65.7	1.66	0.48
Should adoptive parents have access to the original birth certificate?	69	yes no	25 44	36.2 63.8	1.64	0.48
Should confidentiality of birth parents be safeguarded through sealed adoption records?	68	yes no	34 34	50.0 50.0	1.50	0.50

SUMMARY

Based on the analysis, some conclusions about the values held by the organizations surveyed as specific to adoption could be drawn. There were some areas of complete and majority agreement among the organizations and some areas in which agreement could not be achieved or that were rife with contradictions. Shared standards included the professional's role in society, client-employee relations, diligence and due care, communication, and contractual relationships.

Areas in which shared standards could not be established were some aspects of objectivity and independence, integrity, and confidentiality. These areas of conflict are discussed in Chapter 5.

Part III

Contentions

Chapter 5

When Professional Values Collide

In the highly competitive adoption scene it is more crucial to *look* good than to *be* good.

—Jim Gritter

ETHICAL CONFLICTS AFFECTING MEMBERS OF THE ADOPTION TRIAD

Ethical areas that adoption agency licensors and organizations could not agree about were aspects of *objectivity and independence* (including conflicts of interest and defining and serving the client), *integrity* (honesty, disclosure, misrepresentation), and *confidentiality* (disclosures, access to adoption records). There were also problems in the area of *diligence and due care.* In each area, the disagreement involved direct service to the client, whether that service involved actually defining who the client was, or the release of accurate (or any) information to adoption service recipients. The following sections discuss these problem areas and how the lack of clear values and resulting practice standards affect members of the adoption triad and the professionals and agencies serving them.

OBJECTIVITY AND INDEPENDENCE

Defining and Serving the Client

Most adoption groups were interested in the ethical practice of adoption, stating that adoption practice should be based upon values or a code of ethics rather than research and clinical findings or traditional adoption principles. They said that the primary client in an adoption should be identified clearly, for the sake of both the client and the professional. Groups disagreed, however, about who the client is in an adoption, a finding supported by other research (Dukette, 1984; Voss, 1985; Valentine, Conway, & Randolph, 1988).

Some respondents considered an unborn child in a proposed infant adoption the client, while others considered the expectant mother the client. Still others considered the mother and the child the clients, while 45 percent considered the expectant parents, the unborn child, and the prospective adoptive parents the clients. Expectant and birth fathers were most at risk of being overlooked and underserved as clients. Table 5.1 shows the responses to this question.

When respondents were asked who the client is prior to an adoption, state licensors were more likely than others to state that the expectant parent(s) or the birth mother, adoptee, and adoptive parents were the client(s) and less likely to state that the unborn child was the client. Special needs adoption groups were more likely than others to identify the child or the adoptive parents as the client. These groups may have chosen the child as the client because special needs adoption usually involves the adoption of a child whose parents' rights have already been terminated, and often that of an older child. In such cases, usually the birth parents are not part of the adoption process as they are in many infant adoptions.

Birth parent groups were more likely to say that adoption professionals should not define the client in a relationship. Additional comments by

Table 5.1
Before an Adoption, Who Is the Adoption Worker's Client? (N = 73)

Response	Responses (100)	Percent
A - Expectant Parent(s)	10	13.7
B - Unborn Child	17	23.3
C - Adoptive Parents	—	—
D - A & B	10	13.7
E - A & C	3	4.1
F - B & C	—	—
G - A, B, & C	33	45.2

M 4.32, SD 2.47

Concerned United Birthparents clarified the answer by stating that a code of ethics in adoption should be established that would identify who the client is during each phase of the counseling process when an adoption is a possibility but has not yet occurred. Thus, a code rather than an individual's preference would define and identify the client.

Considering more than one party to an adoption as the client, especially when only one adoption professional serves those clients, presents many opportunities for conflicting interests and values. In a proposed infant adoption, for example, if an unborn child is seen as the client, by what standard does the adoption professional serve the child? What values guide the professional? Because the unborn child has no voice and does not even exist as a person legally, the professional cannot apply general professional ethics established for work with adult clients. The danger that subjective standards, driven by something other than ethical codes, will be used in serving the (unborn) client is thus great.

Adoptees placed as older children fare differently as clients. State agency licensors tended to see such children as the client (instead of the birth or adoptive parents or unborn child), possibly because child welfare adoption specialists working for state agencies most often serve older children awaiting adoption as their primary clients. Special needs adoption groups tended to see either the birth parents, the child, or all three parties to an adoption as the clients, rather than seeing adoptive parents as the primary clients. When older adoptable children are the primary clients and are identified as such, less confusion exists and the means of serving the child through casework services become somewhat simpler. If one client, and one client alone (the child), is being served, then the professional can consider the child's need for permanency and work to find ways of meeting that need through various means, such as a fost-adopt programs facilitating the adoption of foster children by their foster parents, adoption, long-term foster care, or group care.

Expectant and birth parents have not fared as well as clients. When they enter an adoption counselor's office, expectant parents considering adoption generally consider themselves to be the clients (Babb, 1996). If such clients knew that nearly one-fourth of adoption organizations or professionals consider their unborn child the client, and another 45 percent consider more than one party to the adoption as clients, they might be surprised. Does the adoption professional tell the expectant parent(s) that he or she considers their unborn child or the prospective adoptive parents the client(s), and that she is ethically bound to serve the client's best interests, rather than the best interests of the expectant parents, if those interests conflict?

Young, single mothers are most at risk of suffering adverse consequences when professionals do not clearly define and serve the expectant mother as the client. Of such women, Merry Bloch Jones writes, "Most young, single women with modest incomes and average educations are destined to remain among the least powerful people in our society. It is no coincidence that this is the group which most frequently relinquishes children for adoption" (1993, p. 13).

The problem of conflicting interests also arises in child welfare system situations involving parents and their children who have been removed from the home judicially. Caseworkers who serve the children and the parents may find that at some point the value of permanency for the children collides with the value of preserving the birth family. Workers need a way of resolving ethical tensions and making values-based decisions.

Respondents agreed that adoption professionals should let the client know who they are serving in an adoption and what relationship the professional will have with each person involved. The majority of respondents also agreed that separate social workers and attorneys should be provided to birth and adoptive parents who are party to the same adoption when the legal processes for both sets of parents are concurrent. These findings concurred with other research showing that adoption is replete with conflicts of interest, which can in part be avoided through providing birth and adoptive parents with separate adoption and legal workers.

There was a relationship between attitudes toward release of the original birth certificate to the adult adoptee and the definition of the client in an adoption. Results showed that respondents who said that adult adoptees should receive their original birth certificate were significantly more likely to identify the expectant mother or the unborn child as the adoption worker's client before an adoption than to identify more than one party to the adoption, such as the expectant parents, the child, and the prospective adoptive parents, as the clients. Table 5.2 shows these results.

INTEGRITY

Integrity as an ethical value supports honesty and fairness in practice and enjoins the use of unfair tactics, undue influence, violations of law, fraudulent practice, misconduct, and misrepresentation. The majority of respondents (76.5%) said they had received complaints about misleading or dishonest behavior among adoption professionals, while 23.5 percent said they had not. This finding suggested that complaints about misleading or dishonest behavior among adoption professionals were common among

Table 5.2
Relationship between Identified Client before an Adoption and Adult Adoptee Access to Original Birth Certificate

In Rows: Before an adoption, who is the adoption worker's client?
In Columns: Should adult adoptees have access to their original birth certificate?

	Yes	No	Total	Percent	$\underline{M}$	$\underline{SD}$	$\underline{V}$
A-Pregnant Woman	(++) 10 14.5%T	(-) 0.0%T	10	14.5	1.	0	.08763
B-Unborn Child			16	23.2	1.38	0.48	0
C-Adoptive Parents	0.0%T	0.0%T	0	0	0	0	0
D-A & B	9 13.0%T	1 1.4%T	10	14.5	1.1	0.3	.04729
E-A & C	1 1.4%T	1 1.4%T	2	2.9	1.5	0.5	.00187
F-B & C	0.0%T	0.0%T	0	0	0	0	0
G-A, B, & C	— 13 18.8%T	+++ 18 26.1%T	31	44.9	1.58	0.49	.07949
Total	43	26	69	100	1.38	0.48	
Percent	62.3	37.7	100				
$\underline{M}$	3.77	5.65	4.48				
$\underline{SD}$	2.39	2.11	2.46				

$c^2 (6, N = 69) = 16.11, p < .05$
+++ $\underline{p} < .01$ Observed $\underline{f}$ greater than expected.
— $\underline{p} < .01$ Observed $\underline{f}$ less than expected.
++ $\underline{p} < .05$ Observed $\underline{f}$ greater than expected.
— $\underline{p} < .05$ Observed $\underline{f}$ less than expected.

all the groups surveyed, whether the groups represented birth parents, adoptive parents, adult adoptees, or other constituencies.

The results supported a need for honest disclosure of background and medical information in domestic and international adoptions and particularly in special needs adoptions. Most of the complaints received by study participants involved failure on the part of professionals to offer or release accurate information, or the withholding of critical information during the adoption process. Four groups, the National Resource Center for Special Needs Adoption, the Academy of Adoption Professionals, the Council for Equal Rights in Adoption, and Concerned United Birthparents also commented that they had received many complaints from all corners of the triad about "baby selling" or child trafficking among private attorneys and other independent adoption facilitators.

Adoptive Parents

The most common complaint against professionals received by adoption groups was the failure of adoption workers to fully and accurately disclose the complete history of the adoptee to the adoptive parents. Special needs adoption groups in particular reported that adoptive parents often expressed discontent over critical information being withheld by professionals or such information simply being unavailable, a finding echoed by other research. Rosenthal and Groze wrote that "the desire of many special-needs parents . . . for more depth in background information seems to us to parallel the search that many adopted at infancy undertake to learn about or make contact with their birth families. Neither adoptive parent nor child desires that the child exist without a past. Instead, knowledge of the past strengthens the adoptive family system" (1992, p. 208).

The second most commonly received complaint by all groups surveyed was about the failure of adoption agencies and professionals to give adoptive parents accurate information about their legal rights, particularly about their right to access financial benefits such as adoption assistance payments and medical assistance for their children.

The groups surveyed more often received complaints from adoptive parents than from birth parents and adoptees combined. This finding might be explained by the comfort adoptive parents feel working within the system, or the entitlement they feel as clients. Special needs adoption groups and state licensors received more complaints from adoptive parents than did other groups, the special needs groups significantly more so.

The tort of wrongful adoption resulted in recent years when adoptive parents and legal professionals began to address the legal implications of professional and agency failure to disclose critical adoption information. Adoption attorneys and professionals should apprise their clients of their rights to receive information as well as of their rights to seek relief in the event that the adoption agency or professional is found to have intentionally withheld information or given misleading information.

Information specific to the prospective adoptee is not the only information that professionals may fail to disclose to adoptive parents. Dixie Davis, of the Adoption Exchange Association, commented that adoptive parent preparation and preplacement counseling is critical. Indeed, the study results showed that 100 percent of respondents agreed that adoptive parents should be given accurate and complete information about the types of adoption available and about the possible risks resulting from adoption, and that prospective adoptive parents should be helped to understand the consequences of decisions they make regarding adoption. Because the majority of complaints received by state licensors and special needs adoption organizations were from adoptive parents, adoption professionals should pay closer attention to their preparation and training of adoptive parents, especially in special needs adoption. More research into effective training programs, materials, and permanent support systems for adoptive parents should also be helpful (Groza & Rosenberg, 1998).

Birth Parents

The lack of information offered by professionals is not only harmful to adoptees and adoptive parents: birth parents also complained about the failure of adoption professionals or agencies to disclose information to them, particularly about adoption alternatives or the psychological and emotional consequences of surrendering a child, which supported the findings of others that birth parents have not been well served in this and other areas of adoption counseling (Brodzinsky, 1990; Jones, 1993). Groups also said that professionals often failed to offer necessary information to birth parents, particularly birth fathers, about their legal rights, including the right to notice about placement and adoption proceedings involving their children.

One of the most common complaints of birth mothers was that professionals and adoption facilitators had failed to give them information about alternatives to adoption. Concerned United Birthparents reported that their members complain that no information or support is given during the counseling process to help expectant mothers in potential infant adoptions feel valued, important to their children, or capable of parenting their unborn children. They said that the message to expectant mothers inherent in most adoption counseling has been, "You don't have any value; your child's adoptive parents do" (Babb, 1996, p. 190). CUB pointed out that the pregnant woman dealing with a crisis pregnancy is at the worst stage of her life and presents her worst self to the adoption agency, while prospective adoptive parents are presenting their best selves to the agency. This would be likewise true of birth parents facing involuntary termination of parental rights through our court and child welfare systems and the adoptive parents adopting waiting children.

In order to avoid coercion and unnecessary adoptions, adoption professionals should take more care to explore and offer adoption alternatives to birth parents and to completely explain the possible long-term effects of adoption surrender to expectant parents considering adoption, including the emotional and psychological consequences for birth parents. As Gonyo and Watson (1988) suggested, agencies can work together with lay adoption search and support groups in order to inform and support adoption clients and to train adoption workers. Expectant parents considering adoption who have the opportunity to talk with adult adoptees and birth parents who have lived with the effects of adoption for many years, as well as with adoptive parents, will doubtless be able to make better informed decisions than those who simply were counseled by an adoption agency social worker or an independent adoption facilitator. This is especially true when the survival of the adoption agency depends upon adoption placement fees, which some say indicates a conflict of interest (Watson & Brown, Summer 1994). Concerned United Birthparents agreed, stating that adoption agencies and professionals who serve two or more clients in an adoption but charge a fee to only one client have an obvious conflict of interest (Babb, 1996).

Information handouts similar to those used at The Family Tree (1994) could prove helpful to other adoption professionals (see Appendix B). Birth mothers Laura Lewis and Victoria Camp also offered guidelines for serving expectant mothers in their work (Lewis & Camp, 1994). A tool for use in child welfare system (special needs and older child) adoptions is the risk-assessment matrix developed by Katz and Robinson (1991).

Finally, birth parents also complained that once their children were grown and they initiated searches for them, agencies and professionals were unresponsive to their requests for help with searches and reunions.

Adoptees

When adoptees complained about a lack of integrity, they most often complained about the failure of professionals or records repositories to release identifying information or accurate background information to them. The participating groups reported fewer complaints from adoptees than from birth and adoptive parents. The groups that received the most complaints from adoptees were state licensors, adoption professional groups, triad organizations, and private adoption agency associations. Birth and adoptive parent groups, special needs adoption organizations, ethnic minority advocacy groups, legal professionals, and medical professionals reported that they received fewer complaints from adoptees than from adoptive parents, birth parents, and other professionals.

Adoptees were most likely to complain about the lack or inaccuracy of information given to them by professionals during the process of the search for, and reunion with, their birth parents. Many were dissatisfied with the accuracy of the nonidentifying information that adoption professionals gave them and considered the judicial sealing of their original birth certificate to be a violation of their civil rights. Along with adoptive parent groups, adoptee groups complained that the nonidentifying background information they had received from professionals was inadequate, incomplete, or incorrect.

Since a high percentage of adoptees in a variety of studies said they wanted identifying information, and since over one-third or more actually seek it, there is a discrepancy between the number of adoptees who expressed the need to have such records in other research and those who complained to the participating groups in this study about not having received it. Since no groups that had memberships of more than 50 percent adoptees were surveyed, the finding may be a result of sampling bias. Or, adoptees who search may recognize that, while they consider the sealed record a moral and civil wrong, it is most often a legal reality. Adoption professionals who abide by sealed record laws are thus acting lawfully, even if the sealed record itself is a moral wrong.

More research exploring this particular finding and explaining it would be helpful, especially since there is no dearth of research or documentation about the wrong adoptees perceive when their records are withheld from them. As adoptee and college president G. William Troxler has written,

> It is an awkward thing to have your birth turn out to be a crime. I had no say in the matter but I am the one whom society has elected to punish. The sentence for the heinous crime of adoption is to be declared incompetent; incompetent to deal with the knowledge of my birth. The sentence is life; a life of aggressive governmental intervention to prevent me from learning anything about my birth or parents.

I hope the government guards nuclear waste with the same enthusiasm and care. (1994, p. 10)

Differences Among Groups

Most of the groups surveyed (birth parent, adoptive parent, professional, triad, medical association, and private adoption agency) received the majority of complaints about unethical professional behavior from adoption triad members rather than from professionals themselves.

Special needs adoption groups were more likely to receive complaints from adoptive parents than were the other groups. Although the other findings were not statistically significant or surprising, the research showed that the birth parent group received complaints mainly from birth parents, the adoptive parent groups received complaints mainly from adoptive parents, and the associations of private adoption agencies and professionals received complaints equally from birth parents, adoptees, and adoptive parents. The adoption triad groups received complaints mainly from adoptees.

CONFIDENTIALITY

The area of confidentiality describes authorized disclosures, including what kinds of information may be disclosed, to whom, and under what circumstances. Groups agreed that confidentiality as a value should be upheld, but disagreed about what is meant by the term in adoption work. Types of information to be disclosed, to whom it should be disclosed, and when it should be disclosed were areas in which disagreement occurred.

The disagreement over areas surrounding disclosure of confidential information—and even which information is to be considered confidential—is not surprising. As in other fields of professional practice, problems surrounding client versus professional control of information and how confidential information ought to be protected are common (Beauchamp & Walters, 1994).

All the respondents agreed that birth and adoptive parents should be told that the adoptee may search for the birth family in the future.

Disclosure of Identifying Information

An interesting and surprising finding was that, while a little over half the respondents said that adoption records should be kept confidential, over half the respondents (58.8%) said that adoptees should be given identifying information about their birth parents after the finalization of an adoption. A surprising 54.4 percent said that identifying information about the adoptee should be given to birth parents. Identifying information was available to birth parents, adoptees, and adoptive parents (the parties to the adoption) prior to the judicial sealing of adoption records in most states (Baer, 1995).

Mutual Consent Release of Information

Only 8.5 percent of respondents said that identifying information should be shared only through mutual consent after an adoption finalization. Groups who supported release of information by mutual consent included three special needs adoption organizations who expressed concerns that there be safeguards for adoptee abuse survivors whose birth parents seek reunions. Adoptive Families of America, Catholic Charities USA, and the American Academy of Pediatrics also supported release of identifying information only through mutual consent.

Confidentiality and the Original Birth Certificate

The majority (62.3%) also said that adult adoptees should be given access to their original birth certificates (see Table 5.3). Most agreed that birth parents should not have access to the adoptee's amended birth certificate and that adoptive parents should not have access to the original birth certificate. This finding, along with the majority opinion that adoptees should receive their original birth certificates, suggests that the original birth certificate is regarded as the property of the birth parents and the adoptee, while the amended birth certificate is seen as the property of the adoptee and the adoptive parents.

These results also supported the idea that sealed adoption records result from myths and tradition more than from ethical principles or sound professional practice (Feigelman & Silverman, 1986; Baran & Pannor, 1990; Watson, 1992). Adoption and helping professionals, legal professionals, and medical professionals tended to favor more, rather than less, openness in responding to the question regarding adult adoptee's access to their original birth certificates, whereas state licensors, charged with upholding the laws of the 50 states, tended to support the sealed record.

Adoptee Access to the Original Birth Certificate

The study's finding that the majority of respondents supported open access of adult adoptees to their records supplemented previous research that showed that many adoptees have a normative desire to have identifying information regarding their biological parents. Adoptees placed as infants and those placed when older express similar desires to have information and documents to which nonadopted Americans are already entitled (Sorosky, Baran, & Pannor, 1989).

Perhaps the most controversial area involving confidentiality is the conflict between the assumed need of birth parents to have their identities kept secret and the needs of adult adoptees to know their identities at birth and to have access to the original birth certificate. Some professionals and many detractors of open records say that birth mothers and fathers were given an implied promise of ongoing confidentiality that cannot be violated except for compelling need, simply to satisfy the adoptee's desire to know his or her identity at birth (National Council for Adoption, 1996). Birth parents, and birth mothers in particular, argue that not only were they never promised perpetual confidentiality of identity, but they had never wanted it (Jones, 1993; Sorosky, Baran, & Pannor, 1989). Maintaining secrecy (complete confidentiality) past the time when it has served a useful social purpose has been experienced by many birth parents as destructive (Brodzinsky, 1990).

Table 5.3 shows the responses to the question, "Should adult adoptees have access to their original birth certificate?" There were four nonresponses. State licensors were significantly more likely to say that adult adoptees should not have access to their original birth certificates than were other groups.

The tendency of state licensors to observe stricter confidentiality was also reflected in the responses to a question about the confidentiality of birth parents and sealed adoption records. Again, state licensors were more likely to say that such confidentiality should be preserved. Adoption and helping professionals most often supported openness, as did special needs adoption groups. The Association of Juvenile and Family Court Judges and the American Academy of Pediatrics also tended to favor more openness rather than less.

The analysis appeared to show that state licensors were more likely than other groups to adhere to strict confidentiality in the adoption process, whether that confidentiality related to all adoption records, the adoptee's original birth certificate, or the confidentiality of birth parents. These findings were significant in all three questions about confidentiality. Based on these findings, substantial opposition to adoptee access to the original birth certificate is most likely to come from public adoption agency administrators.

The issue of confidentiality and how to apply it to adoption clients is clearly a challenge to adoption professionals and the agencies employing them. Professionals must seek to balance the rights and responsibilities of clients, accounting not only for present circumstances, but also for what may happen in the future. The challenge to professionals and agencies is

Table 5.3
Adult Adoptee Access to Original Birth Certificate (N = 69)

Type of Organization	Yes	No	Percent (100)
State licensor	26	24	72.5
Over 50% birth parents	1	–	1.4
Over 50% adoptive parents	–	–	–
Over 50% professionals	5	–	7.2
Divided among triad	2	–	2.9
Private adoption agencies	1	1	2.9
Special needs adopt group	6	–	8.7
Ethnic minority services	1	–	1.4
Legal professionals	1	–	1.4
Medical association	–	1	1.4
Total	43	26	100
Percent	62.3	37.7	

$c^2 (9, N = 69) = 20.94, \underline{p} < .05$

great, underscoring the need for ethical competencies and the availability of professional services throughout the lifespan of an adoption. A clear definition and understanding of the meaning of confidentiality in legal and professional practice contexts is desperately needed in the adoption field.

DILIGENCE AND DUE CARE

Diligence and due care, as we have seen, deals with areas of professional competence, duties, maintenance of competence, knowledge, and accurate and objective reports. Respondents to the research described in Chapter 4 expressed agreement in most areas relating to this ethic.

The respondents favored three primary means of ensuring competence among adoption agency workers: generalized education in a helping profession, in-service training, and on-the-job training or experience. The literature, however, showed that only 2 percent of master's degree level social workers who were field instructors in the discipline could identify ethical dilemmas in their case studies or based their interventions on ethical issues that had been correctly defined (Conrad & Joseph, 1991). The literature also showed that the lack of ethical decision making had negative consequences in terms of service delivery to clients and that professionals need special education and preparation in the area of application of ethical standards since these are rarely taught or mastered (Kugelman, 1992; Dukette, 1984; Pine, 1987; Rest, 1988).

Sachdev recognized the value of expert education and called for professional, specialized training in adoption, just as Rest called for professional education in ethics (Sachdev, 1984; Rest, 1988). The findings of this research thus agreed with the literature that adoption workers require professional training, but also found that groups did not go far enough in recommending adoption-specific training other than whatever training a professional is given during the course of his or her education. Most respondents (79.7%) agreed that adoption-specific training should be required of those working in adoption, and all agreed that such professionals should receive continuing education in adoption. There was disagreement as to how and when such training should be undertaken and by what means, which supported previous findings. Fewer respondents considered adoption conference attendance, a child welfare course with an adoption unit, or work with lay search and support groups as of value to the adoption worker, although all of the latter means of education are adoption-specific. Thus, although respondents agreed that professionals need expert training and education in adoption, there was disagreement about how it was to be achieved. Furthermore, other research has indicated that professional preparation, particularly in ethics and particularly for social workers, those most frequently involved in adoption placements and counseling, is woefully inadequate. Clearly, this is an area needing further attention if we are to offer expert and ethical services in adoption to those who need them.

SUMMARY

The literature reflected professional thought and recommendations regarding professional adoption practice but provided little research or commentary regarding ethical standards for adoption; only one research study offered data regarding what constitutes ethical adoption practice in the United States. The literature did not provide clear criteria for applying ethical decision making in adoption or any way of determining when an action promotes or detracts from the best interest of a child or any adoption client. The data gave scarce attention to how the adoption professional may identify or ethically serve his or her client(s), and presented a dearth of adoption-specific ethical standards or ethical decision-making models.

Professionals who must operationalize the best interests of the child and "communicate ... about ethical adoption practice" need a standard against which they can measure their behavior (Hughes, 1993). If left without clear guidelines and models for such decision making, practitioners will fail to utilize ethical analysis (Pine, 1987; Joseph, 1983). In the absence of ethical standards and models, adoption workers exert a power that is without professional authority. Severson explains:

> Under normal circumstances when such power is wielded, it is done so only within a context of multiple checks and controls. This is simply not so in adoption social work. . . . Power corrupts and absolute power corrupts absolutely, so runs the old truism. Over the last century, adoption work has become corrupt in all too many cases. Unfortunately, the corruption is not flamboyant or excessive in ways that would make it easily identifiable. Rather it is the more pernicious form of laziness, inertia, institutional smugness, mediocrity, poor and undemanding preparation of the professional, hypocrisy and complacency, and widespread polite collusion in platitudes and clichés. . . . It is the corruption that weeps with sentimentality but remains dry-eyed when the suffering is real. (1994, p. 212)

Part IV

Recommendations

Chapter 6

Recommended Model for Ethical Standards in Adoption

Always do right. This will gratify some people, and astonish the rest.
—Mark Twain

Professionals who practice adoption have long been considered to be the most competent among adoption practitioners because of their professional and child welfare training and experience, and the most principled because of their adherence to a professional code of ethics (Barth, 1987; Child Welfare League of America, 1938, 1976; NASW, 1996; Sachdev, 1989; U. S. Children's Bureau, 1961; Walden, Wolock, & Demone, 1990).

Among professionally trained adoption workers, however, there has been a problem of persisting lay attitudes, positions based on cultural values and personal experience rather than professional knowledge, ethical values, or research (Cole & Donley, 1990). In addition, professional adoption workers bring with them into their adoption work a profusion of personal beliefs and common knowledge about what children need and what types of parents will act in the best interests of their children. It is such personal beliefs and knowledge "which they, as adults moved by an urge to 'rescue' children, are tempted to impose. The risk that actions and decisions in child placement will rest on personal values presented in the guise of professional knowledge is therefore great" (Goldstein et al., 1986, pp. 16–17).

Adoption practice has increasingly come under scrutiny and attack by recipients of adoption services, including birth parents, adoptees, and adoptive parents, for actions that they say run counter to their best interests (Babb, 1996; Gonyo & Watson, 1988; Sorich & Siebert, 1982). Throughout the industrialized world, the practice of adoption as a specialty of child welfare has been reformed in law and social policy as a result of pressure brought to bear by social changes and by the dissatisfied recipients of past adoption services (Cole & Donley, 1990; Sachdev, 1992; Sorosky, Baran, & Pannor, 1989).

The reform of adoption in other countries and an increased scrutiny and criticism of adoption practice in the United States have caused several U.S. professional organizations to establish or revise standards for adoption practice as well as to call for the professionalization of adoption as a specialized human service. Another result of the increased scrutiny of adoption practice has been that organizations concerned with professional adoption practice have uniformly opposed the facilitation of adoptions through intermediaries such as medical doctors and attorneys who are neither trained nor licensed to provide child-placing services (Babb, 1994; Barth, 1987; Child Welfare League of America, 1976; NASW, 1996, 1990; Sachdev, 1989; United States Children's Bureau, 1961).

Although the majority of state licensors of adoption agencies and professional and adoption-related groups say that a code of ethics should underlie adoption practice, there is no uniform code of ethics in adoption (Babb, 1996). Most organizations base their adoption practices on general professional ethics which are, according to research, ill understood and poorly applied by professionals. The value of establishing an adoption specific professional code of ethics can be seen. The second most embraced foundation of adoption practice, professional practice principles, are so ill defined as to be nearly useless to any adoption professional grappling with questions about who is the client in an adoption, for whom should the worker advocate, to whom, why, and how adoption information should be disclosed, or how the best interests of a child can be served in complex human situations.

Professionals, though bidden by their respective codes of ethics to base their practice on research and clinical findings, have problems in this foundational area as well. The professional organizations and their various directorates neither publish adoption-specific journals nor host adoption-specific conferences. Such efforts had to be undertaken by other groups. In addition, only about one-third of adoption licensors, groups, and professional organizations considered adoption conferences in their current form—hosted by grassroots, lay, or state organizations—to be of any value in educating adoption professionals in spite of the inclusion of workshops and research-oriented meetings for professionals at most such conferences (Severson, 1994; Babb, 1996).

Adoption professionals have until very recently had only general means by which to exchange information specific to adoption, dialogue concerning adoption standards, or obtain a comprehensive picture of what is happening in adoption today. To this end, the establishment of an association for adoption professionals would be helpful. A professional adoption association might consider the certification of adoption professionals in order to ensure adoption-specific training and competencies. Promising efforts at such professionalization have come about through the publication of *Adoption Quarterly* by Haworth Press in conjunction with the Adoption Studies Institute, and the establishment of the Evan B. Donaldson Adoption Institute in 1996 (see Appendix A). Additionally, a handful of states, including Texas, have proposed or initiated child protective services certification for workers or supervisors that could provide valuable information to those investigating certification in an adoption specialty (Birmingham et al., 1996). An example of proficiencies suggested for Texas child protective services supervisors is included as Appendix C.

Professionals tend to favor generalized education in a profession and state that such preparation is sufficient to ensure competence in adoption work; lay adoption groups, membered by the recipients of professional adoption services, disagree (Severson, 1994; Babb, 1996). Professionals who seek to better serve their clients would do well to heed what adoption triad members have to say about competence in adoption work. The literature showed that professionals are, in general, ill prepared in the area of ethics, and that ethical complaints are common. If adoption-specific standards and education were developed, perhaps we would find that birth parents, adoptive parents, adoptees, and children needing adoption and adoption-related services would all be better served. To that end—that of truly serving our clients—and based on adoption history, literature, and research, the following standards for serving the adoption triad (birth parents, adoptive parents, and adoptees) are proposed. The standards are divided according to the values invoked by eight ethical principles: responsibility to clients, integrity, diligence and due care, confidentiality, communication, objectivity and independence, fees and finances, and contractual relationships.

PRINCIPLE 1: RESPONSIBILITY TO CLIENTS

The first ethical area to be considered is that of client-professional relations, or the professional's responsibility to the client. Responsibility is an ethical concept embodying the values of accountability, self-restraint, and pursuit of excellence. Professional behavior as it relates to responsibility to clients includes several of Levy's (1973) preferred instrumentalities in dealing with people, such as respecting client self-determination, autonomy, and dignity and relieving power imbalances, including those inherent in the professional-client relationship or those between the client and the agency. How responsibility to clients should influence services to adoption triad members is described below.

Responsibility to Birth Parents

Adoption professionals have ethical obligations to expectant parents considering adoption for born and unborn children, to birth parents who voluntarily surrender their rights to parent their children, and to those whose parental rights are terminated by the state.

Nondiscrimination should be observed in counseling expectant and birth parents. The professional should not discriminate against the adoption client or condone such discrimination on the basis of any personal characteristic of the client, including age, race, color, sex, marital status, sexual orientation, mental or physical handicap, national origin, or any other basis or condition. If adoption professionals apply the same standards of service to all clients, regardless of the social mores or personal beliefs of the professional, those professionals have achieved the goal of nondiscrimination.

Foster client self-determination. The adoption professional should foster maximum client self-determination.

Preserve the birth family whenever possible. Adoption professionals should take care to explore and offer adoption alternatives to expectant parents considering adoption for an unborn child and to parents whose children have been involuntarily removed from them through the judicial process. Expectant and birth parents should be taught about the worth they have to their children and helped to understand practical aids available to help them raise their children. Every attempt should be made to preserve the family of origin, and when family preservation is not possible, to safely place the child in the extended family.

When offering adoption alternatives to parents experiencing crisis, adoption professionals should educate parents about how they may receive help to raise their own children. The education process may be accomplished through the use of orientation classes, recommended readings, video lending libraries, support through on-line computer resources, free newsletters, organizational membership, local support and parent assistance groups, parenting classes, psychotherapy, family counseling, and drug and alcohol treatment programs.

The availability of financial aid should be discussed and printed information given to clients about Temporary Assistance for Needy Families (TANF) (formerly AFDC), Medicaid, local social service organizations, church programs, Generalized Education Diploma (GED) and other educational programs, and assistance for secondary education available through government grants and loans, legal and financial aid, and need- and achievement-based scholarships. The adoption professional should also give birth and expectant parents written information about and referrals to other professionals and agencies regarding job training programs, unemployment benefits, Social Security Income (SSI) for children with special needs, food stamps, and subsidized housing. In addition, psychological testing and treatment should be offered as needed, along with vocational testing and planning.

Value birth fathers and treat them with respect. Birth fathers in our society have often been regarded as unnecessary or even as threats to the adoption process. The adoption professional should consider fathers as important and treat the birth father with respect, considering him to be of vital importance to the child whose family is in crisis. The adoption professional should serve birth fathers by offering written information specific to fathers and parenting (articles, magazines, books, pamphlets), access to discussion and support groups, dad-only groups, men's groups and organizations both locally and nationally. Expectant fathers and fathers of born children should be fully considered in service delivery and their rights supported and protected. Birth fathers should be taught about the worth they have to their children and should be helped to understand how they can raise their children and act responsibly as parents.

Value parents as parents. Adoption professionals should value the birth parents as parents. With regard to pregnancy, becoming a family, childbirth and child rearing, parents should be educated about the development and needs of unborn and born children. Expectant mothers should be taught about the changes pregnancy brings to one's body and emotions, and the considerable amount of research regarding the lives of unborn children and their prenatal attachment to their mothers as well as their dependence upon the mother for nutrition. Both parents should be given information about childbirth and infant and child care and should be referred to other agencies and professionals as needed.

When parents are in crisis or a child has been removed from them or is in danger of being removed, professionals should educate parents about the developmental, psychological, and emotional needs of children and about attachment-inducing behavior. Both parents should be given information about child care and child development and be referred to other agencies and professionals as needed or as court ordered.

Respect the client's beliefs. If a client is religious, the professional should be respectful of the client's religious beliefs without exploiting the beliefs or using them to support either relinquishment of a child or preservation of the birth family. The duty of the professional is to support the client in making his or her own decisions, not to influence the client in implementing the decision that the professional or any other person believes is best.

Additionally, in any situation in which a child is placed into temporary or permanent care or when adoption is planned, the professional should respect any religious preference of the birth parents. Whenever possible, children should be placed in foster or adoptive families of the birth parents' religious preference. When such a placement is not feasible or hinders the placement of a child, information about the child's religious heritage should be a permanent part of the information that travels with the child.

Inform the client about legal rights. The adoption professional should encourage birth parents to obtain legal counsel independent of the public or private adoption agency or adoption professional and should give birth parents written information about their legal rights in the state of relinquishment and that of placement of a child.

Adoption professionals should also assist attorneys in informing birth parents of their legal rights, if any, to reclaim their surrendered children, the legal procedures for doing so, and the time frame in which reclamation must occur. In states imposing a best interest of the child standard upon contested adoptions, birth parents should be notified in writing of their legal rights and of the possibility that an attempt to reclaim their children may pit them against agencies, professionals, or adoptive parents in a contest of fitness.

The adoption professional should also advise birth parents of their right to have copies of all legal documents related to their children's births, the consent to adopt, court proceedings, and termination of parental rights, including the right to have their children's original birth certificates.

Finally, the adoption professional, unless also an attorney, should recognize his or her limits of expertise and should advise adoption clients that they should seek independent legal counsel, and advise clients of how to obtain free or low-cost legal assistance from legal professionals when income or resources prevent the client from paying legal fees.

Explain the opportunity of open adoption. The adoption professional should educate all parties to the adoption regarding research results in open adoption, the need of adoptees to know their biological histories, name at birth, and identities of their birth parents, and the risks and benefits of ongoing contact. Clients should be informed of the availability of open adoption as a possibility for birth and adoptive parents in infant and older child adoptions.

When birth and adoptive parents have established or seek to establish ongoing contact in an adoption while the adoptee is still a minor, the adoption professional should make every effort to help establish, support, and maintain such contact and to communicate the desire for such contact as expressed by any party to the adoption.

The adoption professional should provide ongoing support and professional counseling to adoptive and birth parents in open adoptions as requested. The possibility of ongoing contact in intercountry adoptions should also be discussed and the rights and opportunities of all parties to an intercountry adoption explained before a child is placed.

Right to information about adoptee and adoptive parents. Birth parents should be given accurate and complete nonidentifying information about the adoptive parents prior to finalization of an adoption and ongoing nonidentifying information about the adoptive parents and adoptee after an adoption has been finalized when requested. The information should comprise social, psychological, medical, educational, and emotional content. The right of birth and adoptive parents to contact one another and develop ongoing relationships, releasing whatever information to one another they choose in the best interests of the adopted child, should also be recognized, explained, and facilitated by the adoption professional.

Continue to serve the client. The adoption professional or agency serving birth parents should not abandon or neglect birth parents after an adoption has been finalized. Ongoing programs of support, counseling, and education should be provided to birth parents throughout the lifespan, as well as programs offering support during search and reunion when requested by the birth parent. Postrelinquishment support to birth parents can include referral to support or grief groups for birth parents, and for provision of grief counseling, reading materials, and information about organizations serving birth parents and other adoption triad members after an adoption has been finalized.

Responsibility to Adoptive Parents

In support of the ethical guidelines governing *client-employee relations* and the *responsibility to clients*, the following standards are suggested for adoptive parents:

Nondiscrimination should be observed in serving prospective adoptive parents and adoptive parents. The adoption professional should take special care to be nondiscriminatory in working with prospective or other adoptive parents who do not fit the traditional model for adoptive parents (those who are single, older, gay or lesbian, etc.). Placement decisions should be based on research and sound practice principles.

Foster client self-determination. The adoption professional should foster maximum client self-determination.

Prepare adoptive parents. Adoptive parents should be taught about the adoption process, prepared to live with the differences between the adoptive and biological family, and prepared to deal with adoption-related grief, loss, and other adoption issues as part of the adoption process for themselves and the adoptee. Prior to and during an adoption placement, the professional should serve adoptive parents with consistent devotion and the maximum application of professional skill and competence.

Respect the client's beliefs. If a client is religious, the adoption professional should be respectful of the client's beliefs without exploiting the beliefs or using them to support adoption in general or the adoption of certain children. The duty of the professional is to support the client in making his or her own decisions and determining his or her own limits when adopting a child or children.

Inform the client about legal rights. The adoption professional should encourage adoptive parents to obtain legal counsel independent of the adoption agency or adoption professional and should inform adoptive parents about their legal rights. When the parental rights of one or both birth parents have not been terminated and a child is placed with a prospective adoptive family, the adoption professional should apprise the adoptive parents of their rights and the legal and emotional risks inherent in such a placement.

The adoption professional should advise adoptive parents of their rights to have copies of all legal documents related to a child's postsurrender care, the petition to adopt, the final adoption decree, and the original birth certificate.

Finally, the adoption professional should recognize the limits of his or her competence and advise adoptive parents to seek and utilize legal counsel from an attorney.

Child-parent matching. The adoption professional should take great care to base placement decisions on research and clinical findings related to infant and older child adoptions, measures of temperament, ability, and fit for both prospective adoptive parents and prospective adoptees; the desires, wishes, and needs of both the prospective adoptive parents and the prospective adoptees; and the wishes of families of origin.

In older child adoptions, when adoptive parents are knowledgeable and motivated, the adoption professional should foster the participation of parents in identifying the waiting child or children best suited to the adoptive parents' gifts and the family's configuration.

Full disclosure of adoptee history. Adoption professionals, workers, and agencies should disclose all known background information concerning prospective adoptees to adoptive parents prior to placement. The adoptees' histories should include complete and accurate social, psychological, developmental, medical, educational, and emotional facts as well as information about and access to all former caretakers and the birth families, including birth parents and grandparents.

Provision of postplacement services and information. The adoption professional should be able to provide adoption-aware and family-oriented postplacement counseling and support to the adoptive family, or be able to refer the adoptive family to such professionals locally. Such services should include, but not be limited to, respite care, access to support groups, reading materials (books, newsletters, magazines), parent training, conference information, training on behavior management with difficult children, basic child care appropriate to the age of the child, child development, ongoing counseling and support in open adoptions, and counseling and support during the adoptee's search and reunion or when adoptive parents seek to open an adoption or increase contact with the birth family.

The adoptive family should be given complete and accurate information about adoption assistance payments, medical assistance for the adopted child with special needs, and the assistance necessary for completion and approval of the adoption assistance application.

After an adoption is finalized, adoptive parents should be given nonidentifying information about birth parents as available and identifying information as allowed by law or by the birth parent(s) prior to the adoptee reaching the age of majority.

Explain the opportunity of open adoption. The adoption professional should educate all parties to adoption regarding research results in open adoption, the need of adoptees to know their biological histories, name at birth, and identities of their birth parents, and the risks and benefits of ongoing contact. Clients should be informed of the availability of open adoption as a possibility for birth and adoptive parents in infant and older child adoptions.

When birth and adoptive parents have established or seek to establish ongoing contact in an adoption while the adoptee is still a minor, the adoption professional should make every effort to help establish, support, and maintain such contact and to communicate the desire for such contact as expressed by any party to the adoption. The adoption professional should provide ongoing support and professional counseling to adoptive and birth parents in open adoptions as requested.

The adoption professional should not abandon or neglect adoptive parents. After an adoption has been finalized, the adoption professional should be available for ongoing counseling and consultation as described above and should inform adoptive parents about ongoing professional services and support. The need of adoptive families for professional support, information, and education does not end with the finalization of the adoption: adoption professionals should thus make themselves accessible to adoptive families long after the adoption has become legal.

Responsibility to Adoptees

In support of the ethical guidelines governing *client-employee relations* and the *responsibility* to clients, the following standards are suggested. First and foremost, the adoption professional should regard adoption as a service to children who need permanent families.

Nondiscrimination should be observed in counseling adoptees and in the adoptive placement of children needing the service. The adoption professional should neither practice nor condone discrimination on the basis of race, gender, sexual orientation, age, religion, national origin, mental or physical handicap, or any other preferential or personal characteristic of children entering into the adoption process, except insofar as such qualities can be *demonstrated* to have a negative impact on a particular proposed or actual adoptive placement and with regard to a specific child. The adoption professional should not allow any such characteristic to unreasonably postpone or prevent the permanent adoptive placement of a child needing the service of adoption.

Protect the child's right to grow up in his or her family of origin. The adoption professional should, to the best of his or her ability, see to it that children can be cared for by their own parents, or, in the case of failing parental care, by a member of the extended family.

Protect the child's right to grow up with his or her siblings. The adoption professional should value the sibling relationship of children living in foster and adoptive families and, to the best of his or her ability, see to it that children are placed with their siblings. When placement with siblings is not in the best interests of a child, the professional should foster ongoing contact between siblings whenever possible. Information about the existence and whereabouts of siblings and half-siblings should be a permanent part of the information that travels with the child.

Protect the child's right to grow up in his or her own community. The adoption professional should safeguard the child's right to grow up in his or her own community, culture, race, nation, and religion and should support inter-country adoption only when adoption within the child's own community is unavailable.

Oppose black and gray market adoptions. The adoption professional should not participate in adoptions in which illegal, illicit, or unethical behavior occurs among adoption facilitators, whether those facilitators are professionals or not. The professional should not condone the behavior or policies of others, including agencies and attorneys, that treat adoption service as an industry and adoptees as commodities.

Provide age-appropriate adoption counseling. The adoption professional should explain the adoption process to the child needing the service in an age-appropriate way through the use of words, pictures, videotapes, the Life Book, play, and any other means available to him or her.

Allow for the child's consent and participation in adoption when possible. When a child cannot remain with his or her birth parents, the adoption professional should consider the child's wishes and opinions and encourage him or her to participate in the adoption process and give consent to being adopted verbally and in writing, as appropriate to the child's age, circumstances, emotional health, cognitive abilities, and development.

Facilitate grieving. When a child older than infancy leaves his or her birth family, the adoption professional should give the child the opportunity to say good-bye to his or her parents, siblings, pets, neighbors and friends, and other loved ones and should help the child through counseling for grief, separation, and loss. The adoption professional should be prepared to address the adoptee's developmental needs to recycle through the grief process throughout the lifespan.

Give adoptees information about themselves. The adoption professional recognizes and supports the right of the minor adoptee, with the permission of the adoptive parents, and the adult adoptee to have information about him or herself, including his or her name at birth; social, medical, psychological, educational, cultural, and racial background; birth parents' history; and reason for relinquishment.

The adoption professional understands the adoptee's need for a personal history and supports the need by safeguarding informational narratives, videotapes, photographs, heirlooms, gifts, and clothing given to the child by his or her parents and caretakers, entrusting such items to those who will be equally respectful of the importance of such objects.

Give adoptees information about their culture. In all cases of transracial, transcultural, or intercountry adoption, the adoption professional gives adoptees the opportunity to have information about their culture of origin. The adoption professional works with agencies and organizations to give the adoptee cultural and ethnic activities such as camps, homeland tours, and buddy families of the adoptee's cultural or ethnic background, along with written information and bibliographies that emphasize the child's ethnic group, culture, and original nationality.

Give adoptees information about their rights. The adoption professional should advise adult adoptees of their rights, where legally applicable, to have copies of all legal documents related to their births, including their original birth certificates and adoption (amended birth) certificates and adoption decrees. Where such legal rights do not exist, the adoption professional should advocate for such rights on behalf of adult adoptees.

Adoptee-adoptive parent matching. The adoption professional should choose adoptive parents who will best be able to meet the needs of the adopted child.

Continue to serve the client. The adoption professional should not abandon or neglect the adoptee after an adoption has been finalized. Postplacement services to adoptees should be available, the adoptee and his or her parents advised that they are available, and they should be provided as needed.

Respect the adoptee. The adoption professional should divest him- or herself of adoption mythology and refuse to define the adoptee's reality for him or her by describing the adoptee as "chosen, lucky" or in negative terms, such as "ungrateful," or by using words like "illegitimate, bastard."

PRINCIPLE 2: INTEGRITY

Integrity is a foundational ethical concept, the cornerstone of all other ethical values. Integrity involves moral courage and the "elevation of principle over expediency or self-interest and requires a consistency between words and action" (Josephson, 1993, p. 15).

Over 75 percent of adoption groups and licensors say they have received complaints about misleading or dishonest behavior among adoption professionals (Babb, 1996). Among lay groups serving birth parents, adoptive parents, and adoptees, the lack of integrity among adoption professionals, including adoption attorneys, was cited as a major reason for disillusionment with and mistrust of professionals.

Integrity requires a professional to be, first and foremost, truthful with clients. Adoption professionals should not misrepresent to clients adoption and its benefits or disadvantages. In seeking to be honest with clients, the professional simply must have the "good faith intent to tell the truth"

(Josephson, 1993, p. 13). Because adoption is a complex human service, professionals may find it impossible to serve clients honestly without being informed about current research and developments in the field. The truth as we know it in adoption continues to change as new information and research become available.

Integrity enjoins against any type of dishonesty or cunning aimed at depriving a client of anything of value, including money, favors, or a child. It also requires the professional to avoid using his or her position of influence or power to exploit the client.

Birth Parents

Avoid undue influence. The adoption professional should recognize that parents considering voluntary relinquishment of a child are experiencing a crisis, and should recognize vulnerabilities that precipitated and were caused by the crisis. The professional should regard the birth parent considering adoption, or under court supervision for child neglect or abuse, as a client who needs counseling, practical supports, or therapy *before* adoption is viewed as a solution.

Avoid exploitation of dependency or inexperience. Professionals should take extra care with clients who are making weighty decisions with little experience, be aware of their influence on parents considering adoption, and avoid exploiting or influencing the client in the direction they think best. The adoption professional should foster maximum client self-determination.

Support the kinship system. The extended family of the mother and father should be considered first when adoption is chosen as a plan for a child. The parents, siblings, aunts, uncles, and cousins of the expectant parents should be considered as possible guardians or adoptive parents of the child before strangers are asked to assume such responsibilities. If relative placement is not an option, the adoption professional should make every effort to preserve connections of some kind between children going into adoption and their birth families, including siblings and half-siblings of the child.

Be open about open adoption. Professionals who arrange open adoptions should provide birth parents with complete and accurate information, including the legal enforceability or unenforceability of such adoptions. When exploring open adoption with birth parents, professionals should be careful that the promise of open adoption does not become a coercive means of encouraging the surrender of a child.

Professionals should recognize the manipulative potential of open adoption during pregnancy and childbirth, and should consider the harmful effects of having prospective adoptive parents participate in an expectant mother's prenatal care, or be present at an infant's birth or at the hospital afterward. Birth parents should have the opportunity to experience parenthood without the onus of anxiety or guilt about the feelings of the prospective adoptive parents. The potential heartache of prospective adoptive parents with whom they have developed a predelivery relationship should not be used as a coercive means of obtaining the relinquishment of an infant.

Professionals should continue to support the birth parents when a child is adopted and emphasize the need for birth and adoptive parents to keep their commitments to ongoing contact. Adoption professionals working with legal professionals and the birth and adoptive families party to open adoptions may also want to devise a legally binding open adoption contract between the parties when state laws do not protect open adoption arrangements.

Most important, adoption professionals should advise birth and adoptive parents that their ongoing relationships with one another and the adopted child should always be undertaken in the best interests of the child. Adoption professionals should assist birth and adoptive parents in putting the child and his or her needs first.

Caution in use of time for consent to adoption and revocation of consent. Adoption professionals who work in infant placements should not expect or encourage expectant parents to make a binding adoption decision until after an infant is born. Such professionals should provide birth families with encouragement and the opportunity to spend time with their babies after birth, and should allow birth families sufficient time after birth to consider their options prior to legally committing to adoption plans. The Association of Open Adoption Agencies suggests at least a two-week time period (Catholic Charities USA, 1994). Other groups suggest that two weeks to six months is a reasonable time for consent to adoption or revocation of consent without cause (Babb, 1996).

Professionals working with parents who are under court supervision for child mistreatment should help parents understand the necessity of complying with court supervision and the consequences of noncompliance to themselves and their children. They should inform parents of time limitations for compliance with the service plan and of any statutory basis for the state's exemption from its obligation to make reasonable efforts to reunify children and their parents.

Professionals should encourage families to maintain regular and frequent contact with their children living in out-of-home placements and explain the importance of spending time with their children. Parents and extended families should be given sufficient time to consider the options before legally committing to voluntary termination of parental rights.

Adoptive Parents

Avoid undue influence. The adoption professional should recognize that prospective adoptive parents have probably come to adoption through crisis and loss and should recognize the vulnerabilities caused by infertility (if applicable) and by the adoption process itself, and avoid exploiting such vulnerabilities. The adoption professional should not pressure adoptive parents to accept a child that the parents feel unable to raise. The adoption professional should be aware that because of the competitive nature of U.S. adoptions, adoptive parents may be vulnerable to pressure from the professional and should refuse to exploit the adoptive parents in order to place a child. The promise of a child should not be used as coercive means of obtaining more money from adoptive parents in in-country or intercountry adoptions.

Disclosure and truthfulness in recruiting. Adoption professionals should disclose complete and accurate information to prospective adoptive parents during the process of recruiting families for children awaiting adoptive placements.

While recruiting families for waiting children through the use of profiles, photolistings, "matching parties," or other means, the adoption professional should not exploit the emotions of the adoptive parents or their desires to have a child. Critical information about the needs of waiting children and the responsibility of raising them should not be minimized through the use of such recruiting tools or through exploitation of the prospective adoptive parents.

Full disclosure of adoptee history. Adoption professionals, workers, and agencies should disclose all known background information concerning the prospective adoptee to the adoptive parents prior to placement. The adoptee's history should include social, psychological, medical, educational, and emotional histories as well as information about and access to all former caretakers and the birth family of the child.

Be open about open adoption. Professionals who arrange open adoptions should provide adoptive parents with complete and accurate information about open adoption, including the legal enforceability or unenforceability of such adoptions, other legal means of enforcing open adoption agreements or contracts, and the moral obligation incurred by birth and adoptive parents who become party to an open adoption. The adoption professional should also educate adoptive parents about the risks, responsibilities, and benefits of open adoption, particularly about the benefits to the adopted child and the importance of considering the child's needs as of primary importance.

Adoptees

Support the kinship system. The extended families of the mother and father should be considered first when adoption is chosen as a plan for a child. The parents, siblings, aunts, uncles, and cousins of the birth parents should be considered as possible guardians or adoptive parents of the child if adoption is chosen, before strangers are asked to assume such responsibilities. If relative placement is not an option, the adoption professional should make every effort to preserve connections of some kind between children going into adoption and their birth families.

Explain and offer open adoption. Professionals who arrange open adoptions should provide older waiting children with complete and accurate information about open adoption and guardianship, including the legal enforceability or unenforceability of such arrangements and the enforceability or unenforceability of continued contact with the children's birth and former foster families. Older children should be given information about the effect of adoption on their ongoing contact with siblings and relatives.

Be respectful of the waiting child during adoptive family recruitment. The adoption professional regards the child in need of permanency through adoption as of equal value to other children and uses respect, care, and caution through efforts to recruit an adoptive family for a child or sibling group. Children should not be advertised or families recruited for them in such a way that a child might be subjected to ridicule or judgment by his or her peers or otherwise harmed through such recruitment efforts.

When considering the use of photolisting, videotape recruitment, and "matching parties," the professional should approach all efforts by asking how the professional would want his or her own child to be presented to the world. When a child is old enough to consent to recruitment efforts, he or she should participate in the decision making and have the opportunity to review materials advertising his or her availability for adoption.

Avoid undue influence. The adoption professional understands the adoptee's search for his or her birth relatives as a normative aspect of having been adopted. The adoption professional avoids putting any responsibility on the adoptee for the feelings of the adoptive parents. Instead, the adoption professional provides printed resources and referrals to other professionals or groups who can help the adoptive parents cope with the adoptee's search, possible reunion, and possible ongoing contact with the birth family.

PRINCIPLE 3: DILIGENCE AND DUE CARE

This ethical standard speaks to the professional's competence, improvement of knowledge, impairment, obligations, and maintenance of competence. The diligent professional is interested in excellence, in doing his or her best work in the service of adoptees, birth parents, and adoptive parents. The diligent professional maintains and improves his or her competence and works to improve the profession. Diligence and due care apply to services supplied to birth parents, adoptees, and adoptive parents and can be achieved through the following means:

Adoption-specific education and training. Professionals who work in adoption should receive education and training specific to adoption in order to best serve their clients. Such preparation should include generalized education in a helping profession, in-service training, on-the-job training and experience, attendance at adoption conferences, and work with lay search and support groups.

Culturally sensitive education and training. Professionals who work in adoption, particularly in adoptive placement, should understand the influence of culture and ethnicity on families.

Continuing education. Adoption professionals should maintain competence in the field of adoption and child welfare through adoption conferences and continuing education not only with those with whom they can agree philosophically, but also with those who are fundamentally different in their approaches to adoption and the treatment of women and families.

Competence and knowledge. Adoption professionals should maintain knowledge of current adoption research and literature, and base practice decisions on such information as well as on their professional codes of ethics. They should furthermore transmit current information to their clients in an understandable way.

PRINCIPLE 4: CONFIDENTIALITY

The ethic of confidentiality (sometimes called privacy) addresses disclosure of information obtained during the course of professional service. This

ethic governs what information may be disclosed, under what circumstances, and to whom. Observance of this ethic requires a consistent commitment on the part of the professional to protect information obtained in
client-professional relationships.

Disclosures regarding identifying information. Prior to an adoption, the
adoption professional should tell birth parents and adoptive parents that in
the future the adoptee may conduct a search for the birth parents, and that
birth parent identifying information may be released to the adoptee either
under court order or by law.

The adoption professional should inform adoptees of their right to
search for their birth parents and what their responsibilities and rights are
while conducting a search, including all rights or privileges to nonidentifying and identifying information. The adoptee should be told of limitations
to the release of information, including any right of refusal the birth or
adoptive parents may have under the law, including under the laws of the
country in which the child was born or legally adopted.

Limits to confidentiality. The adoption professional should inform birth
parents, adoptive parents, and adoptees of the limits of confidentiality in
adoption practice both under current laws and, potentially, under future
laws regarding release of identifying information and adoption records.
Confidentiality laws in the country of origin in the case of a child adopted
internationally ought also to be explained and written information given
to the birth parents, adoptive parents, and adoptee. The adoption professional cannot and should not guarantee confidentiality to birth parents,
adoptive parents, or adoptees in any adoption.

Use of information. The adoption professional should inform birth parents, adoptive parents, and adoptees of the circumstances under which
confidential information may be released, the use to which such information might be put, and the purposes for which it might be obtained.

Existence of records. The adoption professional should inform birth parents, adoptive parents, and adoptees of the existence, extent, and location
of official records concerning them. Birth and adoptive parents should be
informed of their rights and opportunities, if any, to obtain copies of the
adoption home studies with appropriate releases or under the law.

The adoption professional should also sign releases allowing the adoptive parent(s) access to adoptee records and should advocate for and with
the adoptive parent(s) in obtaining such records from other professionals
and agencies prior to the finalization of an adoption.

Access to records. The adoption professional should give birth parents,
adoptive parents, and adoptees reasonable and lawful access to all professional records concerning them, taking care to protect the confidentiality

of others mentioned in such records. Observing confidentiality of professional records is not the same as barring the adult adoptee from access to his or her official birth certificate and records (Babb, 1996).

Assistance with search. The adoption professional should inform adult adoptees, birth parents, and adoptive parents about legal barriers to the release of identifying information, where applicable, and how they may obtain help with adoption search and reunion apart from the adoption agency or adoption professional. Such help could include referral to an area search and support group for triad members, information about national and international triad or adoptee groups, or recommended readings.

PRINCIPLE 5: COMMUNICATION

This ethic governs disclosures and warnings of adverse consequences of a professional service rendered. It requires professionals to give clients accurate and complete information about the extent and nature of the services available to them. Communication is akin to integrity in that it requires candor, "the obligation to affirmatively volunteer information" that the client needs or wants to know (Josephson, 1993, p. 14). The ethic includes a professional responsibility to allow and foster communication between the client and other professionals, community groups, or other supports who can provide information to the client about adoption (or the professional service rendered), including individuals and groups whose philosophies conflict with those of the professional. Ways in which professionals can operationalize this ethic include the following:

Define the client. When an adoptee or parent (expectant, birth, or adoptive) presents him- or herself to the adoption professional for adoption-related counseling, whether voluntarily or in the case of parents under court-ordered supervision for child mistreatment, the professional should discuss with that person the definition of the client, the standards identifying the client, the primacy of the client's interests, and the nature of the services to be provided to the client. If an adoption professional serves more than one client in an adoption, the professional should inform each client of this and warn the clients of the possibility of conflicting needs and values, offering solutions to possible conflicts of interest before they arise.

Explain adoption realistically and fairly. The adoption professional should explain adoption realistically, along with its potential positive and negative outcomes, and give parents considering voluntary adoption for their child or under court-ordered supervision for child mistreatment, the opportunity to learn from others who have faced similar situations or crises as well as from adult adoptees, former foster children, and adoptive parents.

The adoption professional should prepare adoptive parents for the part that grief and loss play in the formation of all adoptive families and for the reality that adoption is experienced differently by adoptive parents, adoptees, and birth parents. Both the positive and negative aspects of adoption for the adoptive parents and adoptee should be explained by the adoption professional. The adoption professional should give adoptive parents, birth parents, and adoptees the opportunity to learn from other adoptive parents, adult adoptees, and birth parents.

Warn of adverse consequences of adoption. The adoption professional should completely explain the possible long-term effects of adoption surrender to parents, including the possible and probable emotional and psychological consequences of surrender or Termination of Parental Rights (TPR), both for the birth parent(s) and for the child.

The adoption professional should warn prospective adoptive parents about the possible adverse consequences of adoption, especially in special needs, transracial, and international adoptions. The adoption professional should completely explain the possible long-term effects of separation, loss, and adoption to prospective adoptive parents, including the emotional and psychological effects of adoption for both the adoptee and for the adoptive parents. The adoption professional should provide written information, recommended reading, counseling, and other resources to help adoptive parents understand adoption dynamics.

Inform birth fathers of their rights and responsibilities. Birth fathers should be full participants in the counseling process and in any prospective adoption proceedings. The adoption professional should inform birth fathers in writing of their rights and responsibilities and afford birth fathers every opportunity to participate in raising their children or participating in adoptive placements.

Inform grandparents of their rights and opportunities. In some states, grandparents can retain grandparental rights after an adoption is finalized. Grandparents, birth parents, and adoptive parents should be informed about the rights and opportunities of the biological grandparents when an adoption is planned by the birth parents or the courts.

Utilize lay adoption support and search groups. The adoption professional should encourage parents considering adoption for their child to attend support group meetings not associated with an adoption agency or adoption attorney of adult adoptees, former foster children, and postadoption birth parents as soon as possible as they consider their options. Birth parents should also have access to support groups for adult adoptees and adoptive parents who have positive outcomes.

Adoptees should be referred to available local, regional, and national groups that can give them support for issues specific to their individual circumstances (e.g., groups for adolescent adoptees, internationally adopted persons, transracially adopted persons, adoptees searching for birth parents, etc.).

Fully disclose adoptee history. Adoption professionals, workers, and agencies should disclose all known background information concerning the prospective adoptee to the adoptive parents prior to placement. The history should include social, psychological, medical, educational, and emotional histories as well as information about and access to all former caretakers and the birth family of the child. This same information should be available to the adult adoptee or to the minor adoptee with the agreement of the adoptive parent(s).

Provide information about specialized treatment. Some children who are older at the time of adoption and who have emotional or psychiatric problems will need residential treatment or other specialized mental health help. Prior to placement, the adoption professional should teach adoptive parents about such needs and about resources for treatment in the community, state, and surrounding regions. The adoption professional should tell adoptive parents about what financial assistance, if any, is available for such treatment, how much it will be, and its duration. The adoption professional should also inform adoptive parents about costs not covered by assistance programs, if any, and what the cost of such treatment would be in the event that adoption assistance payments, Medicaid, and other federal or state programs are reduced or eliminated.

The adoption professional should inform birth parents and adoptees about specialized services available in the community that will assist them with issues surrounding adoption, grief, loss, identity formation, and other adoption-related concerns.

Warn of adverse consequences of adoption search and reunion. The adoption professional should completely explain the possible long-term effects of adoption search and reunion to adult adoptees, birth parents, and adoptive parents, including the potential negative reaction of the adoptive parents, or a rejection by the birth parents or family upon being found. Professionals should be able to provide their clients with information, resources, and referrals on how to assist family members in dealing with the positive and negative consequences of search and reunion.

PRINCIPLE 6: OBJECTIVITY & INDEPENDENCE

Conflict of interest, adverse positions, and the duty of the professional to maintain objectivity are all issues arising from the ethic of objectivity and independence. This ethic requires the professional to avoid personal relationships with clients, students, supervisees, or research participants when such relationship might impair the professional's objectivity, interfere with the professional's ability to carry out his or her professional duties, or could harm or exploit the other party. The objective professional avoids relationships or commitments that conflict with his or her clients' interests. When institutional or organizational commitments conflict with the professional's duty to clients, the needs of the client are of prime importance. The following standards of professional conduct in serving adoption clients support this ethic:

Avoid dual roles. The adoption professional should avoid commitments or relationships that conflict with the interests of the client. If the client is a parent considering adoption for a child, or a parent under court supervision for child mistreatment, the adoption professional should avoid serving both the birth parents and prospective adoptive parents or others with a vested interest in the custody of the child.

Support separate legal counsel for clients. Adoption professionals should encourage birth and adoptive parents who are party to the same adoption to obtain independent legal counsel. Parents should be encouraged to retain legal counsel independent of the adoption professional or adoption agency. Adoption professionals should see to it that minor children entering adoptive placements are assigned a guardian *ad litem* or separate legal counsel from that of the birth or adoptive parents.

PRINCIPLE 7: FEES & FINANCES

The ethical use of fees involves setting fees that are fair, reasonable, and commensurate with the service performed and with consideration of the client's ability to pay. In addition, the ethical professional acknowledges the real impact of finances on adoption clients and seeks to assist those clients with appropriate information and supports.

Discuss financial aid. Birth parents considering adoption for a child and those receiving family preservation services as a result of court involvement should be educated to know that they can receive financial assistance without any influence or intervention of an adoption agency, attorney, or professional.

Adoption professionals should tell adoptive parents about the expenses they are likely to incur as a result of adopting a certain child and disclose accurate and complete information about Adoption Assistance Payments, Difficulty-of-Care payments, Medicaid, Crippled Children's Services, SSI availability, and other resources available to help the child and the adoptive family after the adoption is finalized.

Adoptive parents adopting intercountry should be informed about all potential costs before the adoption is undertaken.

Adoption placement fees should not be charged. Children needing the service of adoption should be considered the responsibility of the local, state, and federal governments and service fees for their care and placements charged to the appropriate governmental agencies. The costs of adoption should be subsidized through tax deductions, adoption assistance, nonrecurring expense reimbursement, or other means. Adoption professionals should advocate for such legislative changes through their local, state, and federal governments.

Adoption professionals should see to it that financial limitations of the foster or adoptive family do not prevent the permanent placement of a child with special needs. Adoption outside a child's family should not be based solely on the inability of birth family members to pay adoption service fees or care for a child with special needs.

When adoption service fees are charged, they should be disclosed to the person responsible for paying them prior to matching with a child and should be based on the client's ability to pay.

Fees for release of information. Fees for adoption search or release of identifying or nonidentifying information should not be charged by agencies.

Fees charged to birth parents. When the potential for an infant adoption exists, fees for services to expectant parents should be paid by the expectant parents according to their ability to pay. In no case should the payment or nonpayment of fees be used to leverage the relinquishment of a child for adoption.

Expectant parents should be responsible for their own counseling, housing, food, transportation, and clothing needs before a child is relinquished for adoption. The inability to pay for adoption and other counseling fees should not prevent appropriate services from being rendered.

PRINCIPLE 8: CONTRACTUAL RELATIONSHIPS

This ethic requires that professionals represent the client's interest first and foremost at all times. Professionals or others outside the client-professional relationship should be consulted when it is in the best interest of the client, and adoption clients should be allowed or encouraged to seek advice, information, or support from other groups even when the philosophy of the group differs from that of the primary counselor. Contractual relationships are closely related to the ethics of objectivity and independence, and also are influenced by that of communication.

Outside consultation. Professionals or others outside the organization should be consulted when it is in the best interest of the adoption client or when the client requests such a consultation.

Encourage clients to seek other advice. Adoption clients should be encouraged to seek advice, information, or support from other professionals, even those with differing philosophies.

Information about adoption organizations. Adoption service recipients should be given written information about local, regional, and national adoption groups when they seek advice or counseling from the adoption professional.

Ongoing contact and representation of the client's interest. The adoption professional should serve his or her adoption clients on an ongoing basis or arrange for such service after parental rights have been terminated or an adoption has occurred.

In the event of the need for the disruption or dissolution of the child's adoption and subsequent adoptive placement, the adoption professional should apprise adoptive parents of their rights and responsibilities and continue to serve the adoptive family through family preservation services. Every effort should be made to preserve the adoptive family. In the event of a failed adoption, the adoption professional should continue to serve the adoptive parents through crisis and grief counseling and obtain separate professional counseling and supports for the adoptee.

If an adoption fails, the adoption professional should inform the older child about the rationale behind the decision and the options for the child's subsequent placement. The adoption professional should give the adoptee the opportunity to say good-bye to his or her adoptive parents, siblings, pets, neighbors and friends, and other loved ones as age appropriate.

In the event of the disruption or dissolution of the child's adoption, or other events (such as adoptive parents' divorce or death) leading to the child's subsequent availability for new adoptive placement, the adoption professional should, whenever possible, inform the birth parents about the situation, including the birth parents' rights, if any, to contact or adopt the child themselves.

If notified of the death of the surrendered child (adoptee), the adoption professional should make every effort to inform the birth parents about the child's death, the location of the adoptee's burial, and the opportunity, if any, for contact with the adoptive parents.

If notified of the death of the birth parent(s), the adoption professional should inform the adult adoptee, or the adoptive parents in the case of an adoptee who is a minor, about the birth parent's death and any opportunity for contact with the birth family as well as the location of the birth parent's burial.

Part V

Challenges

Chapter 7

Challenges to Change

We are responsible. If we keep doing the things we've been doing, we're going to keep getting the things we've got.

— Judge David Grossman

CHALLENGES TO CHANGE IN ADOPTION PRACTICE

It is not enough to identify our problems in applying values-based ethical codes to the professional practice of adoption, or to propose professional standards that may or may not ever be codified or formalized. Even when professionals train themselves with enough vigor to insure ethical competence, it is not enough to merely understand and apply ethical principles. These same ethical principles must be communicated to the larger society as professionals seek to fulfill their ethical responsibilities to that society.

The helping professions most often involved with adoption—social work, law, psychology and other counseling professions, nursing, and medicine—all acknowledge the individual professional's ethical obligations to society. Such obligations include social and political action to prevent and eliminate discrimination; to ensure that people have access to the resources, services, and opportunities they require to meet basic needs; and to foster respect for a diversity of cultures in society. The professional also has an obligation to act in ways that "expand choice and opportunity for all persons, with special regard for disadvantaged or oppressed groups and persons" (NASW, 1990, p. 9). Finally, this ethic of social responsibility demands that professionals advocate changes in policy and legislation to improve social conditions and promote social justice—weighty requirements for professionals already working to apply professional standards in adoption as they compete with nonprofessional, lay practitioners of adoption operating with a market mentality.

CONFLICTING VALUES

What challenges to change in adoption values and ethics do we face? The essential issues have remained unchanged since early times and involve conflicting values. Such conflicts can be clearly seen in the controversy surrounding the U.S. failure to ratify the United Nations Convention on the Rights of the Child, an international treaty defining minimal standards for the protection of children. On February 15, 1995, Madeleine Albright, then the United States Ambassador to the United Nations, signed the U.N. Convention on the Rights of the Child on behalf of the United States, signaling an intent to ratify. Ratification involves receiving advice and consent from the U.S. Senate, followed by congressional legislation which would ensure uniform implementation of the Convention. As of late 1998 the United States had not yet ratified the Convention, expressing reservations about it in several areas. Only the United States and Somalia have failed to ratify the Convention, whereas 192 other nations have ratified it, making the Convention the most rapidly and widely adopted human rights treaty in history.

The Convention provides for the protection of children from discrimination, torture, unlawful arrest, unlawful confinement, abuse, mistreatment, exploitation, and kidnapping and instructs states to consider the best interests of children in all actions and provide for the care of children when parents fail to do so. Provisions for access to information, education, and social welfare are also set forth. Over these provisions, Americans have no arguments with the Convention.

The Convention addresses areas specific to adoption, foster care, and child welfare. It recognizes the rights of the child to a name at birth, the right to acquire a nationality, and, as far as possible, the right to know and be cared for by his or her own parents. If children cannot live with their parents, they have the right to maintain contact with one or both parents. Parents are given the right to raise their children; the State is instructed to assist them in doing so and also to respect parents and the extended family. Children are to be protected when living away from their parents and have the right to social security and social insurance. Minority race and indigenous children have the right to enjoy their own culture, religion, and language. It is these provisions that have been divisive for Americans.

In America, we cannot agree that children have a right to a name at birth. We wonder whether having the right to a name at birth means that the adoptee has a right to his or her birth name—identifying information that is concealed or altered under most of our state laws governing adoption. Americans cannot agree that children who cannot live with their parents have the right to maintain contact with one or both parents. Do adopted children have the right to open an ongoing contact with one or both birth parents? If so, do these values of identity and of blood-relatedness conflict with the value of human relatedness in the context of families, including adoptive families? Does giving an adopted child the right to ongoing contact with his or her parent(s) compromise the right of that child to a safe, secure, and permanent adoptive family?

The Convention upholds the right of minority race and indigenous children to be raised in their own culture, religion, and language. Does such a right preclude transracial adoption, or challenge American laws that specifically prohibit postponing an adoptive placement solely based on race?

The U.N. Convention asserts that adoption, when recognized or allowed, should be carried out in the best interests of the child, and then only with the authorization of competent authorities and safeguards for the child. Such safeguards include the following:

1. Children have the right to be protected from being sold.

2. Parents must give informed consent to adoption on the basis of competent counseling.

3. Intercountry adoption may be considered an alternative means of placement.

4. If adopted intercountry, the child should be given the same safeguards and be adopted under standards equivalent to those in the country of origin.

5. If adopted intercountry, the placement should not result in improper financial gain for those involved.

6. Bilateral or multilateral agreements between nations shall occur, ensuring that adoption is carried out by competent authorities or organs.

Whereas adoptions are accomplished in several modern nations solely through government agencies employing truly professional adoption workers, in America adoptions are facilitated through professionals, licensed public and private agencies, and also through lay facilitators. Does authorizing "competent authorities" threaten the unregulated, nonlicensed, or lay placement of children that has coexisted with professional adoption practice since America's first child welfare laws were passed? What does "informed consent to adoption on the basis of competent counseling" mean? When U.S. laws support adoptions through licensed and nonlicensed agencies, professionals, or facilitators, will the imposition of possibly higher or more demanding international standards on American adoption practice have an adverse effect on those who favor adoption as an industry (rather than adoption as a human service)?

Under the U.N. Convention, if adopted intercountry, a child should be given the "same safeguards and be adopted under standards equivalent to those in the country of origin." Does this mean that children born in open-records countries such as South Korea, but adopted by U.S. citizens in closed-records states should be given the right to have their birth records at the age of majority? Would imposition of such standards violate American interpretations of ethical values of confidentiality or privacy for the birth parents? Would violation of international standards conflict with the adoptee's right to self-determination and equal access to information under the law?

For intercountry adoption, the U.N. Convention states that the placement should not result in improper financial gain for those involved. How do other nations define "improper gain"? Are infant adoption fees of $20,000 or more to be considered improper? Who will set such standards? Will the imposition of such standards conflict with values respecting the legal processes our nation?

AGENCY VERSUS INDEPENDENT ADOPTION

Today a debate rages between agency-regulated and nonagency adoption facilitators about which type of adoption is better. Independent adoption facilitators claim that America's method of matching waiting parents with available children after extensive adoptive parent preparation and screening is outdated, unfair, and inadequate (Bartholet, 1993). On the other side, professionals and organizations concerned with professional adoption practice have uniformly opposed the facilitation of adoptions through intermediaries, such as medical doctors and attorneys, who are neither trained nor licensed to provide child-placing services (United States Children's Bureau, 1961; Child Welfare League of America, 1976; Barth, 1987; Sachdev, 1989; NASW, 1996). One-third of adoptions in the

United States take place through such independent or private adoption facilitators, with the other two-thirds of adoptions facilitated through public or private licensed child placing agencies (Child Welfare League of America, 1993; Bartholet, 1993).

Each of America's 50 states provides for the licensing of voluntary, private adoption agencies in addition to administering child welfare services through a public child welfare agency. All 50 states mandate the possession of certain qualifications for directors, child placement supervisors, and adoption workers who are entrusted with the foster care and adoption placements of children through licensed agencies (Babb, 1994). Such qualifications require that the worker has child welfare education, training, and experience and at least a bachelor's degree in a social science. Child placement supervisors are often required to possess at the least a master's degree in a social science such as social work, psychology, or counseling, along with one or more years experience in the child welfare field (Babb, 1996). These educational and experiential requirements, combined with mandatory continuing education, are designed to ensure competence among agency personnel.

Adoption specialists employed by each state's public child welfare agency must also meet minimal educational requirements, usually a bachelor's degree in any discipline, and receive in-service and continuing education in child welfare and adoption. Thus, although the frontline state agency adoption specialist may possess a bachelor's degree in history or journalism, hardly relevant to adoption, the in-service training and continuing education provided through such agencies presumably guarantees better service than can be provided by independent facilitators.

Unfortunately, in spite of the contention that agency adoption more ethically and competently serves adoption clients, little evidence exists to support this argument (Zelizer, 1985; Bartholet, 1993). Though we lack empirical evidence supporting the superiority of professional, agency-facilitated adoption over independent adoption, professionals who practice adoption under the authority of licensed agencies have by many been considered to be the most competent because of their child welfare training and experience, as well as the most principled because of their adherence to a professional code of ethics (U.S. Children's Bureau, 1961; Child Welfare League of America, 1976; Pine, 1987; Sachdev, 1989; Barth, 1987; Babb, 1994; Walden, Wolock, & Demone, 1990; NASW, 1996; Vitillo, 1991; Fenton, 1994; Babb & Laws, 1997). Even so, when adoption failure rates range from 5 percent to 25 percent through public and private licensed adoption agencies (Rosenthal & Groze, 1993), one has to ask how much more poorly independent adoption serves waiting children. But because the idea of profit-based motivations in child placement is so loathsome, we suspect that they must be worse for children.

Rather than arguing over which is better, independent or agency adoption, we should be exploring what must be done to try to place children needing parents in the best possible home the first time, so that children who have already lost their original parents need not lose subsequent parents due to lack of competence among adoption facilitators. Whether an adoption facilitator has a master's degree in social work or no degree at all, we must ask how we can keep children from waiting needlessly for adoptive parents, how we can place them in families as quickly yet safely as possible, and how we can keep them in those families in a healthy environment until their majority. Unfortunately, because the issue has not been adequately researched, no one can say for certain that the MSW practicing adoption through a licensed adoption agency is certain to produce better results than an attorney, minister, or adoption facilitator practicing independently of a licensed adoption agency. We may guess that the professional is more likely to have better results based on education and experience, but we cannot prove it with certainty.

What is certain, however, is that without a national standard for the training of adoption facilitators and counselors of all varieties, we cannot even begin to discuss what constitutes excellence in adoption practice. Without universal standards, we cannot measure how well we are serving our clients and our clients cannot know how well they are being served. And as long as we persist in debating over which is better, agency or independent adoption, we waste energy that would be much better spent establishing and legislating standards of competence and ethical behavior in the field of adoption.

THE ADOPTION INDUSTRY

Although adoption agencies claim to provide superior services and better outcomes for their clients, as long as agencies operate through fees and donations based on completed adoptions, any promise of unbiased professionalism can only be self-serving. Indeed, the private, licensed adoption agency and independent adoption facilitator are both supported by fees paid by prospective adopters. As Harvard law professor and adoptive mother Elizabeth Bartholet (1993) has pointed out, American adoption practice is thus largely driven by money or, more accurately, by those who have money and those who want to get it from them. When money is as central to a human service as it is in adoption practice, money not only drives the process, but it shapes the results.

It is no coincidence that the flow of children "is always in one direction, from the less affluent to the more affluent countries internationally, socioeconomically from lower to middle and upper class within any one country, and from minority groups in the United States to the majority group" (Sachdev, 1989, p. 11). Thus, higher fees continue to be justified for the adoptions of children in high demand, while lower fees and even subsidized adoptions continue to be the norm in adoptions of children who are in low demand. Not only does this mean that homes are selected on a questionable basis but also that "adopted children may come to view themselves as commodities" (Watson & Brown, 1994, p. 8). Analyzing the insinuation of commercial norms into parental relationships, Anderson writes that "whereas parental love is not supposed to be conditioned upon the child having particular characteristics, consumer demand is properly responsive to the characteristics of commodities" (1994, p. 235).

It is not only unadopted children who suffer in such a system—prospective adoptive parents suffer also. Consider the situation faced by America's prospective single adopter. Although agencies and professionals may say that no discrimination exists in practice, and that single adoptive parents are welcome to adopt America's waiting children, the truth is that oftentimes married couples are preferred and single adopters passed over for consideration of the most easily placed children. Single parents are then offered the children who are most difficult to place and raise—older children, children with severe handicaps, children with emotional problems—even though single parents usually have fewer emotional and financial resources then their married counterparts upon which to draw. In a field so often driven by commerce rather than caring, it seems that the least 'valuable' children are reserved for the least moneyed prospective adopters to the possible detriment of both.

Money has become the critical variable for determining who gets a child. Bartholet writes that since many parents who surrender infants do so independently, prospective adoptive parents with enough money can easily circumvent the extensive screening process employed by agencies and "find their way to a healthy newborn" (1993, p. 74). Because prospective adopters with money can (and often do) bypass the agency process, Bartholet concludes that the entire American adoption system of parental screening and matching fails: "Together with the rule against baby buying, parental screening is supposed to ensure that children are assigned not to the highest bidder but to those deemed most fit to parent. The fact that money enables those deemed least fit to buy their way to the children who are most in demand makes a farce of the entire system" (p. 74).

Because of the system's failure, Bartholet calls for the deregulation of America's current adoption system in favor of one that guarantees that waiting children receive nurturing parents as soon as possible, that reimburses and subsidizes many of the costs of adoption, and gives adoptive and biological parents equal insurance and employee benefits.

Psychologist and author Randolph Severson agrees with Bartholet's assessment of our adoption system as one driven by the wants of prospective adopters seeking children and adoption agencies seeking profits, writing: "The ostensible respect for social science among adoption professionals conceals a form of collusion between sociology and social work, between the academy and the agency, that maintains them both in business to the detriment of the clients that adoption ought to serve" (1994, p. 188)

Severson challenges Bartholet's assertion that deregulation is the answer, though, suggesting that her

> vision of an adoption world where agencies would mainly be recruiters and empowerers of prospective adoptive parents is really not so far from the truth that is already in place as more and more adoption agencies recreate themselves in the image of facilitators who merely assist adoptive parents in networking in order to find birthparents who are then referred to the agency or directly arrange placement with the couple who found them. (1993, p. 230)

Severson concludes that the old school social workers who match children with parents "have in reality almost vanished" (1994, p. 230), replaced by professionally trained social workers who nevertheless function as mere facilitators of adoptions engineered largely by prospective adopters out hunting for children. Rhodes agrees, pointing out a systemic conflict in social work between the profession's "traditional ethical concerns for the most needy and vulnerable with a market economy based on profit" (1992, p. 45).

Many of those who are concerned about the ethical implications of America's commercial approach to adoption have written and spoken openly about our practice of essentially selling children to the highest bidder, while whitewashing the practice by passing laws making baby selling illegal and calling the payments adoptive parents make to agencies and attorneys "fees for service." Many who think about these things would agree with Jim Gritter that "when adoptive parents pay $25,000 for 10 hours of service, it is difficult to pretend that they are paying for services rendered. They are obviously buying an outcome. They are buying a product" (1997, p. 258). Gritter's solution? Regulation—regulation soon and regulation proper.

Children as Chattels

Although on opposite sides of the adoption fence philosophically, Severson and Bartholet—and those in their respective camps—seem able to agree on one issue, which is that America's child welfare system is supposed to function in ways that serve the best interests of children—and often fails. "Everyone knows," writes Bartholet, "that [children's] best interests require nurturing homes and parenting relationships, but it is painfully obvious that children have no enforceable rights to those things" (1993, p. 77). Severson agrees and goes beyond identification of symptoms to the root problem, "the error, or rather, the outrage of thinking of children as property" (1994, p. 246).

In support of Severson's child-as-chattel theory, one has only to return to America's early days of child placement, when the orphans in most demand were healthy boys over age ten who could provide cheap labor to adoptive families. Today we shake our heads at a society that produced such a utilitarian and objectifying approach to child placement. But we continue to live in such a society. Today, the practical utility of hardy 10-year-old boys has been replaced by the sentimental utility of the healthy infant. Only the characteristics of the adoptable children have changed: our collective soul has not changed.

Reproductive Technologies

We also see evidence that one's offspring—that is, embryos that may become children, nowadays euphemistically referred to as "preembryos"—are often considered property in situations involving artificial means of reproduction. In vitro fertilization (IVF), artificial insemination donor (AID), and surrogacy arrangements have increased over the past twenty years as a result of the rise in infertility and the standardization of IVF and AID techniques (Beauchamp & Walters, 1994).

In her discussion of the moral questions surrounding reproductive technologies, Ruth Macklin (1994) identifies three possible answers to questions about which parent or parent figure has the presumptive right to parent the child produced through reproductive technologies:

1. Gestational parent. This view states that the primary criterion for parental right, regardless of the contributors of the child's genetic

material, is the gestational mother. The gestational mother should have the legal responsibility and right to raise the child because of the gestational mother's "sweat equity"—she contributed to the child's development in the womb, was present at birth, and during the neonate period to care for the child (Macklin, 1994, p. 195). According to Macklin, this position "focuses on what the gestational mother deserves, based on her investment in the child . . . [and] on the interests of the child during and immediately after the birth" (1994, p. 195).

2. Genetics. This position states that the parents contributing their genetic material to the creation of a child—the sperm and ovum donors—are entitled to parenting rights because people own their genetic products (sperm and ova) and because it is in the best interests of children to be raised by parents to whom they are genetically related. In her defense of this position, Macklin (1994) comments that evidence of the importance of genetic relatives is the fact that adoptees so often undertake searches for their biological parents.

3. Gestation and genetics. Those who adopt this position say that surrogates who contribute both the ovum and the womb have more compelling claims to being the primary mother than does the surrogate whose womb alone is used.

Arguments in favor of the genetic parents have implications for adoption that illustrate how conflicting our ideas about parents and children really are. In the adoption world, the "real" parent is the parent who invests what Macklin called sweat equity in the child, generally the adoptive parent. Laws, religious institutions, and popular opinion may favor the genetic parents in the realm of reproductive technologies, though, since experts in these areas fear that

our conception of humanness will not survive the technological permutations before us, and that we will treat these new artificially conceived embryos more as objects than as subjects . . . , unable to track traditional human categories of parenthood and lineage . . . this loss would cause us to lose track of important aspects of our identity [because it] violates the rights of the child; it deprives him of his filial relationship with his parental origins and can hinder the maturing of his personal identity. (Sherwin, 1987, p. 225)

The argument in favor of the gestational parent favors the positions of adoptive parents, in that it recognizes the value of the investment of time, energy, and resources in the life of a child. This respect for the investments of adoptive parents has accrued not only to adoptive parents who have raised their adopted children or cared for them for any length of time, but it has also been extended in recent years to prospective adopters before a child is even born. In planned open infant adoptions, for example, the exercise of the adoptive parents' presumptive rights has occurred earlier and earlier in the child placement continuum. Twenty years ago, infants whose adoptions had been planned in advance were born, placed into foster care, and remained in foster care pending the termination of parental rights of the birth mother, if not the birth father also. Birth and adoptive parents understandably objected to this practice, wanting the child to have the earliest possible opportunity to attach to the adopting parents. Thus, the practice of placing children from the hospital ensued, which, while presenting emotional risk to the adoptive parents was believed to better serve the interests of the child.

Open Adoptions

As open adoption developed and the relationships between relinquishing mothers and the prospective adoptive parents of their unborn children with it, the adoptive parent-infant relationship took another step closer to conception when adoptive mothers began to attend prenatal classes, medical appointments, and even childbirth with the birthing mother. In numerous cases, adoptive parents not only coach the expectant mother through labor, but cut the umbilical cord and are the first to hold the newborn infant. Sometimes hospitals allow adoptive parents who can afford it to stay in the hospital for the three to five days of confinement for the birth mother and baby, bringing the baby to the adoptive mother for feedings while the birth mother recovers from childbirth in a room just down the hall. One wonders when such eager adoptive parents will find a way of taking up residence in the womb with the prospective adoptee.

Critical of attempts to undermine the place of genetic and gestational ties in favor of a more commercial and utilitarian view of children, Anderson wrote: "By upholding a system of involuntary (genetic) ties of obligation among people, even when the adults among them prefer to divide their rights and obligations in other ways, we help to secure children's interests in having an assured place in the world, which is more firm than the wills of their parents" (1994, p. 236).

Macklin rightly asks where the child's interest is in all of the hoopla surrounding conflicting parental claims, quoting Alison Ward, a birth mother who testified before the New Jersey legislature about the possible effects of surrogacy arrangements on the children resulting from them:

> There will always be pain for these children. Just as adoptive parents have learned that they cannot love the pain of their adopted children away, couples who raise children obtained through surrogacy will have to deal with a special set of problems. Donor offspring . . . rarely find out the truth of their origins. But, some of them do, and we must listen to them when they speak of their anguish, of not knowing who fathered them; we must listen when we tell us how destructive it is to their self-esteem to find out their father sold the essence of his lineage for $40 or so, without ever intending to love or take responsibility for them. For children born of surrogacy contracts, it will be even worse: their own mothers did this to them (1994, p. 197).

What Is a Person?

Controversy surrounds the question of whether or not sperm or ovum donors are really parents or preembryos and embryos really human. Is Alison Ward's analysis of what "their own mothers" (and fathers) have done to children brought into this world through surrogacy contracts correct? Or is it more true that the preembryo is nothing more than what is, under United States law, abortable tissue and not a child or a person in any sense of the term? The American Fertility Society (1994) discussed ethical problems of reproductive technologies by suggesting three possible conceptions of the preembryo, preembryo referring to the fertilized egg that has not reached the ninth to fourteenth day of implantation in a woman's womb:

1. The human preembryo is a human being entitled to protection as such from the time of fertilization onward. Any manipulation, research, freezing, or other potentially damaging treatment of the human preembryo is thus considered unethical in this perspective. The view bases the definition of the preembryo as human by noting that during fertilization a new genotype is created, and that given the proper environment, the human preembryo may become a person in his or her own right.

2. The human preembryo is not a person and has no moral status because "the biologic individuality of the preembryo is assured only toward the end of the first 14 days of development" (American Fertility Society, 1994, p. 202). In addition, matter without organs,

limbs, or cognizance cannot be a person and, therefore, has no moral status.

3. The preembryo has some moral status because it has a unique genotype and has potential to become a person. On the other hand, the moral obligations of scientists to infertile couples or pregnant women outweigh their obligation to the preembryo.

And what of the moral obligations of scientists to infertile couples and pregnant women? Answers to this question rely upon the answer to another question: is the preembryo human, or not? If not, then experimentation with the preembryo would be, in most views, moral. If so, then experimentation with the human preembryo would be as morally wrong as experimentation with human infants and children. What has in fact occurred is that frozen embryos not used in IVF procedures are used for research related to IVF or for other medical purposes (Caplan, 1994). In many areas related to children we seem to have gotten the cart before the horse, asking questions about morality and developing ethical standards long after our circumstances have demanded, or our technology has allowed, that we take action in order to solve problems or sometimes merely to satisfy the appetites of consumers.

Money: The Root of All Sorts of Evils

The specter of money in the fertility industry causes us to return to the issue of children as chattels, particularly so when each IVF attempt costs $3,000 to $5,000 in fees. Infertility treatment is to the medical field what healthy, same-race infant adoption is to the adoption field—an expensive, often humiliating, and usually losing proposition, since IVF fails 90 percent of the time (Sherwin, 1987; Rothman, 1994). Healthy infant adoption is at least as disappointing: adoption experts and adoptive mothers Mary Martin Mason and Amy Silberman (1993) estimate that only 60,000 of the 6 million prospective adoptive parents who try to adopt annually actually succeed. Such dismal odds produce competition, anxiety, and despair among prospective adoptive parents, for whose dollars scrupulous and unscrupulous adoption facilitators in turn compete, creating the climate of commercialism we have in adoption today. Ethical adoption practitioners, facilitators, and agencies resist this. Conscientious and virtuous adoption practitioners "resist from the bottom of [their] hearts any trend that reduces children to commodities" and work to interject a spirit of servanthood into adoption practice (Gritter, 1997, p. 280). The final sections of this book will explore ways of improving adoption practice in the United States by considering professions—what they are, why they exist, and why we need them.

IS ADOPTION PRACTICE A PROFESSION?

One of the most misleading and potentially damaging aspects of adoption work in the United States is that the public, and even many professionals, have come to believe that a professional who works in the adoption field, and often anyone who facilitates adoptions, is an adoption professional. Throughout this book, the term *adoption professional* has been used to refer to individuals, educated and trained in a profession, who specialize in adoption work. Unfortunately, although adoption facilitation deals in some of the most sensitive issues of the human heart having many lasting effects, adoption practice as a profession does not exist in the United States.

In spite of the increased demand for child protection and child welfare workers because of increased case loads, the number of professionals trained in these areas has actually decreased over the past 10 years. In Texas, for example, one of the country's top five states placing waiting children, only 28 percent of the child welfare workers have undergraduate or graduate social work degrees, in spite of the fact that child welfare supervisors in the state support efforts to professionalize child welfare services through certification (Birmingham, Berry, & Bussey, 1996).

Because as many as one-third of the individuals employed by public and private adoption agencies actually might qualify as professionals in a field such as social work or counseling, the assumption might be made that adoption practice has been professionalized. A closer look at the assumptions many make about adoption practice will illustrate their folly.

Physicians specializing in the treatment of children are educated and trained in pediatrics. The medical profession, in fact, trains many specialists in areas as diverse as geriatrics, psychiatry, and urology. Neither the public, particularly patients seeking treatment, nor the medical profession assume that general medical education and training prepares the physician to become an expert in a specialty area simply because he or she has become licensed as a physician.

Likewise, in other professions and occupations, licensing or certification in a specialty must be earned before an individual can offer expert services in an area. The certified manicurist may not give facials; the certified hair stylist may not offer manicures. In most specialties other than adoption, the very idea—much less the practice—of employing any "professional" claiming expertise would be ludicrous, if not illegal. Yet in contemporary adoption practice in the United States, individuals with professions as different as social work and law, marriage and family therapy and medicine may call themselves "adoption professionals." And in most states of the union, anyone with enough money to advertise him- or herself as an independent adoption facilitator can claim expertise and get into the business of moving children from family to family.

In spite of the development of practice standards for child placement, adoption has not developed into a profession as many child welfare experts and organizations have hoped, judging by the measures usually employed in defining professions (CWLA, 1976; Catholic Charities USA, 1989; National Association of Social Workers, 1979, 1987).

As we have seen throughout this book, adoption specialists have been unable to translate the ethical principles of their respective professions into behavior, a failure at the root of many of the problems with adoption services in the United States (Conrad & Joseph, 1991). In the adoption field, the first (and only) professional quality adoption journal was published in 1997. There remains no national professional organization for adoption specialists, no professional recognition of adoption practice as a specialty of any discipline, no established education and training requirements, and no regular professional meetings and forums for adoption "professionals." In fact, professionals working in adoption have only general means by which to exchange information specific to adoption, dialogue concerning adoption standards, or obtain a comprehensive picture of what is happening in adoption today. Adoption work is not a profession, not even a professional specialty; but it should be.

Serving Whole People

The fact that adoption work has not been professionalized reflects society's unchallenged assumptions about children and families, if not its prejudices. Indeed, specialty areas serving children, such as child protection and even child counseling, have only recently become recognized as deserving professional merit (Melton & Flood, 1994). Does the struggle child protection specialists have faced in obtaining professional recognition reflect a peculiarly American indolence about recognizing the inherent worth of children? Or are the adoptable children of 1999 much like the adoptable children of 1899, adoptable only because they may satisfy the wants of an adult?

American society is, supposedly, based on an unqualified "respect for the rights and needs of each individual" (U.S. Advisory Board on Child Abuse and Neglect, 1990, p. 3). Unfortunately, many Americans have had to establish their personhood before rights and needs attendant to personhood were applied. Children remain one of the last groups of Americans who have yet to become politically recognized as whole people, even if they are not wholly adult. Adopted children, in particular, face many societal barriers to wholeness. And here we find the crux of the problem in American adoption: what Randolph Severson (1994) calls the idea of the person:

> The key to a fair, true and compassionate adoption system is the idea of the person. Developed during the fifth century by Christian theologians and philosophers in an effort to explain the dual divine-human nature of Christ, in this century the idea has proved its richness and relevance to philosophical grasp of the essentials of the human condition. As a person, each of us is an individual who combines within our existence two natures—body and soul, matter and spirit, brain and consciousness, nature and nurture, etc. Neither element can be denied without diminishing our humanity. (pp. 235–236)

Diminished humanity is one of the primary results of an adoption system built on what Jesus called "unrighteous mammon," because systems arising from material interests alone can scarcely hope to serve spiritual needs too. When American adoption does serve the whole person, it seems almost to do so by happenstance. We meet birth parents at a point of crisis and resolve the crisis by creating a bigger disaster for most of these parents, especially mothers—disasters Brodzinsky describes as "profound and protracted grief reactions, depression, and an enduring preoccupation with and worry about the welfare of the child" (1990, p. 304). We create childless parents who are forever barred from knowing what happened to their children, and whether or not the system delivered on its promise to give them better lives.

We also meet adoptive parents at their point of need, give them children after requiring much hoop-jumping and posturing, and then act as though our work is finished. An Illinois couple, for example, adopted a sibling group of five from a Russian orphanage and received only two calls from their adoption agency social worker, a so-called "adoption professional," in the following nine months of placement! Especially in special needs adoptions, we demand that adoptive parents produce children who will become citizens who are as solid as bricks, without giving parents the information and supports they need to do the job well. We are like Pharaoh, demanding that the Israelites make more bricks without straw.

And we talk about adopted children as if they occupy the most important corner of the adoption triangle, yet when they grow up we withhold the very information and documents from them that can flesh out their pasts—and thus their presents and futures, making them whole persons in the sense Severson describes.

On a grand scale, the American adoption system recreates in adoption-affected families the very disconnectedness it seeks to overcome. It does so because the system is rife with traditions of secrecy and control instead of the ethical values of self-determination, informed consent, and unconditional regard for the whole person. It is these values and others like them, long part of ethical codes of conduct among professionals, that must be brought into the forefront of the adoption practice arena if we hope to ever elevate adoption practice to the professional level.

ELEVATING ADOPTION PRACTICE

Characteristics of Professions

We have already seen that adoption of and adherence to a code of ethics is the cornerstone of a profession, differentiating between professional and quasi- or semiprofessional practice (Greenwood, 1957; Etzioni, 1969; Poppendieck, 1992). Other characteristics of professions or professional subspecialties include professional recognition of the specialty, development of a specialty journal, and regular professional meetings and forums. Another fundamental characteristic of a profession is entry requirements based on experience or a combination of experience and academic or training qualifications, along with measurement of proficiency of knowledge and state or other formal licensing (Scheer, 1984; Gilley & Galbraith, 1986).

In America, professionalism generally means the provision of specialized, high quality services to clients (Greene, 1983). Because they serve the public interest by offering expert services at a fair price, professionals are entitled by law to regulate themselves. The professional's primary interest should be the client's welfare, not financial profit. Thus, professionals do not sell services or goods to consumers; they provide services for clients. And because professionals focus on service and not profits, they do not solicit new clients and neither do they compete with colleagues through advertising or price-cutting.

Professionalism is wonderful in theory. What could be better for the client than receiving the best services available from experts interested not in profits but in people? Unfortunately, in practice professionals are subject to the same forces of supply and demand as anyone else. Like everyone else, professionals have bills to pay and are as driven by the pressures of the profane as everyone else. Instead of being surprised that adoption practice is so unprofessional in the United States, perhaps we should be surprised when agencies and individuals approach adoption practice like public servants instead of industrialists.

Adoption Practice as a Profession

In spite of a national adoption tradition steeped in consumerism, agencies and individuals have wanted and tried to elevate adoption practice to the professional level. To be sure, approaches to the professionalization of adoption practice have been piecemeal and leave something to be desired when compared with the development of other professions or sub-specialities. However, in the late 1990s some positive developments occurred through the establishment of an adoption journal, *Adoption Quarterly*, by the Adoption Studies Institute and a number of efforts on the part of the Evan B. Donaldson Adoption Institute, initiated through the efforts of the Spence-Chapin adoption agency. The Evan B. Donaldson Adoption Institute plans to focus on ethics in adoption, host institute conferences and issue postconference proceeding publications, and provide professional training and education in the adoption field—all actions that, if implemented, will contribute to the professionalization of adoption practice. Still absent from the national picture, though, are integrated efforts related to recognition of adoption practice as a specialty of any discipline and establishment of entry qualifications and proficiency measurements for individuals hoping to be identified as "adoption professionals."

Adoption-specific training and education would have to occur, and a series of adoption-specific courses developed if adoption work is to be professionalized. Students would need supervised experience working with adoption triad members. Faculty members teaching the courses would be most effective if they also had training and experience in the child welfare and adoption fields. Course work, practicums, and internships could result from cooperative efforts among schools of social work, psychology, counseling, marriage and family therapy, human relations, and law.

Individuals working with children who are never adopted, but who age out of the foster care system or who live out their youth in institutions also need specific training. Perhaps instead of calling ourselves adoption professionals we should instead be known as child placement professionals. Whatever we call ourselves, as social worker, therapist, and author Annette Baran says, we should have more than a business license qualifying us to amputate children from one family tree and graft them onto another one

(A. Baran, personal communication, October 30, 1997). "Dry cleaners and beauticians need more licenses than adoption facilitators," Baran says, "and nobody except those in adoption thinks it is disgraceful to permit lawyers and middle men to buy and sell babies" (1997). These failures extend, too, to the American foster care system, where our country's most dependent children rely on the services of quasi-professional and professional social workers whose earnings are among the lowest in the nation, who are inadequately trained, prepared, and supported in their demanding jobs, and whose case loads are alarmingly high (Select Committee on Children, Youth, and Families [SCCYF], 1990).

REGULATION OF PROFESSIONS

In the adoption world, those who facilitate adoptions or treat families and individuals affected by adoption have not, as we have seen, been able to qualify themselves as professionals in the same way other professionals are qualified. We have no professional associations or academies, no certification or licensing procedures, no professional recognition as adoption specialists, and no training or educational qualifications. The nation's only adoption journal is in its infancy, and the first professional meeting and forum specifically aimed at adoption professionals occurred in 1997, through the Evan B. Donaldson Adoption Institute.

But perhaps most important, there is no professional standard for or regulation of adoption practice. Thus, although nearly one thousand occupations are regulated in some or all of the states, nearly anyone in the country can obtain a business license and hang out a shingle as an adoption "facilitator" and overnight become an adoption specialist—and considered by some, particularly adoption clients, as a professional. As long as adoption can be practiced without government or self-regulation, this will continue to be the case.

Types of Government Regulation

There are three levels of government regulation in the United States: registration, certification, and licensure. *Registration* requires that the registrant list his or her name on a roster, offer a character reference in some instances, and obtain bonding. There are 643 registered occupations in the United States (Greene, 1983). *Certification* requires that the practitioner obtain a certificate before he can use certain titles. Certification depends on a person's meeting certain qualifications such as graduation from an approved training program, a certain amount of work experience, and passage of qualifying examinations. Sixty-five occupations are certified in at least one of the fifty states (Greene, 1983). *Licensure* is the third level of regulation imposed by the government, requiring a state-provided license before a person can engage in a trade or profession. The difference between certification and licensing is that certification does not prohibit a person from practicing a trade; it only prohibits her from presenting herself to the public as a certified practitioner. Licensure prohibits practice without the license. In the United States, 490 occupations are licensed (Greene, 1983).

Purposes of Regulation

The goal of regulation is to protect consumers (or clients) from frauds, incompetents, and snake-oil salesmen masquerading as experts. Through tort law, regulation allows clients and consumers to receive compensation for harm they suffer as a result of professional incompetence or negligence. Regulation also provides for standardization of a profession and the establishment of credibility for practitioners (Gilley & Galbraith, 1986, p. 61). Finally, regulation increases the relative supply of high quality practitioners in a field and makes consumers able to more easily access high quality services.

Shimberg and Roederer (1978) write that regulation should meet a public need and protect the public, not the economic interests of the occupational group. Furthermore, government should provide only the minimum level of regulation and requirements, and evaluation procedures for entry into the regulated occupation should be clearly related to safe and effective practice.

Occupations are regulated when the public demands greater accountability of practitioners, or when the practitioners want to improve their status through regulation. Sometimes a group seeks licensure so that practitioners can be reimbursed under federal and state programs or by private insurers.

If individuals practicing in the adoption field were certified or licensed for adoption-specific work, they would have experience, academic, and training qualifications for work with birth parents, adoptees, and adoptive parents. They would be able to demonstrate their knowledge of the psychology and practice of adoption through proficiency examinations. In an ideal situation adoption service recipients—whether receiving adoption-related counseling, adoption search and reunion support, or adoption facilitation services—would receive dedicated and expert services at fair prices. If adoption practice was regulated and professionalized, our traditional consumer-oriented approach to adoption might be replaced with a more respectable approach that considered the best interests of the client first in philosophy, if not in practice. Practitioners could measure themselves against a national standard rather than against their competitors' bottom lines.

Criteria for Regulation

Based on a Department of Labor grant, in conjunction with the Council of State Governments and the Educational Testing Service, Shimberg and Roederer (1978) developed and published several criteria for determining whether or not an occupation should be regulated. The nine criteria were:

1. Does the person perform a service for individuals involving a hazard to the public health, safety, or welfare if unregulated?

2. Do a substantial number of people who do not practice the occupation demand its regulation?

3. How many states already regulate the occupation or practice?

4. Is there sufficient demand for the service by a substantial portion of the population, and no substitute for the service?

5. Does the trade require a high standard of public responsibility, character, and performance of each person engaged in the occupation, as evidenced by established and published codes of ethics?

6. Does the occupation require such skill that the general public is not qualified to select a competent practitioner without some assurance that he has met minimum qualifications?

7. Does the trade or its organizations adequately protect the public from incompetent, unscrupulous, or irresponsible members of the trade?

8. Are current laws pertaining to the trade, occupation, or profession inadequate?

9. Does the practitioner perform a service for others which may have a detrimental effect on third parties relying on the expert knowledge of the practitioner?

As we will see, based on these criteria and others suggested by experts in the field of professional regulation (Greene, 1983; Gilley & Galbraith, 1986), it seems that the time is ripe for the professionalization of adoption practice. When child placement and adoption services are performed by unscrupulous, incompetent practitioners, children, their families, and the public are harmed.

Arguments Against Regulation

Regulation is not a panacea for the ills that beset adoption practice or any other occupation. Critics of professional regulation say that professional groups use the coercive power of government for their own economic advantage by using regulation to restrain competition and line their own pockets (Gilley & Galbraith, 1986, p. 61). Because price advertising is restricted in most professional groups, competition might also be restricted and the occupational group may, through regulation, control the supply of practitioners (Shimberg & Roederer, 1978).

Another problem is that regulation of an occupation might prevent practitioners from other occupational groups from providing services for which they are qualified by training and experience. Another disadvantage of regulation is that consumers who prefer lower-priced, lower-quality service will not be able to receive them, since such practitioners will not be allowed to practice. This could be particularly problematic in the United States, where the lay practice of adoption has coexisted with its quasi-professional practice for generations. Since regulation can decrease the availability of practitioners (Shimberg & Roederer, 1978), prospective adoptive parents in particular are likely to initially experience a negative result if adoption practice is professionalized. On the other hand, since regulation may standardize fees in an occupational field, adoptive parents and other adoption service recipients may find that they receive higher quality services at lower prices than before.

Regulation does not guarantee protection from incompetents, and enforcement of regulatory rules is difficult. Some regulatory systems certify or license the practitioner and then fail to periodically reassess the practitioner's ongoing competence. While continuing education (CE) requirements can ameliorate this problem, problems with insufficient funding and resources for CE program oversight, ambiguous grading standards, and the lack of empirical evidence linking formal CE requirements to competence compromise the benefits. Since training curricula in adoption are largely nonexistent in the United States, development and delivery of CE courses in the adoption field would be a considerable undertaking.

Gilley and Galbraith (1986) write that regulation can also cause division among practitioners. This could further fragment a field like adoption, already diverse and suffering from identity problems. In addition, the chore of identifying, defining, and measuring competencies in a field is daunting.

Measurable standards must be established before applicants can be evaluated. Appropriate and comprehensive qualification criteria must be created, requiring a knowledge of the field that few possess.

The financial and human costs of establishing regulation are high, particularly in the early stages of execution. In order to implement certification or licensing standards, groups must also recruit and choose qualified certification or licensing experts and develop, design, and test competency instruments. Once established, regulatory programs must be promoted and maintained. And in the final analysis, there is always a risk that professionalizing a practice area will fail to improve the quality of the services actually offered to clients.

Poppendieck (1992) warned that professionalism and specialized knowledge and language may "diminish the client's self-esteem and sense of competence to deal with the problem at hand," which would also diminish the client's "ability to deal with life, its problems, and challenges and thus make the client more dependent upon professionals" (p. 41). Fostering dependency and even pathology so that therapists and adoption counselors can continue to practice may also lead to increased helplessness and victimology among adoption clients (Poppendieck, 1992; Severson, 1994). This could be a particular problem in the adoption field, where much of the self-determination and control of the client is compromised by professional control, legal requirements, the restraints of confidentiality, and traditions of secrecy in adoption practice.

TRAINING AND REGULATING ADOPTION PROFESSIONALS

Contemporary adoption practice in the United States is undertaken mostly by public and private adoption agencies practicing alongside independent adoption practitioners such as attorneys, facilitators, ministers, and others. Agency licensing depends upon organizational, financial, and structural requirements more than human resource requirements, although most states enjoin agencies to employ directors, child care directors, and field workers with minimal amounts of education and training (Babb, 1996).

We have already seen that three types of regulation exist in the United States: registration, certification, and licensure. Requiring that a practitioner obtain a certificate before she can use certain titles, certification depends on a person's meeting education, work, and training requirements as well as demonstrating knowledge through a written competency exam. Unlike licensing, certification does not prohibit a person from practicing a trade; it only prohibits her from presenting herself to the public as a certified practitioner. Thus, a noncertified adoption practitioner could practice side by side with a certified adoption professional. Given our history of encouraging lay and quasi-professional adoption practice to coexist in the United States, it seems that if we are ever to professionalize adoption work as a specialty in itself, or as a sub-specialty of another profession, we should consider certification.

The Case for Certification

Certification promotes professionalism in practice areas, enhances the prestige of a profession, protects clients and employers from incompetent practitioners, and distinguishes individuals from their peers and colleagues (Gilley & Galbraith, 1986). In addition, certification encourages individuals to remain in a profession, prevents cannibalism (the recruitment of individuals from other professional associations in order to strengthen one's own), produces income, stabilizes an individual's job security, improves academic programs, and—when achieved through professional organizations—avoids external government regulation (Gilley & Galbraith, 1986).

Adoption legislation and government regulation have increased in recent years, while nongovernment sources of regulation have remained static (Vick, 1997). In general, one of the results of increased scrutiny of an occupation is increased government regulation. Thus, the Baby Jessica case resulted in changes in termination of parental rights laws in a number of states; the Tennessee Children's Home child selling scandal resulted in comprehensive changes in Tennessee's adoption laws; increasing wrongful adoption lawsuits nationwide resulted in legislation in several states that improved access to information about adoptable children by their prospective adoptive parents. While such changes are usually beneficial, such a piecemeal approach to adoption regulation may also have a deleterious effect, arising as it does from crisis and scandal rather than from the thoughtful, educated approach possible when occupations regulate themselves.

One advantage to professionalizing adoption practice from within the occupation, then, is that government control—and any of its unwanted results—can be minimized or prevented. In addition, by self-regulating, professionals can approach certification armed with knowledge, a solid philosophical basis, good theory, proven practice methods, and empirical evidence. Such an approach to professionalization would serve our clients far better than the crisis- and complaint-oriented reactions of our legislatures to problems affecting only some adoption clients. Self-regulation would also provide the basis for a unified, integrated body of adoption knowledge, preferable to what we have today, which, like a scarecrow planted in a crow-beset field, has been created piecemeal from public perception, myths, cultural values, and personal experience.

Preventing Harm

Another reason for professionalizing adoption practice is to prevent harm to clients. Because adoption workers have, by and large, not been regulated in the United States we have a long tradition of inflicting injury on the very people we are supposed to help. Whole books have been written about adoptions gone awry, child stealers and child sellers, celebrity adoptive parents who abused their adopted children, and adoptees murdered by their adoptive parents. Less public but no less heartbreaking are the stories of countless adoptees, birth parents, and adoptive parents who have been scammed, deceived, and abused by so-called "adoption professionals." Talk shows, Internet newsgroups and email mailing lists, grassroots adoption magazines, and newsletters from all corners of the adoption triad are full of these stories. Examples of unethical behavior in the adoption field unearthed during the research for this book include:

- A California adoption facilitator advertised through Usenet newsgroups that a number of babies were immediately available for adoption. When prospective adoptive parents called, they were required to send several thousand dollars in "application fees" along with their home studies and promised that they would receive a child within a matter of weeks. The facilitator collected the money, never delivered a child, and has been sued. She continues to facilitate adoptions.

- A Maryland agency promised to place a nonexistent child with a couple who did not discover that he didn't exist until they had flown to Jamaica to adopt him. The agency was later closed.

- An attorney lied in court, stating that a birth mother's letter revoking her consent to adoption was forged. He was proved wrong and fined but is still operating.

- A facilitator working for an agency used the agency's license to place children from a foreign country without the agency's knowledge. The agency knew nothing about the adoptive parents chosen by the facilitator but would have been liable had the adoptions gone sour. The agency is out of business, but the facilitator contin-ues to charge fees and place children.

- The head of a Washington, D.C., agency attempted to obstruct the finalization of an adoption she had arranged by threatening to tell the court that the adoptive parents were unfit unless they paid her more money. That agency has since closed.

- A prominent Oklahoma adoption attorney charged $15,000 in fees for the adoption of a special needs child whose birth and adop-tive mothers had found one another and came to him for help ar-ranging the adoption. Unbeknownst to the adoptive parents, the attorney submitted a sworn affidavit to the court stating that he had accepted only a few thousand dollars in fees for the adoption. The attorney continues to practice adoption.

- An adoptive mother undertaking her fourth adoption decided to dissolve her third child's adoption. Fearful that the agency wouldn't give her a new child if she told them about the dissolu-tion, she placed her son with another family across state lines. Though the placement violated Interstate Compact placement laws, the new family's attorney and social worker collaborated with them to facilitate the adoption. In the meantime, believing the first adoptive mother's story that her son was visiting relatives and unavailable for an interview, the adoption agency placed a new child with her.

- A college freshman planned adoption for her unborn child and contacted a large Texas adoption agency. When she later changed her mind, the agency social worker told her that she would have to repay thousands of dollars in medical and living expenses to the adoption agency and that she would be prosecuted for fraud for failing to place her baby. The young mother tearfully signed away her rights to her child.

- A large agency operating in several states shuffled a birth mother's relinquishment—and the promised placement of her child—among its branches, charging one adoptive couple after an-other legal fees for each "relinquishment." The agency lost its li-cense in one state for this practice but continues to place children through its other branches.

- The state supervisor of adoptions in a midwestern state acknowl-edged at a public meeting that the state's practice of racial matching violated federal law but bragged that the state had never been caught and would continue to violate the law.

- An independent facilitator in Arizona took money from adoptive parents but never placed children with them. This same adoption facilitator persuaded a Mexican mother to turn her children over to the facilitator, supposedly for medical care and education. The facilitator then placed the children in separate adoptive families without the mother's knowledge. Eventually, the facilitator and one of her colleagues went to jail.

- In California, San Diego Pregnancy Services was ordered to pay a young woman $650,000 for coercing her into relinquishing her child for adoption. While the young mother was in labor, the adoption facilitator forced her to choose adoptive parents from a notebook full of prospective adopters before the facilitator would take her to the hospital. This pregnancy clinic and at least four others in southern California face legal actions from birth parents alleging fraud (Baer, 1995).

- Another large agency with branches in several states incurred some heavy expenses and began using the adoption fees paid by clients to defray these costs—but didn't place children with the clients. The agency eventually went bankrupt, and the adoptive parents were unable to recover the fees.

- A state subsidy administrator and officer of a national organization of adoption administrators defrauded hundreds of special needs children in one state of federal and state financial assistance to which they were entitled by submitting false information to adoptive parents and the state's adoption assistance committee.

- An independent facilitator in Massachusetts used an attorney in a South American country to locate and place children. Eventually it was discovered that the children had been kidnapped by a woman working for the attorney. The Massachusetts facilitator was forced out of business, but the attorney was not punished by his country.

- A foster mother of a severely emotionally disturbed child with a history of parental abuse returned him to the state of Illinois but did not reveal the extent of his problems. He was placed with a family with several other children. The family could not cope with his behavior and returned him to the state. The child had another failed foster placement and is now in residential care.

- An adoption agency separated newborn twin girls and placed them in adoptive families on the east and west coasts of the United States, knowing that their birth mother expected them to be placed together. Six years later, the adoptive parents were horrified to learn that the twins were separated so that the adoption agency could charge each adoptive couple the full adoption fee for a healthy infant's adoption, in effect doubling the fee that they would have received had the twins been placed in the same family.

One needs to exert very little effort to discover that the public has been harmed because adoption practice has been unregulated. While most adoption triad members want to avoid what Randolph Severson (1994) calls *victimology*, were Congress to convene a congressional committee to investigate and document the effects of nonregulation of adoption on adoption clients, there is no doubt that the written testimony of those affected would fill volumes.

Professionalization is necessary because the general public lacks the knowledge needed to evaluate the qualifications of people offering adoption services. This is true whether the services offered are adoption placement services, counseling, or search and reunion help. Especially problematic is the fact that adoption practitioners themselves are confused about who the client is whenever they are called upon to serve more than one adoption triad member (Babb, 1996). It should come as no surprise, then, that clients seeking adoption-related services are themselves ill prepared to evaluate the quality of the services and advice they receive. This is as true for the unwed teen mother considering adoption for her unborn child as it is for the neglectful parents whose children have been placed in protective custody. It is as true for the birth mother seeking a meeting with the child she relinquished 28 years ago as it is for the adoptee asking for his adoption records. None of these clients can be sure whether the advice and information being offered by an adoption counselor is based on personal opinion, cultural values, economic demands, or professional competence arising from research, training, and education. In fact, if the general public understood the research on ethics and the professional practice of adoption, they would probably be surprised to learn that the people they view as professionals actually operate from a nontheoretical, lay perspective (Conrad & Joseph, 1991; Kugelman, 1992).

Professionalization is also needed in adoption because adoption is practiced as often as a business as it is a human service. The competition for the prized healthy adoptable infant has, to use Jim Gritter's words, created desperation and intense competition, a circumstance ripe for exploitation. If any practice in the country merits regulation, it is adoption. That is not to glorify the merits of regulation—it is difficult for auditors to get beyond the scrutiny of a program's mechanical process and measure its heart and spirit—but some form of toothy accountability is necessary to protect consumers. (1997, p. 259)

Adoption involves some of the most sensitive, fragile, and complex aspects of all human services (Silverman & Weitzman, 1986). Adoption practitioners need a high degree of independent judgment requiring skill and experience not possessed by the lay person. Such judgment should be developed through adoption-specific training and education and perpetuated through competency exams and continuing education. When adoption practice is evaluated in the same light as other regulated occupations in this country, the nature and seriousness of the need are at least as great as those in other certified occupations. Given the sensitive and compelling nature of adoption work, one has to ask why we have failed to attempt professionalization, even if through self-regulation.

Laying the Foundation

Before adoption practice can be professionalized, adoption practitioners must lay the foundation. Our occupational group must establish a code of ethics and practice standards through the integrated efforts of philosophers, practitioners, and researchers in the field of adoption. We have long needed a professional organization through which we can communicate our research findings, discuss ideas, educate, and train one another and those who want to work in the adoption field. An adoption-specific code of ethics would need to be nationally promoted, accepted, and enforced.

Once established, a code of ethics would provide adoption practitioners with nationally accepted standards of behavior defining the professional's obligations to clients, colleagues, and society. A code of ethics is particularly important in a field like adoption, which is governed by sometimes strikingly different state laws in addition to federal laws applicable to specific situations. In addition, an ethical code is important in a service industry that involves much secrecy and potential for harm, greed, and opportunism. Officials having ethical oversight of adoption professionals would need an internal ethical oversight committee that would consider complaints of ethical violations. The adoption association's ethical oversight committee would also need to establish a centralized, accessible, and publicized means of contact so that consumers of adoption services could report possible ethical violations.

A nongovernmental certification program could be established to help the public identify qualified adoption practitioners, whether those practitioners are removing children from their original families and placing them in adoptive families, facilitating adoption search and reunions, or offering adoption-specific counseling to triad members. A means of administering and financing the certification program would be arrived at. If a professional association were to be developed, administrators would have to decide whether nonmembers could be eligible for certification or not.

Standards for granting credentials would be developed, along with training and experience requirements. If a competency examination were to be required, it would have to be created, researched, and administered. A decision about grandfathering would be needed, and the public would need some assurances that adoption professionals would maintain their competence. Thus, a continuing education program or other means of ensuring ongoing competence (such as recertification) would be implemented.

Gilley and Galbraith (1986) write that regulators should decide who will establish the measurable standards by which applicants are evaluated and what qualification criteria should be used in evaluating applicants for certification. Who will determine the list of professional competencies for adult education should also be decided. Finally, a method of handling complaints from the public, adoption clients, and from within the profession would be necessary. A decision would have to be made about whether certification would be revoked for illegal or unethical behavior.

Counting the Cost

Some will ask why, when our unregulated adoption system has worked for so many years, should we even entertain the idea of certifying or otherwise regulating adoption practitioners? What will be the result of maintaining the system we currently have? While considering the question of regulating adoption practice, we ought to count the cost of regulating ourselves alongside the cost of eschewing regulation.

A number of unhappy results will occur if adoption practice remains unregulated. Independent adoption facilitators who approach adoption as a business and children as its product will continue to thrive. We will continue to sustain a legacy of adoptions gone awry, adoptive parents defrauded, birth parents wrongly deprived of their children, and adoptees whose lives have been irreparably damaged by inept, greedy, and corrupt adoption workers.

Because child placement workers will continue to be minimally educated and marginally trained, overworked and underpaid, the services received by America's most needy and dependent children—those awaiting permanency in our child welfare system—will continue to be alarmingly inadequate. America's adoptable foster children will wait longer for families, if they get them at all. They will grow up and "age out" of the system and continue to become, disproportionately, residents of our penal institutions. On their way to jail and prison, they will commit crimes against society. Their numbers will increase as we continue to devalue the importance of working with America's discarded children.

As Congress continues to pour more federal dollars into giving cash bonuses to the public agencies placing these children instead of into preplacement prevention to their birth families or postadoption support to their adoptive families, Americans will get the message that adopting a child is a risky proposition. Instead of adopting or fostering through public agencies, more Americans will become highly paid specialized foster parents for the increasing number of privately contracted foster care provider companies. Instead of adopting, more Americans will become the legal guardians of children they would have adopted if our society valued its adoptive families as much as it values the adoption bureaucracy.

According to our popularized view of adoption, parents who voluntarily relinquish their children for adoption will be able to get beyond the loss of their child—if, indeed, society even acknowledges a loss—then find an end to their grief and go on with their lives. We applaud birth parents as generous souls concerned about the welfare of their children before they relinquish, and then hiss at them afterward: what sorts of people give up their own children? Certainly, as long as we continue to marginalize birth parents by ignoring their postsurrender needs for support, counseling, and ongoing information about their children, we will encourage an increase in the documented problems experienced by postsurrender birth parents (Blanton & Deschner, 1990; Brodzinsky, 1990; Rosenberg & Groze, 1997).

Parents whose rights have been involuntarily terminated fare even worse in our society because they are unfit, and any suffering they subsequently experience is considered the just punishment of bad parents. The dearth of research on the posttermination experiences of these parents and the lack of attention in the professional journals to their treatment and support demonstrate a condemnation that must be as common to professionals as it is to lay people. Ours is a peculiar societal condemnation that ignores the posttermination support and rehabilitation needs of birth parents while we spend tens of thousands of dollars rehabilitating incarcerated criminals.

In spite of a national history of mistrusting and scrutinizing government, we accept without question the assumption that these parents have been rightfully deprived of their parenting responsibilities. Although many involuntarily surrendering parents will continue to fail at parenting their subsequent children and fail at life, some will go on to raise other children successfully. When they do, few ask why or how. Fewer still ask why state agencies sometimes return former foster and adopted children to their original parents years after the parents' rights were terminated for neglect or abuse. What professional services are available to families reuniting in such situations? We cannot know, because states are reluctant to admit to this practice. As more children are removed from their parents, wait too long to be adopted, and become runaways and street kids, we will see more of them return to their original families, with or without the state's blessing. Unattached, embittered, and disappointed by our promises of a better life through foster care and adoption, these kids will exact a frightening penance from society. In a seemingly endless cycle of sowing and reaping, they often produce children who also eat the bitter fruits of neglect, abuse, and eventual separation from their parents.

If adoption practice continues on its quasi-professional, lay course, we can expect to see many more birth parents, whether their rights were voluntarily or involuntarily terminated, experiencing the "traumatic . . . physical, emotional, and psychological implications for the rest of their [lives]" (Rosenberg & Groze, 1997, p. 524). Without practice standards and codes of ethical conduct defining our responsibilities to these parents, we will continue to fail them.

Worst of all, if we continue to build our adoption industry, we will hurt children. We will hurt them while they are little and we will hurt them when they grow up. Though we say they are our clients and we want to serve their interests, our actions often bespeak other motivations. When adoptions fall through because they are ineptly handled, children move along to the next family with ideas about their worth and abilities that are even more firmly entrenched. And when hurt, angry, or unattached children are placed by unskilled workers in unprepared families, the potential for damage to other children in the family through acting-out or predatory behaviors is high. The adopted child is rarely the only victim of an incompetent adoption facilitator.

Unqualified adoption facilitators and counselors, whether professionals or not, cannot remain unscathed by the destruction they leave in their wake. Though their agencies are closed or their agency licenses revoked in one state, those with seared consciences will go on to defraud other families on other days in other states. But what of the adoption practitioner with a conscience? As adoptees, birth parents, and adoptive parents in mounting numbers make public their mistreatment by adoption practitioners and child placement specialists, practitioners with a conscience will also experience the emotional (and perhaps professional) fallout from their ill-advised, inept, or uninformed adoption practice. Then, as they

> become aware of their own behavior and its implications, they confront an ethical dilemma of life: that "the suffering of others is real; one's actions can sometimes irrevocably determine the destiny of others; the mistakes one makes are often transmuted directly into others' pain; there is sometimes no way to undo that pain—the dead remain dead, the maimed are forever maimed, and there is no way to deny one's responsibility or culpability, for those mistakes are written, forever and as if in fire, in others' flesh." (Marin, 1981, p. 74, in Dean & Rhodes, 1992, p. 131)

If we fail to confront the inadequacies in our adoption work, as quasi-professional and lay practitioners of a human service we risk the dire result of writing our mistakes "forever and as if in fire," in the lives of the very people we promised to serve (Marin, 1981, p. 74). Surely there is a better way.

PROFESSIONALS AS PHILOSOPHERS

The recommended model for ethical standards in adoption outlined in the previous chapter cannot hope to resolve every, or even most, of the disagreements that abound in adoption work. Rather, it is hoped that it can help to initiate dialogue among those to whom adoption practice is as much a calling as it is a career.

The many conflicting values in adoption and the shortcomings of our adoption services system have been illustrated throughout this book. There is no doubt that moral disagreements abound in adoption work; but we are filled with doubts when we are asked to provide solutions. Though some professionals have tried to build a basis for dialogue, if not understanding and at least some agreement, many adoption clients would say that our attempts have been a case of too little, too late. Even so, we can take steps toward finding solutions. In spite of the complexity of the field of adoption, we can approach ethical problems and moral disagreements constructively rather than destructively, and manage them if we cannot solve them.

Writing about complex dilemmas and their resolution, Beauchamp offers five methods for managing moral disagreements that can be useful to students of philosophy and adoption alike (Beauchamp & Walters, 1994). Adapted for use in adoption practice, they are summarized in the following sections: Get the Facts, Say What You Mean, Adopt a Code, Be Your Own Best Critic, and Analyze Arguments.

Get the Facts

Beauchamp and Walters (1994) write that the lack of information, rather than true moral disputes, has often caused disagreement that might have been prevented with good information. Complete information can facilitate understanding, negotiation, and compromise, can relieve fears and sometimes even resolve disagreements. For example, accurate statistics on birth certificate access in the United Kingdom and New South Wales have persuaded many legislators that adoptee access to the original birth certificate does not cause an accompanying rise in abortion, as open records critics have wrongly claimed. Though opponents to open records continue to support the sealed record on other grounds, accurate information has resulted in disagreement on fewer issues.

In special needs adoption, accurate information about the successful use of adoption assistance payments (AAP) resulted in increased access of waiting children and prospective adoptive parents to this program through federal legislation and also resulted in clarification of the rights of children in Indian tribal custody and children under guardianship and kinship care to receive AAP (Gilles, 1995).

Say What You Mean

Some disputes have been settled when both parties to a disagreement clarified the terminology they were using. Even when agreement cannot be arrived at through clarifying terms, discussion of the issues involved and the grounds for agreement and disagreement can at least be undertaken once there is clarity about the definitions one is using. To use the open records example again, what do we mean by "open records"? By open records, do we mean that we want adult adoptees to have access to the entire adoption file, including counseling notes and charts, retained by the adoption agency? Or do we mean access to the entire adoption court file? Or does "open records" mean that we want adult adoptees to be given a copy of their original, unamended birth certificate when they request it?

Another controversial area is that of confidentiality. What do we mean by confidentiality? How does the professional value of keeping confidences interact with the professional value of allowing for informed consent, or with that of supporting a client's self-determination? We should define what we mean by confidentiality in adoption services.

Adopt a Code

Some ethical controversies can be resolved if parties on both sides of an argument can agree on a common set of ethical standards. While complete agreement in any field is unrealistic, in adoption practice we can surely arrive at some universally accepted principles. For example, the Child Welfare League of America expressed common standards through its *Standards for Adoption Practice*, and the Hague Conference on International Adoption also arrived at common standards (CWLA, 1988). Standards and codes of ethics "give guidance in a circumstance of uncertainty or dispute," and while they do not apply to every situation that arises, they provide a foundation for decision making (Beauchamp & Walters, p. 5).

Be Your Own Best Critic

Some arguments over morality can be resolved through use of what Beauchamp (1994) calls example and opposed counterexample. To the lay person, this method is akin to analyzing the pros and cons of a situation, except that it sets up arguments that appear irrefutable and then challenges the thinker by utilizing exceptions to the rule. This is often done using the case study, which has been widely employed in the literature, in training, and in continuing education in the social sciences. Use of case studies facilitates moral reflection, development of judgment, and decision making while at the same time illustrating the dilemmas that often accompany moral choices. Reduced to its simplest element, the use of the counterexample to the example might begin with, "But what about . . .?"

Analyze Arguments

Finally, as philosophers and professionals, we must analyze our own beliefs and identify all that is disconsonant about them. Beauchamp and Walters write, "If an argument rests on accepting two incoherent points of view, then pointing out the incoherence will require a change in the argument" (1994, p. 6). Thus, recognizing what is irrelevant, imperfect, or imprecise about our beliefs will only improve them.

Using this method, some years ago psychotherapists Nancy Verrier and Randolph Severson engaged in a published debate over Verrier's theory of the primal wound in adopted children. Although the two could not agree on several fundamental points, they did arrive at agreement in other areas and illuminated the entire discussion of what adoption means in the context of parent-child relationships. The adoption field needs more thinkers, writers, philosophers, and professionals who are brave enough to invite their peers and clients to scrutinize and challenge their most dearly held beliefs and values. Of the sort of moral courage exemplified by those who are willing to bring their values into the public arena of debate, Stephen Carter writes,

> saying publicly that we are doing what we think is right, even when others disagree is made particularly difficult by our national desire to conform. Most of us want to fit in, to be accepted, and admitting to (or proudly proclaiming) an unpopular belief is rarely the way to gain acceptance. But if moral dissenters are unwilling to follow the example of the civil rights movement and make a proud public show of their convictions, we as a nation will never have the opportunity to be inspired by their integrity to rethink our own ideas. (1996, pp. 11–12)

THE PROFESSIONAL'S ROLE IN ADOPTION

Professionals who work in adoption speak of adoption as a lifelong process. We spend years counseling, studying, and writing about our birth parent, adoptive parent, and adoptee clients, and we become adoption experts. We pride ourselves, usually, on our experience and understanding of the adoption triad and adoption dynamics. Many of us spend months and years working predominantly in adoption. We pay dues to our professional associations, write articles and books, and collect salaries or fees based on our adoption research, teaching, counseling, and placements. Yet many professionals who specialize in adoption are now realizing that what we've done has often only marginally served our clients and that our adoption statutes and the institutions or agencies for which we work have done little to help us, as professionals, approach adoption work ethically.

While many experts have called for the professionalization of adoption through various means, these same experts cannot seem to iron out their own philosophical differences with sufficient ease to establish adoption professionally. Many of these same experts nevertheless counsel and admonish birth parents, adoptive parents, and adoptees to view one another as parts of an extended adoption kinship system that must somehow, together, work out their relatedness over a lifetime—with or without professional help.

No thanks to us, adoptive parents, adoptees, and birth parents have done just that, many times giving up on professionals as any source of support, comfort, or guidance. They have established their own support groups and grassroots organizations such as Adopt a Special Kid, Adoptive Families of America, Concerned United Birthparents, the North American Council on Adoptable Children, the American Adoption Congress, Adoptee's Liberty Movement Association, and Bastard Nation, offering to one another what we have failed to give them: a means of living a lifetime with adoption, philosophically, politically, and practically.

While professionals debate in the pages of their publications over whether adoptees have a primal wound or birth mothers want to be found, adoptees and birth parents by the tens of thousands have searched for and found one another. Adoptive and birth families have contacted one another and opened their families to each other largely without professional help. They have done it, often, not because we could not help them, but because we told them such contact was ill advised, or illegal, or that we simply would not help. They have sometimes done it clumsily and at no small harm to themselves and their families because we stood back as if our work had been done the day the adoption was finalized. We did not trouble ourselves to increase our expertise in adoption in order to serve adult adoptees and their families; our clients had to become their own best experts.

Today in America, we speak and write of "adoption specialists" and "adoption workers," but we do not know what qualifies a person to specialize in adoption. Individuals with no adoption-specific training at all are building adoptive families, sometimes at the expense of birth families, and many times at the expense of powerless children. When adoptions go awry, adoptive parents and their kin are also harmed.

If we are to professionalize adoption work in the United States, we must have a uniform standard. We must have ethical codes specific to serving the various triad members and models for ethical decision making. Ethics, values, and morality are inextricably bound to adoption practice because the practice of adoption involves influence, and influence is bound to moral issues, to issues of what we think ought to be.

Though we have been unable to agree on how to work together to define, refine, and perfect adoption practice so that it serves our clients, "it is our commitment to helping that binds us together—and a special kind of

helping that is built on trust, nurturance, and expertise" (Van Hoose &
Kottler, 1988, p. 5).

Hopefully our professional commitment to serve our adoption clients to
the best of our ability will translate, eventually, into rules of ethical
conduct and the professionalization of adoption practice that will assure
our clients that we are ultimately concerned with doing the right thing.

Appendix A

Resources

Adoption Quarterly. Haworth Press, 10 Alice Street, Binghamton, NY 13904–1580

The Adoption Studies Institute, 2924 M. Street, NW, Suite 101, Washington, DC 20007. Tel.: 202–338–1550; Web: http://www.adoption-studies.org/

Education and Policy Council (EPC), Adoptive Families of America, 2309 Como Avenue, St. Paul, MN 55108. Tel.: 612–645–9955 or 800–372–3300; Fax: 612–645–0055. Web: http://www.adoptivefam.org/

The Evan B. Donaldson Adoption Institute, 120 Wall Street, 20th Floor, New York, NY 10005–3902. Tel.: 212–360–0280; Fax 212–360–0283; Email: Knespeco@echonyc.com; Web: http://www.adoptioninstitute.org/

Joint Council on International Children's Services, 7 Cheverly Circle, Cheverly, MD 20785–3040. Tel.: 301–322–1906; FAX 301–322–3425; Email: Mevans@jcics.org; Web: http://www.jcics.org/

Appendix B

Are You Considering Adoption? Information for Expectant Parents

THE FAMILY TREE INFORMATION GUIDE FOR
EXPECTANT PARENTS CONSIDERING ADOPTION

Expectant parents faced with an unplanned pregnancy may consider adoption for the unborn child for many reasons. Often, such parents are young and lack financial and emotional support within their families. If you are an expectant parent considering adoption for your child, you should know some facts about adoption before you make such a life-changing decision.

Thinking about Adoption

Facing an Unplanned Pregnancy. Women who voluntarily relinquish children for adoption are usually single and facing an unplanned pregnancy. Many are young, haven't finished their educations, or lack financial and emotional support from their family or partner. Young single women, especially those who lack support and have limited financial means, are sometimes told that adoption is the most loving plan they can make for their unborn child. And in some cases, adoption is the best plan for the mother and her unborn child. In other cases, adoption can cause more problems for the mother, if not the child. Once an adoption has taken place, it is too late to change your mind. If you are facing an unplanned pregnancy, get as much information as you can about the pros and cons of adoption and other alternatives. You need information and resources to help you make an informed choice about adoption.

You will always remember the child you gave up for adoption. In the past, sometimes mothers who planned adoption for their babies were told that, with time, they would forget the child they gave up for adoption. The truth is that a mother does not forget the child she carried for nine months and then birthed. Birth mothers and fathers often think about the children they gave up, especially on holidays and on the child's birthday. Though the pain may lessen over the years, it will probably never completely go away. Giving a child up for adoption is a major loss for mothers and fathers. Some say it is the biggest loss of their lives.

Adoption may be the best choice for you. There is plenty of information available about what is good about adoption. Some research shows that women who faced unplanned pregnancies while young and who surrendered their children, went on to achieve higher educations and make more money in life than those women who kept their babies. Sometimes adoption agencies, attorneys, and others interested in placing children for adoption use such statistics to show expectant parents that adoption is the best choice. Sources of information about why adoption can be a good choice for you are the Independent Adoption Center, Surrogate Mothers Network, or the AdoptioNetwork.

Adoption can work for adoptees. Research shows that the outcomes for adoptees are generally good—they usually grow up healthy and relatively happy. There's little doubt that most adoptees were dearly wanted and loved by their adoptive parents. And adoptive parents, on average, tend to be better educated and make more money than parents in the general population. All these factors may help to give your child a positive experience in an adoptive family.

Adoption may not work for you. Research with birth parents, especially birth mothers, shows that the long-term effects of having given up a child can be devastating. According to some research, the grief of birth mothers is worse and more debilitating than that of mothers whose children have died. Instead of getting better over time, the grief of many birth mothers gets worse. Some have identified what has been called the "Birthmother Syndrome," which has been described by Merry Bloch Jones in her book, *Birthmothers.*

Adoption may not work for your child. The majority of adoptees grow up in good adoptive families. However, some adoptees are abused physically, emotionally, or sexually in their adoptive families. Although the rate of divorce is lower in adoptive families, adoptive parents, too, sometimes divorce. Adoptive parents may divorce, or a parent may die, leaving your child to be raised by a single parent. There are no guarantees in adoption, just as there are no guarantees in life. Keep in mind that prospective adoptive parents put their very best foot forward when they undergo the home study and interview process with an adoption agency or attorney. But adoptive parents have flaws, too. There are no perfect people!

You are an expectant parent. As you consider your options in facing an unplanned pregnancy, keep in mind that a child—or what will become a child—grows inside you. Treat yourself and your unborn child well if you plan to continue with the pregnancy. Information about pregnancy and childbirth are available through many community organizations. They will be happy to give you more information about having a healthy pregnancy.

Adoption is unique. Being raised in an adoptive family is different from being raised in a birth family. Although most adoptions are successful and most adoptees grow up being dearly loved and well cared for, many adult adoptees describe the pain of being raised apart from their birth families. Others, even though they grew up in wonderful adoptive families, always felt a need to meet and get to know their birth parents and siblings, or simply to have accurate information about them. While adoption can and usually does provide a good family and home life for the adopted child, being raised adopted is not the same as being raised in a birth family. It is very important that you and the adoptive couple understand this, so that everyone can act in ways that are best for the child.

Financial help is available to those in need. These days, no parents should be separated from their child because of money. You can receive help with the costs of prenatal care and delivery, medical care for your baby, and even with the cost of formula and baby food. Through TANF (Temporary Assistance to Needy Families) you can receive monthly income for you and your baby, help paying your rent and utilities, food stamps, and even assistance with furthering your education. You can stay home with your baby for up to one year in most states, and when you return to school, the state can help you with the costs of day care. There are various programs available to help you with job training. Whichever way you choose, you can receive help with tuition costs, along with monthly financial help for yourself and your baby, ensuring a brighter future for both of you.

The consent to adoption. Once you sign the consent to adopt in many states, it is very difficult for you to change your mind and get your baby back. In many states, if you change your mind, you must do it within so many hours or days of signing the consent to adopt. If you change your mind within the specified time and withdraw your consent, in many states the judge will also notify the prospective adoptive parents and the adoption agency or attorney involved and ask them to testify about why the withdrawal of your consent would not be in the best interests of the child.

You may have to prove that you are qualified to raise your own child. Once the interlocutory or final decree of adoption has been entered, you usually cannot change your mind about the adoption. Even if an adoption is illegal, you cannot challenge the adoption once the adoption has been finalized in most states. For all these reasons, it is very important for you to take the time you need to think about adoption before you sign your consent. Many professionals and adoption groups such as the Association of Open Adoption Agencies recommend a waiting period of at least two weeks.

About Fathers

Fathers have rights and responsibilities. Fathers have rights, too. Fathers also have the right to raise their children and must be notified of planned adoptions. In many states, a father can waive his right to appear in court by signing a sworn statement, allowing his child to be adopted. Fathers who are not named in court may be able to claim paternity and even gain custody of the child. It is very important for you to name the child's father during any adoption proceedings so that problems don't take place later on. It is best for your child, for you, and for everyone involved when everyone helping in an adoption plan is honest and open about the facts.

Fathers should help during pregnancy. Most state laws say that the father of a child born out of wedlock is responsible for paying the reasonable expenses of the mother while she is pregnant and after she has the baby and is recovering from childbirth, even if the child is not born alive. (Check with an attorney in your state to learn about the applicable laws.) Fathers who don't help during pregnancy may not have a right to disagree with a later adoption.

Fathers should support their children. You can often establish the paternity of your child by filing a paternity lawsuit in district court. In this petition, you file a document that names the father of your child, asking the judge to rule on whether he is the father or not. The judge then orders the father to appear in court and either prove or disprove that he is the father of your child. If the father does not admit paternity, the judge may be able to order him to have a blood test that will prove or disprove paternity. If the person you name is found to be the father of your child, the law may allow the judge to order him to pay for the costs of the lawsuit. The judge can also order the father to pay child support to you, because many state laws say that fathers must pay for the support and education of their children even if they are not married to the mother.

Child selling. It is against the law for an attorney or adoption agency to pay you money or give you things so that you will give your baby up for adoption. In all states, it is a felony when you accept, or when a person or an agency offers to pay you or give you furniture, clothing, or other items of value so that you will give your baby up for adoption. This crime is known as Child Trafficking, and people who do these things can be fined, lose their professional licenses, or even go to jail. It is also against the law for anyone to induce you to enter a maternity home, hospital, or other home and promise to pay for your maternity care or delivery in exchange for placing your child in an adoptive family. In many states, it is legal for others to help you with expenses while you are pregnant; but it is against the law for anyone to try and buy your baby or child.

Open Adoption

What is open adoption? Open adoption is when the birth parents of a child choose the people who will raise their child, meet them, and stay in touch with the adoptive family and child indefinitely.

What does the research say about open adoption? Open adoption has been traditional in many cultures besides ours. In our culture, it is a relatively new practice (about 15 to 20 years old). The research so far shows good outcomes for birth parents, adoptive parents, and adoptees who are in open adoptions. However, some research has showed that the grief for birth mothers is worse in an open adoption than the grief for closed adoption birth mothers. In the studies available, the vast majority of adoptive parents and adoptees in open adoptions are very happy with the results. However, the research doesn't prove that open adoption is better than closed adoption. If you want to know more about open adoption, the book *The Open Adoption Experience*, by Lois Melina and Sharon Roszia (1993, HarperCollins), is a good one.

When an agency promises you an "open" adoption, it is making a promise it cannot enforce. An open adoption is one in which you may choose, meet, and get to know the adoptive parents of your child. Some agencies promise that they will help you maintain contact with your child until he or she is an adult. They may offer to send letters, photos, and gifts from you to your child, or from the adoptive parents to you. However, once the adoption is finalized (usually six months to one year after you relinquish your rights), no agency or attorney can enforce an open adoption agreement unless state law specifically provides for such agreements. The agreement depends completely on the trust developed between you and the adoptive parents. If you want ongoing contact with your child, be sure that the agency you use is really in favor of open adoption. Be sure to meet the adoptive parents face-to-face and get to know them. The only chance you will have to be sure about your decision will be before you sign a consent to adopt. You are the parent—it is up to you to choose what is best for your child and for you.

Looking Ahead

Adoptees speak. Many adult adoptees worldwide do decide to search for their birth parents, especially their birth mothers. Even if you think you do not want to have contact with the child you give up for adoption, chances are that your son or daughter—or even his or her adoptive parents—will one day search for you. If you choose adoption for your child, you should know that some day he or she may want to know you.

Birth parents wonder about their children. One of the questions birth parents ask most after relinquishing a child for adoption is, "Where is my child, and how is he or she doing?" Even if you think it will be too painful for you to have some contact with your child over the years, you may change your mind. You may want to plan an adoption with an element of openness, working with an agency you can trust, so that you can know about how your child is doing after you relinquish your rights. Your parental rights may end, but your love and concern for your child will not.

Your Rights and Responsibilities

Talking to a professional about adoption does not mean you must place your child for adoption. You are under no obligation to any adoption agency or attorney to place your child for adoption until you have signed a consent to adoption after your child is born. Just talking to an agency or saying you will plan adoption does not obligate you in any way.

You have the right to have your own attorney and counselor. You don't have to rely on the advice of an agency or adoption attorney, social worker, or other professional who works at an adoption agency or who makes money by placing children for adoption. You have the right to have an attorney who doesn't represent the agency or the prospective adoptive parents.

You should be fully informed before making a decision to give your child up for adoption. Most birth mothers who have surrendered children say that they wish someone had told them that the pain of giving up a child often gets worse, not better, with time. Most say they would have benefited from attending a support group for post-relinquishment birth mothers before they gave their children up. Although agency-sponsored support groups can be very helpful, you should also try to attend a support group not affiliated with an adoption agency.

Learn about adoptive families. You may also want to find out if there are adoptive parent support groups in your area, and attend a social event they sponsor so that you can see adoptive families in action, too. The more information you have about adoption, the better a decision you can make for you and your child.

Appendix C

Texas Child Protective Services Supervisor Competencies

I. FOUNDATIONS OF CPS WORK: COMMON KNOWLEDGE AND SKILLS

- Abusive and neglectful families
- Legal system as it affects CPS
- Separation and attachment
- Child development
- Family systems
- Influence of culture and ethnicity on families
- Influence of mental health/mental retardation issues
- Influence of chemical dependency
- Communication and interviewing strategies and skills
- Knowledge of and linkage with resources in PRS, DHS, and the community
- Policy and procedures

II. CPS CASEWORK METHODS AND PRACTICE

- Casework methods

From: Children's Protection Services Training Institute. (1993). *Proficiencies for CPS supervisor competencies*. Austin, TX: Author.

- Stages of service
- Family preservation
- Permanency planning

III. SUPERVISOR AS MANAGER IN PUBLIC SOCIAL SERVICES

- Roles and responsibilities
- Techniques of effective supervision and management
- Staff and/or volunteer selection and retention
- Managing change and conflict
- Complaint resolution
- Crisis and stress management
- Decision making and problem solving

IV. SUPERVISOR AS LEADER

- Styles of leadership
- Use of authority: delegation and assignment
- Group dynamics
- Team building
- Cultural sensitivity
- Advocacy for program and staff

V. DEVELOPMENT OF STAFF

- Providing different types of supervision
- Conducting individual and group conferences with staff
- Conducting unit meetings
- Conducting performance evaluations of staff
- Working effectively with problem employees

Glossary

AAC. American Adoption Congress.

AAP. Adoption Assistance Payments, also known as adoption subsidies. Payments made by state or federal governments to adoptive parents of qualifying children with special needs.

AASK or Aask. Adopt a Special Kid.

Adoptee. The person, usually a child, who is voluntarily or involuntarily removed from his or her birth parents and adopted by parents who then have responsibility for the adoptee.

Adoption. To legally accept the child of other parents to raise as one's own child.

Adoption circle. Refers to the group of people interested in or involved with adoptions; may include the adoptee, his or her birth and adoptive relatives, and professionals.

Adoption disruption. Termination of an adoption prior to legal finalization.

Adoption dissolution. Termination of an adoption after legal finalization.

Adoption kinship system. The birth and adoptive relatives of the adoptee. See extended adoption family.

Adoption professional. A professional who specializes in adoption work.

Adoption reform movement. The nationwide organized effort of adoptees, birth parents, adoptive parents, and others dedicated to achieving reforms of adoption law and social policy that prevent unnecessary family separations, secure equal rights for adoption triad members, extend full disclosure of information to prospective adoptive parents, provide for the informed consent to adoption of expectant parents, and legally open the sealed original birth certificates of all adult adoptees living in states disallowing such access.

Adoption triad. Sometimes called adoption triangle. Refers to all three parties to an adoption: the birth parents, the adoptive parents, and the adoptee (single parent adoptions are included).

Adoptive parents. The individuals (usually, but not always, a couple) who legally adopt a child and raise the child in their family.

AFA. Adoptive Families of America.

AFDC. Air to Families with Dependent Children.

Amoralism. The view that moral truth does not exist, that morality is a complete fiction, and that all moral claims are false. Also known as *moral nihilism*.

Beneficence. A value expressed as those actions which do no harm and express kindness, generosity, compassion, or reciprocity.

Birth parents. The individuals responsible for the conception and birth of the child. Also known as biological parents, original parents, first parents, or singularly as birth mother, birth father, original parent.

Casuistry. Practical decision making about certain cases in which the judgments cannot simply be brought under general norms such as principles and rules.

Child placement. All administrative, legislative, judicial, and executive decisions concerned with establishing, administering, or rearranging parent-child relationships.

Closed adoption. Adoptions in which birth parents and the adoptee cannot maintain contact with each other after the child is placed with the adoptive parents. Also referred to as traditional adoption.

Coercion. Threatening, overtly or covertly, to punish noncompliance by withdrawing resources or services or by sharing negative feelings (McCormick, 1979).

Contested adoption. When a birth parent seeks to regain custody of the child that was previously placed for adoption with an adoptive parent or parents.

Conventionalism. The classic form of ethical relativism that views moral principles as depending on social choice. A principle is not moral unless a society has embraced it.

CUB. Concerned United Birthparents.

Cultural relativism. A descriptive thesis stating that moral beliefs across cultures are widely divergent.

CWLA. Child Welfare League of America.   ·

DHS, DSS. Department of Human Services, Department of Social Services.

Dissolution. Termination of adoptive parent rights following legalization of the adoption.

Duty-based Kantianism. The view, originated by Immanuel Kant, that each person is a rational being and, as such, has fundamental worth. As rational beings, people can use reason to develop a consistent set of timeless, irrefutable moral principles.

Ethical relativism. A normative thesis stating that there are no universally valid moral principles, but that all moral principles are valid relative to cultural or individual choice.

Ethics. Formal, professional rules of right and wrong conduct.

Ethics of care. A philosophical approach that concentrates on character traits that are especially important in intimate relationships, such as friendship, compassion, and so on.

Extended adoption family. Includes those primarily involved (e.g., the adoption triad) and all of the people related to members of the triad, such as children, siblings, aunts, uncles, grandparents, cousins, and others.

Infertile couple. The couple that is unable to conceive, carry to term, and give birth to a living child.

Informed relativism. A philosophical framework that allows an ongoing openness to comprehending approaches and perspectives different from one's own, leading to an enlarged understanding and reevaluation of one's own opinions.

Integrity. Qualities of steadfastness, promise keeping, courage, and moral wholeness.

Intuitionist ethical theories. The theory that the good or the right thing to do can be known directly through human intuition rather than rationally.

ISRR. International Soundex Reunion Registry.

IVF. In-vitro fertilization.

Justice. Fairness and equity.

Kantianism. *See* duty-based Kantianism.

Marxist-based ethical frameworks. The view that the good society is promoted by "social and economic institutions that create respect, freedom, and equality for all persons" and that human happiness is dependent upon productive, cooperative work with other human beings (Rhodes, 1991, p. 37).

MEPA. Multi-Ethnic Placement Act.

Moral absolutism. The view that there is one true morality with a consistent set of nonconflicting moral principles.

Moral nihilism. *See* Amoralism. Attributed to Nietzsche, the view that morality does not exist and is a mere fabrication.

Moral objectivism. The view that moral principles have universal objective validity that may conflict or be overriden by other principles due to circumstances.

Moral skepticism. The view that people cannot know whether there are moral truths.

MSW. Master (Degree in) Social Work, the degree or the individual with a master's degree in social work.

NABSW. National Association of Black Social Workers.

NACAC. North American Council on Adoptable Children.

NASW. National Association of Social Workers.

Nonidentifying information. The information collected and recorded about adoption triad members during the process of adoption that is later made available to the parties involved should they request it. It is "nonidentifying" in that all references to names and places are withheld to insure the anonymity of those involved.

Open adoption. The pre- and postplacement process whereby birth parents and adoptive parents have personal contact with each other. In many cases the birth parents actually select the adoptive parents with whom their child will be placed, and open adoption usually denotes continuing postplacement contact between birth parents, adoptive parents, and adoptee. (There are degrees of "openness," ranging from limited contact to an ongoing relationship including the exchange of letters, pictures, and so forth.)

Placement. Physical placement of a child with prospective adoptive parents or in another setting.

Professionalization. The process whereby an occupation transforms itself into a profession.

Psychological parent. A parent who, on a day-to-day basis, through interaction, companionship, and mutuality, fulfills the child's psychological needs for a parent, as well as the child's physical needs (Goldstein et al., 1973).

Relinquishment. The action of the birth parents which results in the placement of the child with the adoptive family. May also be referred to as "surrender."

Respect for autonomy. A value respecting self-determination, self-mastery, freedom of choice, voluntariness, privacy, and the acceptance of responsibility for one's own choices.

Reunion. The end point of the search process when the searching person locates and has personal contact with the person(s) for whom he or she has been searching.

Rights-based theories. The view that agreement about what is right or good cannot be achieved in society and that the freedoms and interests (or good) of individuals must therefore be balanced against those of others.

Sealed adoption records. The practice of judicially sealing the original birth certificate and adoption records of an adoptee and issuing an amended birth certificate designating the adoptive parents as those who gave birth to the adopted child. The sealed record is inaccessible to any individual except upon a court order opening the file in most states in the United States. Also referred to as "closed records."

Search. The process wherein the adoptee seeks information about and contact with his or her birth parents. The same term is used when birth parents seek contact with the child they relinquished, or when an adoptive parent or other person searches on behalf of an adoptee.

Search Group. A support group of lay people, usually adult adoptees or birth parents, dedicated to providing emotional support, advice, and assistance to adult adoptees, birth parents, or others engaged in a search for biological relatives separated through adoption. Some groups may be facilitated through adoption agencies or by professionals, but most are not.

Special needs adoption. The adoption of children who have experienced trauma such as abuse, neglect, or multiple placements; have developmental disabilities; are intellectually or physically impaired; are members of a sibling group to be placed together; are members of a minority ethnic group; or are older at placement.

Standards. Commonly accepted, but not necessarily formally or professionally adopted rules of right and wrong conduct in a field.

Subjective universalism. The view that moral principles cannot be objectively valid because morality must first be created through human choice.

Subjectivism. The view that moral principles are applicable to individuals only and not to groups of people. Morality is thus a personal decision.

Surrender of child. When birth parents give up their legal rights to raise their child. Also called relinquishment, planning adoption.

TANF. Temporary Assistance for Needy Families.

Termination of Parental Rights (TPR). When the legal parental rights of biological parents are judicially terminated.

Traditional adoption. The process whereby the adopted child, usually a healthy infant, is placed in the adoptive home without prior contact between the birth parents and adoptive parents and with none of the parties having access to identifying information about each other.

Utilitarianism. The view that the well-being of society as a whole, rather than the good of individuals within the society, ought to be promoted. The greatest good for the most people.

Values. Those ideals regarded as desirable.

Values-based open adoption. Developed by James Gritter at Catholic Human Services, a type of open adoption motivated by values of child-centeredness, flexibility, cooperation, respect, and informed consent.

Virtue-based frameworks. The view that ethics are defined through what it means to be a righteous, or good, person.

Virtues. Qualities such as trustworthiness, honesty, fidelity, respect, responsibility, justice, fairness, caring, compassion, generosity, and citizenship.

References

Amadio, C. (1989). Wrongful adoption: A new basis for litigation, another challenge for child welfare. *Journal of Law and Social Work, 1* (1), 23–31.

Amadio, C. (1991). Doing the right thing: Some ethical considerations in current adoption practice. *Social Thought, 17* (3), 25–33.

American Association for Marriage and Family Therapy. (1991). *AAMFT Code of Ethics.* Washington, D.C.: Author.

American Fertility Society. (1994). Ethics and the new reproductive technologies. In T. L. Beauchamp & L. Walters (Eds.), *Contemporary issues in bioethics* (pp. 201–206). Belmont, CA: Wadsworth Publishing.

Amlung, P. (1990). Conflicts of interest in independent adoptions: Pitfalls for the unwary. *Cincinnati Law Review, 59,* 169–189.

Anderson, E. (1994). Is women's labor a commodity? In T. L. Beauchamp & L. Walters (Eds.), *Contemporary issues in bioethics* (pp. 233–243). Belmont, CA: Wadsworth Publishing.

Anderson, P. (1989). The origin, emergence, and professional recognition of child protection. *Social Service Review, 63* (2), 222–244.

Aristotle. (1951). *The Politics.* (Book 7) (T. A. Sinclair, Trans.). Harondsworth, England, Penguin Classics.

Austin, L. T. (1993). *Babies for sale: The Tennessee Children's Home adoption scandal.* Westport, CT: Greenwood Press.

Babb, L. A. (1994, September 30). *The Family Tree model of crisis pregnancy counseling.* Model presented at the annual conference of the Council for Equal Rights in Adoption, New York.

Babb, L. A. (1994, September 30). *Serving our clients, or serving ourselves?* Paper presented at the conference of the Council for Equal Rights in Adoption, New York.

Babb, L. A. (1996). A study of ethics in contemporary adoption practice in the United States. *Research Abstracts International, 21* (3), LD-03361.

Babb, L. A. (1998). Ethics in contemporary American adoption practice. In V. Groze & K. Rosenberg (Eds.), *Bridging the gap: Clinical practice in adoption throughout the lifespan.* Westport, CT: Praeger.

Babb, L. A., & Laws, R. (1997). *Adopting and advocating for the special needs child.* Westport, CT: Bergin & Garvey.

Baer, J. (1995). *The history and consequences of sealing adoption records.* San Francisco State University. (Available from Janine Baer, P.O. Box 8081, Berkeley, CA 94707.)

Baker-Jackson, M. (1979). The impact of legal decisions and trends upon the traditional role of adoption worker. *Social Work Papers, 15,* 36–45.

Baran, A., & Lifton, B. J. (1995). Adoption. In W. T. Reich (Ed.), *Encyclopedia of bioethics* (Rev. ed.) (pp. 71–75). New York: Simon & Schuster Macmillan.

Baran, A., & Pannor, R. (1990). Open adoption. In D. Brodzinsky, & M. Schechter (Eds.), *The psychology of adoption* (pp. 316–331). New York: Oxford University Press.

Barth, R. (1987). Adolescent mothers' beliefs about open adoption. *Social Casework, 68,* 323–331.

Bartholet, E. (1993). *Family bonds: Adoption and the politics of parenting.* Boston: Houghton Mifflin.

Beauchamp, T. L., & Walters, L. (Eds.). (1994). *Contemporary issues in bioethics.* Belmont, CA: Wadsworth Publishing.

Benet, M. (1976). The politics of adoption. New York: Free Press.

Benson, P. L., Sharma, A. R., & Roehlkepartain, E. C. (1994). *Growing up adopted: A portrait of adolescents and their families.* Minneapolis, MN: Search Institute.

Berry, M. (1991). The practice of open adoption: Findings from a study of 1396 adoptive families. *Children and Youth Services Review, 13,* 379–396.

Birmingham, J., Berry, M., & Bussey, M. (1996, November-December). Certification for child protective services staff members: The Texas initiative. *Child Welfare, 75* (6), 727–740.

Blanton, T. L., & Deschner, J. (1990). Biological mothers' grief: The postadoptive experience in open versus confidential adoption. *Child Welfare, 69,* 525–535.

Borgottra, E. F., & Fanshel, D. (1965). *Behavioral characteristics of children known to psychiatric outpatient clinics.* New York: Child Welfare League of America.

Bowlby, J. (1951). *Maternal care and mental health* (Monograph Series 2). Geneva: World Health Organization.

Brinich, P. M., & Brinich, E. B. (1982). Adoption and adaptation. *Journal of Nervous and Mental disease, 170* (8), 489–493.

Brissett-Chapman, S. (1997). Child protection risk assessment and African American children: Cultural ramifications for families and communities. *Child Welfare, 76* (1), 45–63.

Brodzinsky, A. (1990). Surrendering an infant for adoption. In D. Brodzinsky & M. Schechter (Eds.), *The psychology of adoption* (pp. 295–315). New York: Oxford University Press.

Brodzinsky, D., & Schechter, M. (Eds.). (1990). *The psychology of adoption.* New York: Oxford University Press.

Brooks, G. (1995). *Nine parts of desire.* New York: Anchor Books.

Brown, A. W., & Bailey-Etta, B. (1997, January-Feburary). An out-of-home care system in crisis: Implications for African American children in the child welfare system. *Child Welfare, 76* (1), 65–83.

Campbell, T. (1988). Ethical issues in hepatitis b screening. *American Journal of the Disabled Child, 142* (1), 13–24.

Caplan, A. L. (1994). The ethics of in vitro fertilization. In T. L. Beauchamp & L. Walters (Eds.), *Contemporary issues in bioethics* (pp. 216–224). Belmont, CA: Wadsworth Publishing.

Carter, S. L. (1996). *Integrity.* New York: BasicBooks.

Catholic Charities USA. (1989). *Perspectives on adoption.* Washington, D.C.: Catholic Charities USA Department of Social Services.

Catholic Charities USA. (1994). *Perspectives on adoption* (rev. ed.). Alexandria, VA.

Child Welfare League of America. (1938). *Minimum Safeguards in Adoption.* Washington, D.C.: Author.

Child Welfare League of America. (1959). *Child Welfare League of America standards for adoption service.* Washington, D.C.: Author.

Child Welfare League of America. (1960). *Standards for services to unmarried parents.* Washington, D.C.: Author.

Child Welfare League of America. (1971). *Guidelines for adoption service.* Washington, D.C.: Author.

Child Welfare League of America. (1973). *Standards on transracial adoption.* Washington, D.C.: Author.

Child Welfare League of America (1976, 1988). *Standards for adoption service.* (rev. ed.). Washington, D.C.: Author.

Child Welfare League of America. (1993). *The child welfare stat book 1993.* Washington, D.C.: Author.

Cole, E., & Donley, K. (1990). History, values, and placement policy issues in adoption. In D. Brodzinsky & M. Schechter (Eds.), *The psychology of adoption* (pp. 273–294). New York: Oxford University Press.

Conrad, A. P., & Joseph, M. V. (1991). Ethical problem solving skills in social work practice. *Social Thought, 17* (3), 5–15.

Couch, A. J. (n.d.). Explanation of the provisions of the Indian Child Welfare Act. (Available from Judge Alan J. Couch, Cleveland County Courthouse, Norman, OK 73069.)

Courtney, M. E. (1997, November-December). The politics and realities of transracial adoption. *Child Welfare, 76* (6), 749–779.

Davie, L. (1984). Babes and barristers: Legal ethics and lawyer-facilitated independent adoptions. *Hofstra Law Review, 12,* 933–981.

Dawson, C. (1993, February). *A study of the implications of secrecy as imposed by sealed records in adoption.* Unpublished doctoral dissertation. The Union Institute.

Dean, R. G., & Rhodes, M. L. (1992, March). Ethical-clinical tensions in clinical practice. *Social Work, 37* (2), 128–132.

Deutsch D. K., Swanson, J. M., Bruell, J. H., Cantwell, D. P., Weinberg, F., & Baren, M. (1982). Over-representation of adoptees in children with the attention deficit disorder. *Behavior Genetics, 12,* 231–238.

DeWoody, M. (1993, May-June). Adoption and disclosure of medical and social history: A review of the law. *Child Welfare, 54* (3), 195–217.

Deykin, E., Patti, P., & Ryan, J. (1988). Fathers of adopted children: A study of the impact of child surrender on birthfathers. *American Journal of Orthopsychiatry, 58* (2), 240–248.

Dolgoff, R., & Skolnik, L. (1992). Ethical decision making, the NASW Code of Ethics and group work practice: Beginning explorations. *Social Work with Groups, 15* (4), 99–112.

Doxiadis, S. (1989). Children, society and ethics. *Child Abuse and Neglect, 13* (1), 11–17. Paper presented at the Seventh International Congress of the International Society for Prevention of Child Abuse and Neglect, Rio de Janeiro, Brazil.

Dukette, R. (1984). Values issues in present-day adoption. *Child Welfare, 63* (3), 233–243.

Etter, J. (1993). Levels of cooperation and satisfaction in 56 open adoptions. *Child Welfare, 72* (3), 257–267.

Etzioni, A. (1969). *The semi-professions and their organization.* New York: The Free Press.

Everett, J. E. (1995). Child foster care. In R. L. Edwards & J. G. Hopps (Eds.), *Encyclopedia of Social Work* (vol 1.) (pp. 375–389). Washington, D.C.: National Association of Social Workers.

Families for kids of color: A special report on challenges and opportunities. (n.d.). W. W. Kellogg Foundation, P.O. Box 5196, Battle Creek, MI 49016–5196.

Feigelman, W., & A. Silverman, (1986). Adoptive parents, adoptees, and the sealed record controversy. *Social Casework, 67* (4), 219–226.

Fein, E. (1991). The elusive search for certainty in child welfare: Introduction. *American Journal of Orthopsychiatry, 61,* 576–577.

Fein, E., & Maluccio, A. (1992). Permanency planning: Another remedy in jeopardy. *Social Service Review, 66* (3), 335–348.

Fenton, J. (1994, February). Response to NCFA query. *The CUB Communicator,* 12.

Fieweger, M. E. (1991). Stolen children and international adoption. *Child Welfare, 70* (2), 285–291.

Frankena, W. (1973). *Ethics* (2nd ed.). Englewood Cliffs, NJ: Prentice-Hall.

Freundlich, M. (1997–1998, Winter-Spring). Confidentiality becomes political: The new strategy in opposition to open records. *Decree, 15* (4), 1–5.

Gies, F., & Gies, R. (1989). *Marriage and the family in the Middle Ages.* New York: Harper and Row.

Gilles, T. (1995). *Adoption assistance in America: A programmatic analysis fifteen years after federal implementation.* St. Paul, MN: North American Council on Adoptable Children.

Gilley, J. W., & Galbraith, M. W. (1986, June). Examining professional certification. *Training and Development Journal,* 60–61.

Goldstein, J., Freud, A., & Solnit, A. (1973). *Beyond the best interests of the child*. New York: The Free Press/Macmillan.

Goldstein, J., Freud, A., & Solnit, A. (1979). *Before the best interests of the child*. New York: The Free Press/Macmillan.

Goldstein, J., Freud, A., Solnit, A., & Goldstein, S. (1986). *In the best interests of the child*. New York: The Free Press/Macmillan.

Goldthwaite, R. (1972). The Florentine palace as domestic architecture. *American Historical Review, 77*, 977–1012.

Gonyo, B., & Watson, K. (1988). Searching in adoption. *Public Welfare, 46* (1), 14–22.

Goode, W. J. (1957, February). Community within a community: The professions. *American Sociological Review, 22* (1), 194–200.

Greenwood, E. (1957, July). The attributes of a profession. *Social Work, 2*, 45–55.

Gritter, J. (1997). *The spirit of open adoption*. Washington, D.C.: CWLA Press.

Gross, H. E. (1993, May-June). Open adoption: A research-based literature review and new data. *Child Welfare, 72* (3), 269–284.

Grotevant, H., McRoy, R., Elde, C., & Fravel, D. L. (1994, June). Adoptive family system dynamics: Variations by level of openness in the adoption. *Family Process, 33*, 141–142.

Groza, V., & Rosenberg, K. (Eds.). (1998). *Bridging the gap: Clinical practice in adoption throughout the lifespan*. Westport, CT: Praeger.

Hoopes, J. (1982). *Prediction in child development: A longitudinal study of adoptive and nonadoptive families*. New York: Child Welfare League of America.

Hope Cottage. (1996, Winter). Hope cottage adopts new business plan. *Hopeline, 3* (2), 1.

Hostetter, M., Iverson, S., Dole, K., & Johnson, D. (1989). Unsuspected infectious diseases and other medical diagnoses in the evaluation of internationally adopted children. *Pediatrics, 83* (4), 559–564.

Hughes, R. (1993). Child welfare services for the catastrophically ill newborn: I. A confusion of responsibility. *Child Welfare, 72* (4), 323–340.

International adoption statistics released. (1997, December). *Adoptive Families Magazine, 30* (6), 6.

Jackson-White, G., Davenport Dozier, C., Oliver, J. T., & Barnwell Gardner, L. (1997, January-February). Why African American adoption agencies succeed: A new perspective on self-help. *Child Welfare, 76*, 1, 239–254.

Jacobs, L. (1995). *The Jewish religion: A companion*. New York: Oxford University Press.

Jeter, H. R., & Child Welfare League of America. (1963). *Children, problems and services in child welfare programs*. Washington, D.C.: U.S. Department of Health, Education, and Welfare.

Joint Council on International Children's Services. (1997–1998, Winter). Gender and age of children adopted internationally. *Bulletin of the Joint Council on International Children's Services*. Chevely, MD: Author.

Jones, M. B. (1993). *Birthmothers*. Chicago, IL: Chicago Review Press.

Joseph, M. V. (1983, Fall & Winter). The ethics of organizations: Shifting values and ethical dilemma. *Administration in Social Work, 7* (3 & 4), 47–57.

Josephson, M. (1993). *Making ethical decisions*. Marina del Rey, CA: The Josephson Institute.

Kadushin, A. (1984). Principles, values, and assumptions underlying adoption practice. In P. Sachdev (Ed.), *Adoption: Current issues and trends* (pp. 3–14). Toronto: Butterworths.

Katz, L., & Robinson, C. (1991). Foster care drift: A risk-assessment matrix. *Child Welfare*, 70 (3), 347–358.

Keck, G. C., & Kupecky, R. M. (1995). *Adopting the hurt child*. Colorado Springs: Piñon Press.

Kristinsdottir, G. (1991). *Child welfare and professionalization*. University of Umea, Umea, Sweden: Umea Universitets Tryckeri.

Kugelman, W. (1992). Social work ethics in the practice arena: A qualitative study. *Social Work in Health Care, 17* (4), 59–80.

Lawrence-Webb, C. (1997, January-February). African American children in the modern child welfare system: A legacy of the Flemming rule. *Child Welfare, 76* (1), 9–30.

Laws, R. (1995). Special needs adoption support and periodicals: A study of parent-written and adoption professional-written articles. (Doctoral dissertation, California Coast University). Research Abstracts International, 20, 05, LD-03161.

Laws, R. (1998). The history, elements, and ongoing need for adoption support. In V. Groze & K. Rosenberg (Eds.), *Bridging the gap: Clinical practice in adoption throughout the lifespan*. Westport, CT: Praeger.

Levy, C. (1973). The value base of social work. *Journal of Education for Social Work, 9* (1), 34–42.

Lewis, L., & Camp, V. (1994, September 30). Coercion and the cult of adoption from the mother's perspective. Paper presented at the third annual conference of the Council for Equal Rights in Adoption, New York City.

Lifton, B. J. (1988). *Lost and Found*. New York: Harper and Row.

Lifton, B. J. (1994). *Journey of the adopted self: A quest for wholeness*. New York, NY: Basic Books.

Lynch, L. (1997, September-October-November). Open adoption questions and answers. *Adoptive Families, 30* (5), 24–28.

MacIntyre, A. (1995). The nature of the virtues. In L. P. Pojman, *Ethical theory: Classical and contemporary readings* (pp. 357–370). Belmont, CA: Wadsworth Publishing.

Macklin, R. (1994). Artificial means of reproduction and our understanding of the family. In T. L. Beauchamp & L. Walters (Eds.), *Contemporary issues in bioethics* (pp. 191–198). Belmont, CA: Wadsworth Publishing.

Marin, P. (1981). Living in moral pain. *Psychology Today, 15* (7), 68–80.

Markus, A., & Lockwood, M. (1994). Is it permissible to edit medical records? In T. L. Beauchamp & L. Walters (Eds.), *Contemporary issues in bioethics* (pp. 182–187). Belmont, CA: Wadsworth Publishing.

Mason, M. M., & Silberman, A. (Speakers). (1993). *Networking with birthparents: Seeking and finding a match* (Cassette Recording No. 4C-93). Minneapolis, MN: Adoptive Families of America.

McRoy, R. G., Oglesby, Z., & Grape, H. (1997, January-February). Achieving same-race adoptive placements for African American children: Culturally sensitive practice approaches. *Child Welfare, 76* (1), 85–104.

Melina, L. R., & Roszia, S. K. (1993). *The open adoption experience.* New York: HarperPerennial.

Melton, G. B., & Flood, M. F. (1994). Research policy and child maltreatment: Developing the scientific foundation for effective protection of children. *Child Abuse & Neglect, 18* (1), 1–28.

Montalvo, E. (1994). Against all odds: The challenges faced by Latino families and children in the United States. *The Roundtable, 8* (2), 1–5.

National Association of Social Workers. (1979, 1987). Foster care and adoption. *Social Work Speaks: NASW Policy Statement* (2nd ed.). Washington, D.C.: Author.

National Association of Social Workers. (1990). *NASW Code of Ethics.* Washington, D.C.: Author.

National Association of Social Workers. (1996). *NASW Code of Ethics.* Washington, D.C.: Author.

National Council for Adoption. (1996, March-April). Ann Landers under attack again. *National Adoption Reports, 17,* 3/4, 1–2. Washington, D.C.: Author.

National Council for Adoption, Ad Hoc Committee on Ethical Standards in Adoption. (February 1991). *Principles of good practice in infant adoption.* Washington, D.C.: Author.

Neubauer, Peter B. (1990). *Nature's thumbprint: The new genetics of personality.* Reading, MA: Addison-Wesley Publishing Company.

New American Standard Bible. (1977). New York: Thomas Nelson Publishers.

Pacheco, F., & Eme, R. (1993, January-February). An outcome study of the reunion between adoptees and biological parents. *Child Welfare, 72* (1), 53–64.

Pine, B. (1987). Strategies for more ethical decision making in child welfare practice. *Child Welfare, 66* (4), 315–326.

Pojman, Louis P. (1995). *Ethical theory: Classical and contemporary readings.* Belmont, CA: Wadsworth Publishing.

Poppendieck, J. E. (1992). Values, commitments, and ethics of social work in the United States. *Journal of Progressive Human Services, 3* (2), 31–45.

Presser, S. B. (1972). The historical background of the American law of adoption. *Journal of Family Law, 11,* 443–516.

Reitz, M., & Watson, K. (1992). *Adoption and the family system: Strategies for treatment.* New York: Guilford Press.

Rest, J. R. (1988, Winter). Can ethics be taught in professional schools? The psychological research. *Easier Said Than Done,* 22–26.

Rhodes, M. L. (1991). *Ethical dilemmas in social work practice.* Milwaukee, WI: Family Service America.

Rhodes, M. L. (1992, January). Social work challenges: The boundaries of ethics. *Families in Society: The Journal of Contemporary Human Services,* 41–47.

Riben, M. (1988). Shedding light on the dark side of adoption. Detroit, MI: Harlo Press.

Robertson, I. (1987). *Sociology* (3rd ed.). New York: Worth.

Rompf, E. (1993). Open adoption: What does the "average person" think? *Child Welfare, 72* (3), 219–230.

Rosenberg, E. B. (1992). *The adoption lifecycle.* New York: The Free Press/Macmillan.

Rosenberg, K. F., & Groze, V. (1997, September-October). The impact of secrecy and denial in adoption: Practice and treatment issues. *Families in Society: The Journal of Contemporary Human Services*, 522–530.

Rosenthal, J. A., & Groze, V. K. (1992). *Special-needs adoption*. New York: Praeger.

Ross, W. D. (1930). *The right and the good*. Oxford: Oxford University Press.

Rothman, B. K. (1994). Infertility as disability. In T. L. Beauchamp & L. Walters (Eds.), *Contemporary issues in bioethics* (pp. 211–216). Belmont, CA: Wadsworth Publishing.

Rutter, M., Quinton, D., & Liddle, C. (1983). Parenting in two generations. In N. Madge (Ed.), *Families at risk*. London: Department of Health and Social Security.

Sachdev, P. (1984). *Adoption: Current issues and trends*. Toronto: Butterworths.

Sachdev, P. (1989). *Unlocking the adoption files*. Lexington, MA: D.C. Heath.

Sachdev, P. (1992). *Sex, abortion, and unmarried women*. Westport, CT: Greenwood Press.

Saul, S. (1997, October 15). In the name of research: Identical brothers separated at birth were studied, but truth was hidden. *Newsday.com* (http://www.newsday.com/news/ncov1012.htm).

Schaefer, C. (1991). The other mother. New York: Soho Press.

Schechter, M., & Bertocci, D. (1990). The meaning of the search. In D. Brodzinsky, & M. Schechter (Eds.), *The psychology of adoption* (pp. 62–92). New York: Oxford University Press.

Schechter, M. D. (1960). Observations on adopted children. *Archives of General Psychiatry, 3*, 21–32.

Scheer, W. E. (1984). Is personnel management a profession? *Personnel Journal, 43*, 225–261.

Schmeiser, C. B. (1992). Ethical codes in the professions. *Educational Measurement Issues and Practice, 11* (3), 5–11.

Select Committee on Children, Youth, and Families, U.S. House of Representatives. (1990). *No place to call home: Discarded children in America*. House of Representatives Report 101–395. Washington, D.C.: U.S. Government Printing Office.

Severson, R. (1991). *Adoption: Charms and rituals for healing*. Dallas, TX: House of Tomorrow Productions.

Severson, R. (1994). *Adoption: Philosophy and experience*. Dallas, TX: House of Tomorrow Productions.

Sherwin, S. (1987). Feminist ethics and in vitro fertilization. In M. Hanen & K. Nielsen (Eds.), *Science, morality, and feminist theory* (pp. 265–284). Calgary, Alberta: University of Calgary Press.

Shimberg, B., & Roederer, D. (1978). In R. J. Marcelli (Ed.), *Occupational licensing: Questions a legislator should ask*. Lexington, KY: The Council of State Governments.

Sigvaardson, S., von Knorring, A. L., Bohman, M., et al. (1984). An adoption study of somatoform disorders: I. The relationship of somatization to psychiaztric disability. *Archives of General Psychiatry, 41*, 853–859.

Silber, K., & Speedlin, P. (1983). *Dear Birthmother: Thank you for our baby*. San Antonio, TX: Corona Publishing.

Silberberg, A. (1996, November-December). Open adoption: Is it legally enforceable? Should it be? *Adoptive Families, 29* (6), 14–16.

Silverman, A., & Weitzman, D. (1986). Nonrelative adoption in the United States. In R. Hoksbergen (Ed.), *Adoption in worldwide perspective: A review of programs, policies, and legislation in 14 countries.* Lisse: Swets & Zeitlinger, Berwyn: Swets North America.

Silverman, C. (1989). Regulating independent adoptions. *Columbia Journal of Law and Social Problems, 22,* 323–355.

Simon, N. M., & Senturia, A. G. (1966). Adoption and psychiatric illness. *American Journal of Psychiatry, 122,* 858–867.

Solinger, R. (1992). *Wake up, little Susie: Single pregnancy and race before Roe v. Wade.* New York: Routledge.

Sorich, C. J., & Siebert, R. (1982, April). Toward humanizing adoption. *Child Welfare, 61* (4), 207–216.

Sorosky, A., Baran, A., & Pannor, R. (1989). *The adoption triangle: The effects of the sealed record on adoptees, birth parents, and adoptive parents.* San Antonio: Corona Publishing.

Spencer, M. E. (1987). Post-legal adoption services: A lifelong commitment. *Journal of Social Work and Human Sexuality, 6* (1), 155–167.

Sutton, J. R. (1990, May). Bureaucrats and entrepreneurs: Institutional responses to deviant children in the United States, 1890–1920s. *American Journal of Sociology, 95* (6), 1367–1400.

Thomasma, D. C., & Pisaneschi, J. I. (1977). Allied health professionals and ethical issues. *Journal of Allied Health, 6* (2), 15–20.

Triseliotis, J. (1973). *In search of origins.* London: Routledge & Kegan Paul.

Triseliotis, J., & Hill, M. (1990). Contrasting adoption, foster care, and residential rearing. In D. Brodzinsky & M. Schechter (Eds.), *The psychology of adoption* (pp. 107–120). New York: Oxford University Press.

Troxler, G. W. (1994, May 5). State of the sabbatical: Midway to Marianne. Unpublished report to trustees, faculty, and board of Capitol College. (Available from Dr. Troxler or Capitol College at 11301 Springfield Road, Laurel, MD 20708–9759.)

U.S. Advisory Board on Child Abuse and Neglect. (1990). *Child abuse and neglect: Critical first steps in response to a national emergency.* Stock No. 017–092–00104–5. Washington, D.C.: U.S. Government Printing Office.

U. S. Children's Bureau. (1961). *Legislative guides for the termination of parental rights and responsibilities and the adoption of children.* Washington, D.C.: Department of Health, Education, and Welfare.

Valentine, D., Conway, P., & Randolph, J. (1988). Placement disruptions: Perspectives of adoptive parents. *Journal of Social Work and Human Sexuality, 6* (1), 133–153.

Van Hoose, W. H., & Kottler, J. A. (1988). *Ethical and legal issues in counseling and psychotherapy.* San Francisco, CA: Jossey-Bass Publishers.

Vick, C. (1997, December). Foster parents: The heroes of child welfare. *Adoptive Families, 30* (6), 8–13.

Vitillo, R. (1991). International adoption: The solution or the problem? *Social Thought, 17* (3), 16–24.

Voss, R. (1985). A sociological analysis and theological reflection on adoption services in Catholic Charities agencies. *Social Thought, 11* (1), 32–43.

Walden, T., Wolock, I., & Demone, H. (1990). Ethical decision making in human services: A comparative study. *Families in Society, 71* (2), 67–75.

Watson, K. (1992, Winter). Providing services after adoption. *Public Welfare,* 5–13.

Watson, K. (1994). Should adoption records be opened? YES. Unpublished manuscript.

Watson, K., & Brown, D. (1994, Summer). Charging fees undermines process of adoption. *The Decree, 11* (2), 8–9.

Weisman, M. (1994, July). When parents are not in the best interests of the child. *The Atlantic Monthly,* 43–63.

Zelizer, V. A. (1985). *Pricing the priceless child: The changing social value of children.* New York: Basic Books.

Index

Abandonment of clients, 141, 143, 158

Abduction, 36

Abortion, 47

Academy of Adoption Professionals, 97, 122

Access to adoption records. *See* Confidential records access

Adamec, C., 47

Administrative appeals, 15, 18, 19

Adopt a Special Kid (AASK), 57, 97, 199

Adopted person: access to original birth certificate, 110–113; background information about, 122, 125, 140–141, 143, 149, 155; as client, 124; consent to adoption, 145; and culture, 145–146; mental health, 61; notification of birth parent death, 158; respect for, 146; values in serving, 150–151

Adoptee. *See* Adopted person

Adoptees Liberty Movement Association (ALMA), 55, 199

Adoption agencies, 87, 168

Adoption Assistance and Child Welfare Act of 1980, 56, 75

Adoption assistance payments (AAP), 14–16, 19, 56, 122, 143, 196

Adoption Exchange Association, 97, 123

Adoption Quarterly, 137, 180

Adoption Opportunities Act, 56

Adoption professional's role in society, 100

Adoption reform movement, 54–56, 58

Adoption search, 106, 110, 124, 154

Adoption Studies Institute, 137

Adoption subsidies. *See* Adoption assistance payments

Adoption Web Ring, 91

Adoption workers, 92

Adoptive families, 110

Adoptive Families of America (AFA), 48, 57, 97, 127, 199

Adoptive parents: access to information, 112; complaints of, 122–123; exploitation of, 178; responsibility to, 89, 149

Adoptive Placement Agreement, 15, 16
Advertising, 35, 96
Adverse consequences: of adoption, 154; of search and reunion, 155
Advising, 96
African Americans and adoption, 51
Agency adoptions, 39
Aid to Families with Dependent Children (AFDC), 43, 51
Altruism, 77
Amadio, C., 83, 108
American Academy of Adoption Attorneys, 97
American Academy of Pediatrics, 97, 127, 128
American Adoption Congress (AAC), 55, 97–98, 199
American Association of Open Adoption Agencies, 98, 148
American Association for Marriage and Family Therapy (AAMFT), 103
American Fertility Society, 174
Anderson, E., 169
Anderson, P., 36, 40
Apprenticing as adoption, 34
Aristotle, 31, 67
Arizona, 189
Arles, Synod of, 33
Artificial insemination donor (AID), 171
Association of Juvenile and Family Court Judges, 128
Attachment Disorder, 5
Autonomy, 80, 111

Babb, L. A., 49, 57, 60, 83, 85, 86, 88, 90, 95, 99, 119, 124, 136, 146, 153, 167, 185, 190
Baby brokering, 41–42, 45, 55
Baby farmers, 37
Baby Jessica, 186
Babylonian law and adoption, 30–31
"Bad blood" theory of adoption, 41

Baer, J., 41, 55, 107, 127, 189
Balzert, C., 21
Baran, A., 28, 48, 61, 86, 127, 181
Barth, R., 135
Bartholet, E., 60, 68, 166, 167, 168
Bastard Nation, 56, 86, 107, 199
Beauchamp, T., 80, 81, 82, 90, 111, 126, 171, 196, 197
Beneficence, 81, 111
Benet, M., 27, 30
Berry, M., 88
Best interests of the child, 39, 62, 70, 74, 84, 103, 148, 164
Biblical accounts of adoption, 29–30
Birmingham, J., 137, 176
Birth families: preservation of, 110, 138; respect for beliefs of, 140; value of, 139
Birth fathers, 118, 123, 139
Birth parents: as client, 118; complaints of, 123; exploitation of, 147, 178; fees, 105, 108; identity, 110–111; notification of adoptee's death, 158; notification of adoption failure, 158; professional responsibility to, 89–90, 138, 141; separation from child, 61; values related to, 147–149
Birthmothers, 24, 55, 90, 120
Black market adoptions, 41–42, 122, 145
Blackfoot Indians, 36
Blanton, T. L., 89, 90, 193
Blood ties, value of, 62, 63, 65, 104
Borgotta, E. F., 61
Brace, Charles Loring, 36
Brissett-Chapman, S., 52
Brodzinsky, A., 90
Brodzinsky, D., 60, 61, 193
Brooks, G., 31
Brown, A. W., 92
Brown, D., 124

California, 57, 187, 189
Camp, V., 124

Candor, 66
Caplan, A. L., 175
Carter, S., 82, 198
Casuistry, 79
Catholic Charities USA, 40, 44, 46, 58, 98, 127, 177
Catholic church, 37
Caucasians and adoption, 49–50
Certification, 181, 185–187
Chicago Child Care Society, 108
Child placement standards, 70
Child Trafficking, 41–42, 45, 55
Child welfare: development of standards in, 39–40; ethics in, 93; growth of, 36–37, 40
Child Welfare League of America (CWLA), 20, 40, 41, 62, 98, 106, 135, 136, 166, 177, 197
Children as chattel, 40
Children Awaiting Parents (CAP), 98
China, 30, 48
Christianity, 32, 69
Citizenship, 65
Client, defining, 84, 103, 117–120
Client-employee relations, 46, 100, 113
Closed records, 41, 55, 61, 64, 85, 86, 111
Code of ethics, in adoption, 191, 197
Coercion, 89–90, 120, 148, 149, 173
Cole, E., 33, 37, 40, 45, 65, 108, 135
Colonial America, 35–36
Columbus, Christopher, 49
Committee for Hispanic Children and Families (CHCF), 50
Communication, 96, 102, 153
Community: adoptee's right to grow up in, 145; interest in adoption, 64
Competence, professional, 91, 151
Competition in adoption, 107
Complaints by adoptive parents, 122
Concerned United Birthparents (CUB), 55, 98, 103, 122, 123, 124, 199

Confidential intermediaries, 106
Confidential records access: and adoption reform movement, 54–55; as a civil right, 86; defining terms, 196; and definition of client, 120; ethics of, 100–101, 110, 112, 152; illegal, 18; legal, 64; politicalization of, 112
Confidentiality: controversies, 117, 126; defining, 197; as ethical principle, 96, 151–152; legal interpretations of, 64; professional understanding of, 87; research regarding, 110–113
Conflict of interest, 84, 103, 105, 108, 118
Conflicting ethical values, 104, 107, 114–134, 164
Connecticut, 35
Conrad, A. P., 28, 74, 92, 129, 177, 190
Consent to adoption, birth parent revocation of, 109; by adopted child, 145
Consulting, 96
Contested adoptions, 109
Continuing education, 151
Contractual relationships, 96, 108–110, 157
Control of information, 87
Control of unwed mothers, 43
Conventionalism, 79
Council for Equal Rights in Adoption (CERA), 98, 122, 199
Council on Adoptable Children (COAC), 50
Court-Appointed Special Advocate (CASA), 57
Courtney, M. E., 60
Crisis pregnancy counseling, xxv
Cultural relativism, 79

Datheus, Archbishop, 33
Davie, L., 85
Davis, D., 123

Dawson, C., 41
Dear Birthmother: Thank You for Our Baby, 57
Death: of adopted child, 158; of birth parent, 159
DeBoer, Jessica, 186
Demand for adoptable children, in early America, 37
Dependency, exploitation of, 147
Deutsch, D. K., 61
DeWoody, M., 85, 87, 102
Deykin, E., 89
Difficulty-of-Care payments, 156
Diligence and due care, 96, 102, 117, 129, 151
Disabled, adoption by, 101
Disclosure of information, 85, 87, 102, 126, 143
Discrimination, 100–101
Displaced Persons Act, 47
Dissolution or disruption of adoption, 158
DNA testing, 48
Dolgoff, R., 27
Domnitz, Michael, 21–24
Donley, K., 33, 37, 40, 45, 65
Doxiadis, S., 32, 33, 65
Dred Scott Decision, 73
Dual representation or relationships, 103, 120, 140, 156
Dukette, R., 27, 61, 62, 68, 84, 86, 118, 130
Duty to warn, 153, 154

Editing of records, 111
Education of professionals, 151
England, 34–35
Environment v. heredity, 41, 60
Ethical codes, 95
Ethical relativism, 79
Ethics, defined, 28, 73
Ethics of care, 79
Etter, J., 88
Etzioni, A., 179
Europe, adoption in, 33, 34, 48

Evan B. Donaldson Adoption Institute, 137, 180
Everett, J. E., 92
Excellence, pursuit of, 81
Expectant mothers, 118, 119

Fair hearings, 15, 18, 19
Falsification of records, 111
Family preservation, 63–64, 68, 104, 110
Family Tree, The, 124
Fees and finances, 96, 105–108, 156, 157, 166
Feigelman, W., 86, 127
Fidelity, 81
Financial gain and adoption, 65
Fisher, F., 54
Flemming rule, 51–52
Florence Crittendon Association, 40, 44, 46
Florida, 51
Form of practice, 96
Foundling asylums, 33, 34, 35, 69
France, adoption in, 33
Freedom of information, 86
Freud, A., 46
Freundlich, M., 112

Galland, Eddie, 21–24
Gay men, adoption by, 101
Genetic determinism, 60
Gies, F., 33
Gilles, T., 196
Gilley, J. W., 179, 182, 184, 192
Golden Rule, 77
Goldstein, J., 46, 135
Goldthwaite, R., 33
Gonyo, B., 86, 124, 136
Grandparents, 154
Gratitude, 81
Great Britain, 34–35
Great Depression, 39
Greece, adoption in, 32
Greenwood, E., 179
Grief, 89, 145

Gritter, J., 58, 59, 66, 69, 117, 175, 190–191
Gross, H., 88
Grotevant, H., 88–89
Groza, V., 34, 37, 41, 57, 85, 91, 102, 122, 123, 193, 194
Guatemala, 48

Hague Conference on International Adoption, 197
Haley, A., 54
Hammurabi, Code of, 30
Healthy infants, adoption of, 60
Helping the helpless, 67
Heredity, 41, 60
Hinduism and adoption, 31
Hispanic Americans, 50
Holt, Harry and Bertha, 47
Homosexuals, adoption by, 101
Honesty, 66
Hoopes, J., 61
Hughes, R., 131
Humane societies, 36

Identifying information, 64, 126, 128
Identity, value of, 62
Illegal records access, 18
Illegitimacy, 40–41
Illinois, 189
Imbalance of power, 88
Immaturity, as factor in adoption, 120
Immigration and Nationality Act, 48
Improper gain, 166
In vitro fertilization (IVF), 171, 175
Incompetence, 92
Indentured servanthood, 34
Independent adoption, 39, 59, 109, 136, 166
India, 31
Indian Child Welfare Act (ICWA), 50
Industrialization, effect of on adoption, 34, 37
Industry, adoption as an, 60, 168

Infant adoption, 37
Infertility, 59, 60
Information: about adoptee, 122, 140–141; access to, 152–153; existence and use of, 152
Informed consent, 24–25, 66, 90
Informed relativism, 77
Innate worth of humans, 69
Integrity, 65, 82, 96, 117, 120, 146
International adoption, 47–48
International Concerns Committee for Children (ICCC), 98
International Soundex Reunion Registry (ISRR), 54, 106
Irish, 37
Islamic adoption, 31

Jackson-White, G., 53
Jacobs, L., 30
Japan, 30
Jeter, H. R., 52
Jewish law and adoption, 32
Joint Council on International Children's Services (JCICS), 48, 67
Jones, M. B., 24, 55, 90, 120
Joseph, M. V., 28, 74, 131
Josephson, M., 77, 93, 146, 147
Judeo-Christian values, 77
Justice, 81, 112
Justinian Code, 32

Kadushin, A., 108
Kant, Immanuel, 77
Kantianism, 76
Katz, L., 124
Kellerman, David, 21
Kidnapping and adoption, 36
Kirk, H. D., 61
Korean adoptions, 47–48
Kramer, Betty, 48
Kristinsdottir, G., 34, 37
Krugman, Dorothy, 21
Kübler-Ross, Elizabeth, 54
Kugelman, W., 92, 93, 130, 190

Latinos and adoption, 50
Lawrence, Margaret, 55
Lawrence-Webb, C., 51, 52
Laws, R., 34, 36, 45, 48, 49, 57
Legal adoption, 67
Legal profession, 96, 109, 120
Lesbians, adoption by, 101
Levy, C., 138
Lewis, Laura, 124
Licensure: of adoption agencies, 167; of adoption professionals, 181, 185
Lifton, B. J., 48, 54
Limits to confidentiality, 152
Louise Wise Services, 21, 22
Louisiana, 51
Low income, and adoption, 101
Loyalty, 81
Lynch, L., 41, 59

MacIntyre, A., 77
Macklin, R., 171
Marin, P., 195
Market economy in adoption, 107, 168, 171, 175
Markus, A., 111, 112
Maryland, 187
Mason, Mary Martin, 175
Massachusetts, 36, 189
Master's level social worker (MSW), 18
Matching: child with adoptive parent, 142–143, 146; parties, 149
McCarty, Kevin, 91
McRoy, R., 52, 53, 54
Medicaid, 15
Medical professions, 97, 109, 111–112
Melina, L., 41
Melton, G. B., 93, 177
Mental health professionals, 60–61, 96
Mentally ill, adoption by, 101
Michigan, 57
Minority race and adoption, 49
Mississippi, 51

Money in adoption, 105
Montalvo, E., 50
Moses, 29
Muhammad, 31
Multiethnic Placement Act (MEPA), 53, 75
Muslims, 31

Napoleon, 33
Narva, Emperor, 32
Natchez massacre orphans, 35
National Adoption Center (NAC), 98
National Association of Black Social Workers (NABSW), 53, 98
National Association of Juvenile and Family Court Judges, 57, 98, 128
National Association of Social Workers (NASW), 46, 92, 96, 135, 136, 164, 166
National Council for Adoption (NCFA), 46, 97, 128
National Institute of Mental Health (NIMH), 22
National Resource Center for Special Needs Adoption, 98, 122
Native American Child and Family Resource Center, 98
Native Americans and adoption, 33–34, 36, 49–50
Nature v. nurture, 41, 60
Neubauer, Peter, 22, 23
New York Children's Aid Society, 36
Non-agency adoptions, 39, 59, 109, 136, 166
Nondiscrimination: adoptees, 144; adoptive parents, 101, 141; birth parents, 138
North American Council on Adoptable Children (NACAC), 57, 98
Nursing, 96

Objectification of children, 171
Objectivity and independence, 96, 103, 117–120, 155

Oceania, 31
Oglesby, Z., 52
Oklahoma, 188
Older child adoption, 38, 118
Open adoption, 11, 57–59, 87, 89, 110, 140–141, 143, 148, 173
Open records, 18, 54–55, 64, 86, 100–101, 110, 120, 152, 196
Organization for a United Response (OURS), 48
Original birth certificate, 41, 111, 112
Orphan trains, 34, 37
Orphan Voyage, 55
Orphanages, 35, 37, 69
Outside consultation, 158

Pannor, R., 28, 61
Parents of Korean and Korean-American Children, 48
Paton, Jean, 54, 55, 56
Permanency, 66
Philosophical frameworks, 75, 195
Phips, Sir William, 36
Photolisting, 3, 57, 149, 150
Physicians, 97, 109, 111–112
Pierce, W., 47
Pine, B., 93, 130, 131
Plato, 67
Pojman, L., 77
Policy or practice changes, 109–110
Political activities, 110
Poppendieck, J. E., 69, 92, 179, 185
Post-adoption services, 91, 107, 143
Power, 87–88
Practice standards in adoption, 95, 109–110
Preventing harm, 187–188
Prima facie duties, 81
Primal wound theory, 198
Privacy, 112, 151
Private adoptions, 39, 59, 109, 136, 166
Professional excellence, 67, 69, 91
Professionalization of adoption practice, 176–177

Professional's role in society, 96, 198–199
Propriety, 70
Protection of children, 65, 67
Protestants, 37
Psychiatrists, 111
Psychologists, 41
Public Law 87–31, 51
Public Law 95–266, 56
Public Law 95–608, 50
Public Law 96–272, 56, 75
Public Law 103–382, 53, 75

Quality of adoption service, 93
Racial discrimination, 17, 49–54, 100
Reactive Attachment Disorder of Childhood, 5
Records, editing and falsification of, 111; existence of, 152
Recruitment of adoptive parents, 149
Refugee Relief Act, 47
Registration, 181, 185
Regulation: arguments against, 184–185; certification, 186; of professionals, 74, 185; of professions, 181
Reitz, M., 28, 60
Relativism, 77
Religion, 140
Reproductive technologies, 171, 175
Respect, 65, 80
Responsibility to clients, 89, 100, 137
Rest, J. R., 92, 93, 130
Reunion registries, 54, 106
Revocation of consent to adoption, 109
Rhodes, M., 73, 74, 75, 77, 79, 83, 87, 105, 170
Riben, Mirah, 90
Rights-based theories, 77
Rocky Mountain Adoption Exchange, 98
Roe v. Wade, 44, 47
Romantic view of adoption, 42

Rosenberg, K., 34, 37, 41, 57, 91,
102, 193, 194
Rosenthal, J., 85, 89, 122
Ross, W. D., 82
Roszia, S., 41, 58
Rule of reciprocity, 77
Russia, adoptions from, 48
Rutter, M., 61

Sachdev, P., 62, 63, 64, 84, 86, 91,
130, 135, 169
Salvation Army, 44, 46
San Diego Pregnancy Services, 189
Saul, S., 22, 23
Schaefer, C., 90
Schechter, M., 60, 61, 90
Scheer, W. E., 179
Schmeiser, C. B., 80, 96
Sealed adoption records, 41, 55, 61,
64, 85, 86, 111
Search and reunion, 106, 110, 124,
154
Search fees in adoption, 106
Secrecy and adoption, 61, 87, 111
Select Committee on Children,
Youth, and Families, 181
Self-determination, 64, 142
Self-improvement, 81–82
Self-interest among adoption profes-
sionals, 105
Sentimental value of children, 39
Separation of twins in adoption, 22,
190
Severson, R., 108, 131, 137, 170,
178, 185, 190, 198
Shafran, Robert, 20–24
Sherwin, S., 172
Shared Fate, 61
Shimberg, B., 182, 184
Siblings: ongoing contact, 144; place-
ment together, 144; twins, 22, 190
Sigvaardson, A., 61
Silber, K., 44, 58, 59, 88
Silberberg, A., 88, 175
Silverman, C., 85, 86, 92, 191

Simon, N. M., 61
Single parents, adoption by, 101
Sliding scale fees, 105
Social Security Act of 1935, 51
Social work, 70, 92, 96, 129
Solicitation, 96
Solinger, R., 40, 44, 46
Sorich, C. J., 88, 136
Sorosky, A., 28, 34, 35, 36, 128
Special needs adoption, 56–57, 59,
118, 122
Spence-Chapin adoption agency, 180
Spencer, M. E., 91
Standards, adoption, 40; in child wel-
fare, 39; development of, 40; prac-
tice, 95; shared, 114
State licensors of adoption agencies,
109, 118, 127
Subsidies. *See* Adoption Assistance
Payments
Supervision, 96
Sutton, J. R., 40

Talmudic law and adoption, 30
Tennessee, 186
Tennessee Children's Home, 186
Texas, 57, 137, 188
Thomasma, D. C., 93
Time, and adoption, 62, 66; of adop-
tive placement, 20; for revocation
of consent to adoption, 109, 148
Traditional adoption, 89
Training, of adoptive parents, 123; of
professionals, 151, 185–186
Transcultural adoption, 146
Transracial adoption, 49–54, 101, 146
Triseliotis, J., 61
Troxler, G. William, 125
Twins, separation of in adoption, 22,
190

Unborn children, 84, 118, 119
Undue influence, 149
Unethical behavior, examples of,
187–190

United Nations, 62

United Nations Convention on the Rights of the Child, 64–65, 164–166

United States: adoption statutes in, 36; first adoption in colonies, 36; first adoption statutes, 36; first orphanage in, 35

United States Children's Bureau, 39, 44, 135, 166

Unwed mothers, 41, 43

U.S. Advisory Board on Child Abuse and Neglect, 177

Utilitarian adoption, 39–40, 60

Utilitarianism, 76

Valentine, D., 89, 118

Value of children, 39

Values, defined, 28, 62

Van Hoose, W. H., 200

Verrier, N., 198

Vick, C., 186

Vilardi, Emma Mae, 54

Virginia Company, 34

Virtue, 82

Virtue-based frameworks, 77

Vitillo, R., 64

Walden, T., 135

Wallace, Alfia, 107

Watson, K., 28, 60, 86, 108, 124, 169

Weisman, M., 35

Wisconsin, 57

World War II, 47

Wrongful adoption, 3–10, 85, 112, 122, 186

Zelizer, V. A., 37, 38, 39, 41–42, 44, 60

About the Author

L. ANNE BABB is Executive Director of a nonprofit adoption advocacy center, the Family Tree Adoption and Counseling Center in Norman, Oklahoma. She is recognized as one of the country's foremost public servants and adoption advocates for her work on behalf of adoptable children and is the co-author of *Adopting and Advocating for the Special Needs Child* (Bergin & Garvey, 1997).